Recycling
Advanced
English

Fourth Edition (With Removable Key)

Previously published by Georgian Press

Clare West

CAMBRIDGE
UNIVERSITY PRESS

University Printing House, Cambridge CB2 8BS, United Kingdom

Cambridge University Press is part of the University of Cambridge.

It furthers the University's mission by disseminating knowledge in the pursuit of education, learning and research at the highest international levels of excellence.

www.cambridge.org
Information on this title: www.cambridge.org/9781107657519

© Clare West 1995, 2002, 2009, 2013

First published by Georgian Press (Jersey) Limited 1995
Second edition 2002
Third edition 2009
Reprinted and published by Cambridge University Press 2010
Fourth edition 2013
Reprinted 2013

Printed in the United Kingdom by Latimer Trend

A catalogue record for this publication is available from the British Library

ISBN 978-1-107-65751-9 Paperback

Originally produced by AMR Design Ltd (www.amrdesign.com)
Drawings by Martyn Ford

CONTENTS

SECTION 3   VOCABULARY

SECTION 4   WORD STUDY

SECTION 5   WRITING

INTRODUCTION

Recycling Advanced English is for students at advanced level who wish to improve their general English and/or prepare for the Cambridge Certificate in Advanced English (CAE) or the revised Certificate of Proficiency in English (CPE). It can be used to supplement any coursebook at this level, and is suitable for use in the classroom, for homework, or for self-study.

The book aims to provide:
- coverage of the five main areas of difficulty at advanced level – grammar, phrasal verbs, vocabulary, word study and writing
- concise, clearly-presented explanations
- extensive practice of each point covered
- a strong element of recycling
- a user-friendly, attractive layout, so that the material is accessible and a pleasure to use
- a variety of exercise types which are not exam-specific
- examples of all the CAE and CPE task-types for Use of English and Writing
- an appendix of useful reference material.

Recycling Advanced English is divided into five distinct sections:

Section 1 GRAMMAR (25 units)

This large section aims to cover all the major grammatical points at advanced level, with practice and revision exercises for consolidation.

Section 2 PHRASAL VERBS (15 units)

In this section, phrasal verbs are grouped according to their particle, and there is also a focus on three-part phrasal verbs and phrasal verbs as nouns, with extensive practice in varying formats.

Section 3 VOCABULARY (22 units)

Here there are texts and tasks presenting and practising vocabulary from key topics which regularly occur in advanced classwork and examination syllabuses.

Section 4 WORD STUDY (17 units)

This section attempts to get beneath the surface of the language and to delve deeper into the linguistic areas which cause difficulties for the advanced learner, such as idioms, false friends, humour and collocations.

RECYCLING UNITS are an important element in Sections 1 – 4, providing consolidation of each block of preceding units. It is therefore advisable to use the Recycling units in the order in which they appear.

Section 5 WRITING (12 units)

This section offers guidance on a number of different writing tasks and styles, with appropriate phrases to learn, as well as practice exercises. All the types of composition required for CAE and CPE are covered, with model answers in the Appendix. There is also a unit offering help with writing tasks.

The APPENDIX provides additional grammar reference material and model answers for writing tasks.

The Fourth Edition

The book has been revised for a number of reasons: to update some of the texts, to incorporate suggestions made by readers, and to bring the tasks in line with the recent revision to the CPE syllabus. Much of the book remains essentially the same as its predecessor, but there are minor changes to many units, especially in the Writing section.

The Revised CPE Examination

Important changes to Papers 1 & 2 are as follows:

Paper 1

- Use of English and Reading papers are combined in this paper
- it has seven parts and takes 1 hour 30 minutes
- the short multiple choice reading task has been removed
- the gapped sentence Use of English task has been removed
- the summary Use of English task has been removed
- there is a new multiple matching reading task (as in FCE and CAE)

Paper 2

- this is the new Writing paper
- it takes 1 hour 30 minutes
- there is a new compulsory task in Part 1: you are required to write an essay summarising and evaluating the key ideas from two short texts
- in Part 2 you may be asked to write an article, a letter, a report or a review, but not a proposal
- in the set text options there may also be an essay task
- there are new word limits: 240–280 words for Part 1, 280–320 words for Part 2

Papers 3 (Listening) and 4 (Speaking) are outside the scope of this book.

For further information on the revised CPE examination, please go to Cambridge ESOL's website, where specifications and sample papers can be viewed and downloaded.
www.cambridgeesol.org

I would like to thank all the people who have offered their comments and suggestions. Whether you are using this book for exam preparation, or purely to improve your English at advanced level, I hope you will enjoy **Recycling Advanced English** and find that it motivates you and helps you to make progress.

Clare West

Articles and uncountables

No article is used when generalising (with plural, abstract and uncountable nouns) but the or a/an is used when talking about particular examples. The definite article the is used when it is clear which noun we mean, whereas the indefinite article a/an is used when a noun is referred to for the first time.

Singular countable nouns must always have an article (or possessive), except in the following cases: prepositions with *home, school, college, university, church, work, class, hospital, prison, bed, sea, breakfast, lunch, supper, dinner.*

Note also:
- *at night, on foot, by car/bus/tube* etc. (means of transport), *to/in/from town* (when referring to the town we live in, a local large town or the capital), *go to sleep* and *go home*

Notice the difference between *She's in prison* (she's a prisoner) and *She's in the prison* (she either works there or is visiting).

The article is also omitted in certain double expressions:
- *from top to bottom, on land and sea, hand in hand, face to face*

The indefinite article a/an is normally used to indicate someone's profession:
- *He wants to train as a psychotherapist.*

A Complete the sentences by putting *the, a/an* or no article (–) into the spaces.

1 You remember my sister Jane? ____ one who has always been afraid of ____ spiders?

2 She's been studying ____ architecture at ____ university for ____ last three years.

3 At ____ moment she's researching into ____ work of Le Corbusier. Don't you know him? He's ____ well-known French architect.

4 She's pretty busy in ____ daytime, but she finds she's at ____ bit of ____ loose end at night, so ____ last year she joined ____ film club.

5 ____ club members can watch ____ films at ____ very low prices, in ____ disused warehouse on ____ other side of ____ town.

6 So when she gets home from ____ college, she usually goes straight over there by ____ bike, and has ____ drink and ____ sandwich before ____ film starts.

7 One evening she was in such ____ hurry to get there that she had ____ accident.

8 She was knocked down by ____ car and had to spend two months in ____ hospital.

9 When I went to visit her, I was shocked to find her swathed in ____ bandages from ____ head to ____ toe.

10 But luckily her injuries looked worse than they really were, and she managed to make ____ very speedy recovery.

The is also used with

a a unique person or object: • *the President* • *the North Pole*
b musical instruments • *He plays the guitar.*
c some adjectives with plural meanings • *the rich*
d nationality adjectives, ships, geographical areas, most mountain ranges, oceans, seas, rivers, deserts, hotels, cinemas, theatres, plural names of countries, island groups, regions
e when talking about a whole species: • *the African elephant*

No article is used when talking about continents, most countries, towns, streets, etc. (except *the High Street*), lakes, and the main buildings of a particular town:
• *Kingston Town Hall*

The is not used with *most* except with the superlative:
• *most people* • *the most incredible sight*

B Correct the sentences if necessary. Tick any which are already correct.

1 Tony had always wanted to explore the foothills of Himalayas.

2 So when he was offered an early retirement package by his firm, he decided to take advantage of the opportunity.

3 First he needed to get really fit, so he spent a month training in Lake District.

4 When he could run up Buttermere Fell without stopping, he considered he was ready.

5 He booked a trip with a well-known trekking company and flew out to the Kathmandu, the capital of Nepal.

6 His group were planning to trek in Annapurna region, but unfortunately Nepalese were beginning to get worried about the amount of damage being done to their ancient mountains by the constant pummelling of climbers' feet.

7 So they temporarily suspended permission for foreigners to climb or use the footpaths in the area.

8 Group leader was very apologetic, but he laid on rafting on River Trisuli and sightseeing in the capital.

9 After a few days, the authorities lifted their ban, and Tony was able to trek through some of world's most beautiful scenery, with breathtaking views of the Mount Everest and Kanchenjunga.

10 At night, group were accommodated in the simple village rooms and ate with Nepalese.

11 Most of group were more experienced trekkers than Tony, and several of them had visited Himalayas before.

12 All in all, Tony reckoned it was most exciting experience he'd ever had, and vowed to return to the Nepal at very first opportunity.

The indefinite article **a/an** cannot be used with uncountable nouns. Most nouns in English are either countable or uncountable, but the following may be used countably or uncountably:
- *cold, country, taste, wine, coffee, tea, cake, cheese, work, hair, life, death*

C Decide whether the nouns in *italics* are being used countably (C) or uncountably (U).

1 I'll have a *coffee* while I sort my papers out.
2 It's a matter of *life* and *death*.
3 They've always dreamed of living in the *country*.
4 Celebrities and critics flooded into the West End to see Harold Pinter's latest *work*.
5 I like a bit of *cheese* after my main course.
6 The reason he's so bogged down at *work* is that he's had a heavy *cold* for the last fortnight.
7 His *death* came as a terrible shock to his colleagues.
8 She's furnished the flat with such *taste*, hasn't she!

Note especially these **uncountable nouns**:
- *furniture, luggage, news, information, progress, knowledge, research, advice*

Many and **(a) few** are used with countables, **much** and **(a) little** with uncountables.

D Match the two halves of the sentences correctly.

1 Scientists have made little
2 It is doubtful whether we have enough
3 I don't suppose there are many
4 I can guarantee he'll give you some
5 The examiner asked both
6 I had to check every
7 I was hoping you could let me have a
8 She's so well-groomed – she never has a
9 He hasn't got much
10 Could you let me know if there's any

A spanner, if I promise to return it tomorrow.
B applicants for that job, are there?
C news about my sister?
D progress into their research into the common cold.
E natural gas for the next fifty years.
F the candidates to sit down.
G excellent advice.
H hair out of place.
I single connection, before I found the fault.
J luggage, has he?

Present tenses

The present simple is used

a to express what happens habitually or regularly:
  • *I go to Italy every summer.*
b to describe facts that are always or usually true:
  • *That road leads to Oxford.*
c to describe natural and scientific laws.
d with verbs that do not normally take the continuous form, such as *dislike, appear, belong, understand.*
  There is a list of these verbs in **Section 1** of the Appendix.
e in the **if** clause of the first conditional.
f with **if** and **when** for parallel facts and conditions:
  • *When you turn the key, the engine starts.*
g for explanations and instructions.
h to describe the sequence of events in a film, play or book.
i for headlines in a newspaper.

(For the future use of the present simple, see **Unit 4**.)

A Match the different uses of the present simple with the categories in the study box above.

1 Local girl wins national contest

2 First you turn the dial, then you press the ignition switch ...

3 The hero meets a girl in a café, falls in love with her and ...

4 We usually take part in the general knowledge quiz on Fridays.

5 It appears that there was some mistake in the information we received.

6 The earth revolves around the sun.

7 Traffic flows much better outside rush hours.

8 If he saves up, he'll soon be able to afford a new computer.

9 The great monastery library now belongs to the state.

10 When you hear the police siren, you slow down and pull in, to allow emergency vehicles to pass.

11 Fisherman finds treasure trove

12 Wood floats on water.

13 Now that he's retired, he watches football every afternoon on satellite TV.

14 I understand that none of the children actually qualified for the award.

15 You separate the eggs, then whip the whites until they're stiff.

16 If you cry wolf too often, people don't pay attention when you really need help.

The present continuous is used

a to refer to what is happening now. Key words: **at the moment, at present, now, currently, today, this week**.

b to describe a repeated action, sometimes with annoyance:
  • *She's always criticising other people!*

c to talk about a temporary habit:
  • *He's smoking a lot these days.*

d to give a running commentary on an event:
  • *Look, the door's opening ...*

(For the future use of the present continuous, see **Unit 4**.)

B Correct the sentences if necessary. Tick any which are already correct.

1 I'm always forgetting to set the alarm.

2 It sounds a marvellous idea.

3 She's studying hard for her exams at the moment.

4 Are you understanding what the lecturer said?

5 I'm thinking that they made a mistake.

6 I'm seeing my friend Jean tonight.

7 The police aren't knowing why he came here.

8 He's constantly leaving his papers all over the place.

9 She jogs around the park three times a week.

10 He commutes to Paris every day this week.

C Decide whether to use the present simple or the present continuous in these sentences.

1 You (look) very worried. What you (think) about?

2 Listen, he (climb) the stairs! What he (do) now? He (ring) the bell!

3 Thank goodness Barbara (take) more exercise these days! She (seem) much fitter, you (not think)?

4 When water (boil), it (give off) steam.

5 Alex never (break) a promise or (let down) a friend.

6 The house (stand) on its own, on a hill that (overlook) the park.

7 I (know) her husband (look for) a new job at the moment, but I (not suppose) he will find one quickly.

8 When you (heat) the pan, the fat (begin) to sizzle.

9 The Foreign Ministers of several EU countries currently (meet) in Luxembourg, where they (attempt) to negotiate a solution.

10 He always (spill) coffee on his shirt! It (make) me furious!

11 At weekends she frequently (drive) up to her mother's in Liverpool, and (spend) an evening with her sister on the way back.

12 I'm a bit worried about Greg. He (work) too hard in his present job. He really (need) a holiday.

The **present perfect** is used to refer to

a actions in a period of time which is not yet finished.
Key words: **already**, **yet**, **so far**, **up to now**, **for** (a period of time), **since** (a fixed point in time), **ever**, **before**.
b actions in the recent past where the time is not known or not important. Key words: **just**, **recently**, **lately**.
c actions in the recent past with an effect on the present.
d habitual actions which started in the past and are still going on.
e states which began in the past and are continuing.
It is also used
f with verbs that do not normally take the continuous form (see above).

It does not make sense to use the **present perfect** with an adverb of finished time, such as **yesterday**, **last week**, **in 1924**.

The **present perfect continuous** is used to stress that
a a present perfect action is continuing.
b the action is very recent.
c the action has a result in the present.

It is not used with clearly defined, completed or quantified activities:
• *I've written ten letters so far this morning.*
Compare: *I've been writing letters all morning.*

D Correct the sentences if necessary. Tick any which are already correct.

1 I am studying English here since August.
2 I've interviewed five applicants and it's still only 11.30!
3 We have met several fascinating people at the conference last week.
4 Once upon a time a beautiful princess has lived in a castle ...
5 Have you ever read any of Hemingway's novels?
6 I've been owning this answerphone for three years.
7 They haven't been selling all the tickets for the Cup Final yet.
8 My friends are married for a long time now.
9 I haven't been feeling at all well lately.
10 A light plane has been crashing in the French Alps.
11 I've already been speaking to the delegates three times.
12 A barrister in a case which is being heard at the High Court in London has accused the authorities of negligence.

E Complete the following sentences with *for* or *since*, and the correct form of the verb in brackets.

1 I (not have) time to do any typing _____ Monday.
2 Nobody (hear) from Amanda _____ she went to the Seychelles.
3 She (wear) the same old clothes _____ a week.
4 He (not ride) a bike _____ 1970.
5 I don't think I (see) you _____ the sales conference.
6 It (not snow) here _____ ages.
7 They (live) in that house _____ it was built.
8 My neighbour (not speak) to me _____ more than two years.
9 I (not buy) a new battery _____ last year.
10 She (wait) for you _____ an hour and a half.

Modal verbs

The verbs **will**, **would**, **shall**, **should**, **can**, **could**, **may**, **might**, **must**, **ought to** and **used to** are called modal verbs, because they convey a particular meaning or mood. Modal verbs have some important grammatical features.

1 Apart from **can** and **could** they do not have past or future forms, or use any auxiliary verb (e.g. **do/did**) either to make a question or a negative:

- *Will she be there?* • *I couldn't help it.*

An exception to this is **used to**, which often takes **did** as an alternative auxiliary:
- *Did you use to be good at maths?* • *Used you to be good at maths?*

2 Modal verbs (except **ought to** and **used to**) take the infinitive without **to**:
- *They can't have arrived yet.*
- *You must have seen her.*
(See **Unit 7** for the different infinitive forms.)

An alternative to **can** is **be able to**, which is used for all tenses:
- *They'll be able to book the tickets soon.*
Could is used as the past simple or conditional of **can**.

An alternative to **must** is **have to**, which is used for all tenses:
- *Surely you didn't have to pay!*
See the study boxes below for differences in meaning of these verbs.

Note the short forms **will not ~ won't**, **shall not ~ shan't**, **cannot ~ can't**.

Dare and **need** can be used either as normal verbs:
- *I didn't dare (to) mention it.*
- *He doesn't need to borrow any money.*
or as modal verbs: • *She daren't tell him the truth.* • *You needn't cry.*

See the study box below for the different uses of **need**.

A Complete the sentences with the correct verb from the box.

will	dare	may	be able	ought	should	used	have

1 How _____ you speak to me like that?

2 He really _____ admit that he is to blame for the whole affair.

3 When she was younger, she never _____ to wear make-up.

4 _____ I use your phone, please?

5 Do you think he'll _____ to come up with the money in time?

6 Steel yourself – it's just possible you might _____ to pay a heavy fine.

7 The authorities _____ to have investigated the incident more thoroughly.

8 There's every likelihood our candidate _____ win the election.

B Correct the sentences if necessary. Tick any which are already correct.

1 Did you must renew your visa last February?
2 Your accountant ought to have give you better advice.
3 The President can't to be re-elected for a fourth term.
4 You could come on the expedition if you wanted to.
5 I might had returned the book. I just can't remember.
6 Will you can help me with my luggage if I tell you exactly when I'm leaving?
7 They didn't could have a picnic because of the inclement weather.
8 The police must have preferred charges against him by now.

Must/mustn't are used

a to express commands or the authority of the speaker:
  • *You must do what I say in future.*

b to express an internal obligation, from the speaker's viewpoint:
  • *I mustn't forget to phone Jake this evening.*

Have got to can be used in all tenses instead of **must** to express external obligation, especially rules or laws made by someone else:
• *We've got to check in at least an hour before take-off.*

The modal form **needn't** is usually used to express the speaker's own opinion or viewpoint: • *You needn't phone me unless there's any problem.*

Don't need to is less personal and is usually used to express lack of external obligation: • *If you're a UK citizen, you don't need to have a work permit.*

Didn't need to do and **didn't have to do** mean that something was not done, because it was not necessary.
Needn't have done means that something was done, although it was not necessary.

C Complete the sentences, using the correct word or phrase from the pair in brackets.

1 You _____ take flowers to your hostess if you don't want to. (mustn't / needn't)
2 She _____ do all the work herself, because nobody will help her. (must / has to)
3 I'm so tired, I really _____ go to bed now. (must / have to)
4 What a pity you _____ go now! You'll just catch your train if you hurry. (must / have to)
5 Yesterday all the students _____ read a poem aloud. (must / had to)
6 I was going to book the tickets, but Angus bought them on his way home, so I _____. (didn't need to / needn't have done)
7 When I turned up at the hospital and saw Natalia surrounded by visitors, I realised I _____ coming. (didn't need to bother / needn't have bothered)
8 You _____ smoke in here. It's against the rules. (mustn't / needn't)

> **Should/shouldn't** and **ought to/oughtn't to** are both used
>
> **a** to express the idea of duty or strong advice. **Should** gives the speaker's subjective opinion, whereas **ought to** is a little more forceful, based on objective considerations.
>
> Other uses of **should** are
>
> **b** instead of **would** in formal writing:
> - *I should be glad to hear from you as soon as possible.*
>
> **c** to convey an assumption:
> - *Jane should have arrived at the office by now.*
>
> **d** as a formal or literary alternative to an **if** clause:
> - *Should the star be ill, the concert will be cancelled.*
> to express a remote possibility with an **if** clause:
> - *If they should ever ask about it, tell them the truth.*
> and after **in case**:
> - *We'll hide, in case they should see us.*
>
> **e** to make a suggestion or a request for advice:
> - *What should I wear to the wedding?*
>
> **f** after **so that**, **in order that**, verbs like **command**, **insist**, **suggest**, and adjectives like **vital**, **essential**, **necessary**, **anxious**, to show that something must be done: • *I'm anxious that he should feel at home.*

D Match the different uses of *should* with the categories in the study box above.

1 Should there be any difficulty, ring me at home.
2 Do you think I should put in an application or not?
3 I took a book with me, in case I should have to wait.
4 The irate customer insisted that the manager should apologise.
5 By this time my brother should be at the station.
6 You really should start planning for your future.
7 If anyone should inquire, kindly take their name and address.
8 It's essential that this should be kept in the strictest confidence.

> **Could** is used to express general ability in the past:
> - *I could read when I was three.*
>
> For an achievement on a particular occasion in the past, **was able to/managed to/succeeded in** are used instead:
> - *How many letters were you able to write last night?*
>
> **Couldn't** is used for both general and particular ability.
>
> **Used to** and **would** are both used to talk about past habits. **Used to** is used for situations and actions, whereas **would** only refers to repeated actions:
> - *I used to have a guinea-pig when I was younger.*
> - *Lisa would always eat porridge for breakfast.*

E Match the two halves of the sentences correctly.

1 My grandmother would
2 She never used
3 But she could cook
4 Somehow she was able to
5 We all wondered how
6 The only thing she couldn't
7 She'd get
8 But she always managed

A better than anyone else.
B very angry every time it curdled.
C produce a wonderful meal every time.
D select vegetables carefully at the market.
E make was yoghurt.
F to use it up in a cake.
G to consult any recipes.
H she managed it.

F Complete the sentences with *could*, *couldn't*, *was/were able to*, *used to*, or *would*.

1 Unfortunately my cousin _____ see his solicitor that day, as no appointment had been made.
2 When I was a child, I _____ always take the same route to school and back.
3 The boy next door _____ swim when he was five, but he never learnt to sail.
4 In the past people _____ have larger families than they do nowadays.
5 Stephen had to give up half-way round, and _____ finish the marathon.
6 Despite the thunderstorm we _____ climb right to the top of the mountain.
7 I sat on the terrace, drinking coffee. From there I _____ see the vineyards and the olive groves below me.

A **question tag** is composed of an auxiliary verb and a personal pronoun. If there is a modal verb in the main clause, we use this in the question tag:
• *They won't mind, will they?* • *He can swim, can't he?*

Remember that **will you?** is the usual question tag after a command, and **shall we?** after a suggestion with **Let's**.

G Complete the sentences with the correct question tag.

1 We can't see him yet, _____?
2 I ought to pay now, _____?
3 Remember to lock up, _____?
4 You'd rather wait till next week, _____?
5 He must be there, _____?
6 It might rain tonight, _____?
7 They had to do it, _____?
8 Don't tell him about it, _____?
9 Let's have a picnic on the beach, _____?
10 You love him very much, _____?
11 I'd better not say anything, _____?
12 We could stay overnight, _____?

The future

The future simple is used

a in the main clause of a first conditional sentence:
  • *If she passes the test, she'll go up to the next class.*
  But **will** is not normally used in the *if* clause.

b for predictions after certain verbs like **think** , **expect**, **wonder** and **hope**, and after certain adverbs like **probably** and **perhaps**:
  • *I think it'll stay fine for the race.* • *I hope he'll stay in touch.*

c for instant decisions or spontaneous reactions: • *I'll just answer the phone.*

d for offers of help: • *I'll give you a hand, if you like.*

e for promises: • *Believe me, I'll never do it again.*

f for invitations and polite requests: • *Will you come to the theatre with me?*

Except in questions, **will/will not** are usually contracted to **'ll/won't** in spoken English. **Shall** is used mainly in questions with **I/we** to express offers of help, suggestions or requests for advice: • *Shall I give you a lift?* • *Shall we go swimming?*

Avoid using the **future simple** in any situations other than those described above.

A Match the category on the left with the correct sentence on the right.

1	prediction	A	Honestly, I'll work very hard.
2	promise	B	I'm pretty sure he'll win.
3	first conditional	C	Unless it's cheap, I won't buy it.
4	quick reaction	D	Shall we wash up for you?
5	polite request	E	I'll answer the door.
6	offer of help	F	Will you hold the door open, please?

Will is not used after conjunctions of time, such as **after**, **before**, **until**, **when**, **as soon as**. Instead, a present tense is used:
  • *I'll ring you as soon as I find out.* • *He'll turn up before we've finished.*

B Put *shall*, *will* or *won't* correctly into the sentences. Tick any phrases or sentences which are already correct.

1 I'm afraid I _____ be able to attend the wedding.
2 He _____ interview you as soon as you _____ arrive.
3 _____ we try the chicken supreme or the steak pie?
4 There _____ be a lot of trouble when the staff _____ find out!
5 By the way, _____ you please take notes?
6 _____ I change your library books for you?
7 Don't worry, you _____ have to stay for the whole session.
8 Make sure you _____ put the rubbish out before you _____ leave.
9 If I _____ see her, I _____ give her your love.

The present simple is used to talk about timetables, programmes of events and people's schedules:
- *What time does your train leave?* • *The President arrives at 9.30.*

The present continuous is used to talk about planned future arrangements:
- *Tomorrow I'm flying to Hong Kong.*

A future time-phrase should be used or understood, to prevent confusion with the present uses of this tense.

Going to is used to talk about
a firm intentions: • *I'm going to be an actor when I grow up.*
b predictions based on something in the present: • *Look! He's going to fall!*

The future continuous refers to a continuous action which will be happening at a future point in time:
- *I'll be playing football on Saturday afternoon.*

The future perfect is used to talk about an action which will have happened by a certain point in the future. **By** is often a key word:
- *He'll have finished his exams by Friday week.*

The future perfect continuous is used similarly to the future perfect, but stresses that the action is continuous, or not completed:
- *By the end of May we'll have been living here for three years.*

Remember that many verbs do not have a continuous form; refer to the list in **Section 1** of the Appendix for guidance.

C Correct the sentences if necessary. Tick any which are already correct.

1 What time does your badminton class start?
2 'What will you do tonight?' 'Oh, we will have a barbecue.'
3 By this time next week I'm filling in my tax forms.
4 I promise I'm supporting you whenever you will need me.
5 You won't see him this summer. He'll do his military service then.
6 I'm being an architect when I'm finishing my studies.
7 Don't get up. I'll make the coffee.
8 Do you come to dinner with me tonight?
9 I think he shall probably marry the girl next door.
10 What do you do at 3 o'clock next Sunday afternoon?

D Complete the sentences with the most suitable verb form.

1 If you (not object) we (ask) the committee to approve the proposal.
2 By the time Juan (finish) his maths project next week, he (be) exhausted!
3 What our world (be like) in the year 2050?
4 Anne (not be) happy until she (see) the doctor this afternoon.
5 This time next year I probably (live) on the other side of the world.
6 I (not watch) the horror film that's on tonight. I know it (give) me nightmares.
7 By the end of this week we (raise) over £800 for the children's charity.
8 I swear I (do) my best from now on. Things (be) different, you (see).

UNIT 5

Recycling

A Choose the correct word or phrase to complete each sentence. Write the letter in the space.

1 Despite playing under strength, the village team _____ beat their rivals.

a) could   b) were able to   c) couldn't   d) weren't able to

2 She had to do the shopping for her neighbour, _____ she?

a) didn't   b) hadn't   c) does   d) isn't

3 He daren't _____ his boss for a rise just now.

a) asking   b) be asking   c) to ask   d) ask

4 I'll hand over all my files to my assistant before I _____.

a) am leaving   b) leave   c) will leave   d) shall leave

5 By the time Bernard's daughter graduates, _____ retired.

a) he   b) he has   c) he'll being   d) he'll have

6 How long has the property _____ to your family?

a) belonged   b) belonging   c) belongs   d) been belonging

7 Buy me a newspaper on your way back, _____?

a) do you   b) will you   c) have you   d) don't you

8 The noise was so loud that we all _____ wear ear-protectors.

a) must   b) have to   c) should   d) had to

9 This time next year _____ chief translator to the French UN delegation.

a) he is   b) he'll being   c) he'll be   d) he's being

10 It is essential that all top security documents _____ be stamped CONFIDENTIAL.

a) should   b) must   c) will   d) may

11 I suggest Andrea _____ in touch with the organisers.

a) should get   b) to get   c) getting   d) should getting

12 According to _____ surveys, the majority of Britons are in favour of the monarchy.

a) the most   b) most   c) most of   d) the most of

13 The four men who successfully retraced Sir Ernest Shackleton's open-boat voyage across _____ Ocean are resting on South Georgia.

a) Southern   b) a Southern   c) the   d) the Southern

14 You _____ continue. You've made your point clearly enough already.

a) needn't   b) mustn't   c) don't have   d) won't

15 Let's get the house cleared up before he _____.

a) is arriving   b) arrives   c) will arrive   d) arrived

16 In my opinion, the government should _____ action.

a) to take   b) taking   c) take   d) have take

17 Since 1997 my department's work _____ built up considerably.

a) was   b) have   c) is   d) has

18 The bill had already been paid, so I _____ to do it.

    a) hadn't   b) didn't need   c) needn't   d) haven't

19 Only _____ research has been carried out in this field.

    a) a little   b) a few   c) few   d) not much

20 It's 4 p.m. Marc _____ have arrived in Istanbul by now.

    a) would   b) can   c) should   d) ought

21 If Molly _____ to her guns, she'll probably get what she wants.

    a) will stick   b) would stick   c) stuck   d) sticks

22 By December Tim _____ enough to buy a mountain bike.

    a) saves   b) will have saved   c) has saved   d) will be saving

23 _____ anyone object, the plan will be reconsidered.

    a) If   b) Do   c) Should   d) Might

B Complete the text by putting **one** word in each space. The main focus of this task is on grammar rather than vocabulary.

Chile 1) _____ over a hundred potentially active volcanoes. Several teams of international geology experts have 2) _____ collaborating with Chilean colleagues on two of 3) _____ most interesting, known 4) _____ Lascar and Sollipulli. A recent study of Lascar has shown that glaciation seems 5) _____ have had 6) _____ important influence on its eruptions. When the ice retreated at the end of 7) _____ Ice Age 20,000 to 15,000 years ago, Lascar suffered 8) _____ most violent eruption. Scientists hope that further study of this volcano 9) _____ produce valuable data leading to some definite conclusions.

A British team 10) _____ led the investigations into the Sollipulli volcano, where 11) _____ glacier fills the main depression. At 12) _____ moment the ice cap 13) _____ melting at a rate of about 5 cm a day. This 14) _____ indicate a high risk factor for the surrounding countryside, as the ice cover normally plays a useful role 15) _____ preventing the violent release of volcanic gases 16) _____ cause explosive eruptions. 17) _____ the ice cap continues retreating, the volcano is very likely to erupt. This is a serious threat to the rich agricultural lands and tourist areas which 18) _____ Sollipulli.

Work is 19) _____ on both volcanoes, as, fortunately, the teams 20) _____ received a guarantee of international funding for further study for the next two years.

C Think of **one** word only which can be used appropriately in all three sentences in each group.

1 Having had a _____ of cruising last winter, he's been thoroughly bitten by the bug.

You know, this chicken has hardly any _____ at all!

She always dresses with such _____, doesn't she?

2 The club's best player seemed to have lost his _____, and was beaten by a junior.

I'm fine now, thanks – it was just a rather annoying _____ of flu.

Do keep in _____ once you get to Australia, won't you?

3 I _____ say that mobile phones will be superseded in due course.

Kim didn't _____ to move from her seat while the invigilator was watching her.

How _____ you threaten me like that!

4 The books dropped to the floor with a surprisingly _____ thud.

If you're found guilty, you'll have to pay a _____ fine.

Hazel had to drive through _____ rain on her way home.

5 The missing _____ of clothing was later discovered in the lost property cupboard.

I first read about McNulty's new film in a magazine _____.

The _____ is one of the parts of speech that cause most difficulty to students.

6 Jane has just _____ twenty, although you'd never think it to look at her.

As the evening wore on, the conversation _____ to football.

The milk in the pantry _____ rancid in the unaccustomed heat.

7 The opposition party _____ the government for an answer to their questions.

With great daring I _____ the button, and the machine started clicking and whirring.

Henry had to have his suit _____ at the hotel before attending the meeting.

8 You'll be able to _____ the audience's attention if your speech is lively enough.

I realise you're in agony, but just _____ on till the doctor gets here.

How many files is that drawer really supposed to _____?

Past tenses

The past simple is used

a for completed past actions at a known time. The time can be stated or understood: • *He bought his car last month.* • *She worked there as a teacher.*

b with **when**, enquiring about past time: • *When did you last see her?*

c for habitual past actions and states: • *She always wanted to be loved.*

d for a definite period of past time: • *They spent five years in York.*

The past continuous is used for

a continuous past actions sometimes interrupted by the past simple:
• *He was just getting into bed when the phone rang.*
or setting the scene for a story:
• *The sun was shining and the birds were singing as he walked down the lane.*

b simultaneous past actions: • *She was ironing while he was bathing the baby.*

c repeated past actions: • *I was always trying to save my pocket money.*

d past intentions, often not carried out:
• *She was planning to ring her friend, but she forgot.*

The past perfect is used for

a a past action that happened before a past simple action:
• *She had worked in Bonn before she moved to Stuttgart.*

b an action that happened before a stated time:
• *He had completed the work by tea-time.*

But if two past actions are close in time or closely connected, we often avoid the use of the past perfect:
• *When he reached the airport, he checked in immediately.*

The past perfect continuous is used to stress that a past perfect action was continuous or repeated. Remember that many verbs do not have a continuous form; refer to the list in **Section 1** of the Appendix for guidance.

A Complete the sentences with the correct past tense of the verb in brackets.

1 Helena (receive) hospital treatment for a year before the doctors finally (tell) her their diagnosis.

2 The party chairman only (make) a statement after there (be) a lot of speculation in the press.

3 Julia (try) several computer dating agencies by the time she (meet) and (fall in love) with George.

4 Sharon eventually (find) the job she (want) last year, although she (graduate) the year before.

5 The official I (ask) to speak to (not be) there. Apparently he (go) abroad on business.

6 When the doctor (arrive) at the scene of the accident, he (realise) the victim still (breathe).

7 The workmen (spend) all morning digging the trench, and by lunchtime they (finish) it.

8 When the ship (hit) the reef, most of the crew (play) cards, and the passengers (have) dinner.

9 It (rain) and (begin) to get very cold as I (set out) on my long walk home.

10 When she (be) a child, she always (want) to do the most dangerous things.

11 I suddenly (recognise) the town square. I (be) there ten years before.

12 When my friend (open) the door, I (feel) like hitting him. I (ring) his doorbell for at least twenty minutes!

13 When Oscar (go back) into the room, his colleagues still (quarrel) about the coffee.

14 I (not answer) the phone immediately, because I (try) to finish some work.

15 When you (get) your first job?

16 Between 1989 and 2000 they (work) in three different countries, and (move) house five times.

B Correct the sentences if necessary. Tick any which are already correct.

1 My aunt worked in London before she had moved to Norwich.

2 The lawyer had a nervous breakdown because he had been working for years without a break.

3 We were packing the cases while the removal men were loading the furniture into the van.

4 The judge had brought the trial to an end yesterday.

5 The writer spent most of his childhood in abject poverty.

6 Pierre was owning a sailing boat for several years.

7 The company thought of giving their assistant manager the sack, but he resigned.

8 He was delighted with his purchase. He had been saving up to buy the motorbike for months.

9 The Norwegians planted their flag at the summit just before the British team were arriving.

10 A police car was almost knocking me over as I had crossed the road.

11 When did you leave school and go to college?

12 'Who are they?' 'Oh, a group of students who had arrived in Oxford a week ago.'

13 The First World War ended in 1918.

14 Until he explained a second time, I didn't understand what he meant.

15 The mountain was seeming very high as the weary group started to plod uphill.

C Complete the text, which is about a turbulent period in British history, with the correct past tense of the verbs in brackets.

At the Battle of Bosworth in 1485, Henry Tudor (1 defeat) and (2 kill) the reigning English monarch, Richard III, and (3 be) subsequently crowned Henry VII. For the previous thirty years there (4 be) intermittent conflict between two great families, the houses of York and Lancaster. The Wars of the Roses, as they were known, (5 be) thus brought to an end, and Henry, leader of the Lancastrians, (6 aim) to unite the two warring houses by marrying Elizabeth of York. In order to flatter the new monarch, Tudor chroniclers (7 be) at pains to disparage his predecessor, and Richard (8 be) described as a malicious, vengeful usurper, who (9 murder) his innocent nephews two years before.

But did Richard III actually commit this heinous crime? All we know is that sometime in 1483 the two royal princes (10 disappear) from the grim and forbidding Tower of London while in his care. There (11 be) no bodies, there (12 be) no trail of blood, and not a shred of proof. But Richard (13 have) both the motive and the opportunity, and, suspiciously, he (14 seize) the throne even before their disappearance.

However, we know that Henry Tudor (15 want) the crown so much that in 1485 he (16 be) prepared to raise an army and fight for it. It is possible that it was he who (17 arrange) to eliminate the young princes well before the Battle of Bosworth, to give himself a smooth path towards the throne. If that was his plan, it certainly (18 succeed).

D Match these parts of sentences which use past tenses.

1 The little boy had already learnt to read

2 She was planning to finish her homework,

3 Our decorator had painted both garage doors

4 As soon as I saw a space,

5 The taxi had been waiting for twenty minutes

6 By the time the bell rang,

7 I was hoping to see the doctor,

8 When the manager told me the price,

9 She looked miserable, and I realised

10 When the twins were younger,

A I clinched the deal at once.

B but he'd been called away in an emergency.

C by the time he started school.

D she'd been crying into her soup the whole time.

E but then her friend came round and they got chatting.

F by the time the couple came out of the house.

G and put on a second coat by lunchtime yesterday.

H they were always trying to push the boundaries.

I none of us had finished the exam paper.

J I pulled over and parked.

Gerund and infinitive

The gerund (the **-ing** form used as a noun) is used

a as the subject of a sentence: • *Swimming is Dorothy's favourite sport.*

b after certain verbs, including most verbs of liking and disliking. See **Section 3** of the Appendix.

c after all prepositions, including adjective-plus-preposition phrases, and verb patterns ending in a preposition:
  • *I'm tired of not having a garden.*
  • *He drove off without looking in his rear mirror.*
  Remember that **to** has two uses. It can either be used with the infinitive:
  • *They want to pay the bill.*
  or it can be a preposition, in which case it is followed by the gerund:
  • *I'm looking forward to seeing them.* • *You'll soon get used to not drinking coffee.*
  Object to, **be/get used to**, **look forward to**, **in addition to** are all followed by a noun or gerund.

d after phrasal verbs: • *He went on peeling the potatoes.*

e after common expressions such as: **It's (not) worth, waste/spend time, burst out.**

In formal English, possessives (**my**, **her**, **their**, etc.) are used with the gerund:
• *I hope you don't mind my asking.*
but in informal English the pronouns **me, her, them** etc. are more common:
• *I hope you don't mind me asking.*

The passive gerund can be used:
• *I remember being teased by my classmates at boarding school.*

A Correct the sentences if necessary. Tick any which are already correct.

1 To take regular exercise is becoming quite a trend these days.
2 I don't mind to be interviewed in the street by market researchers.
3 Excuse my interrupting, but I can give you the directions you want.
4 Since he's been in Ireland, he's got used to driving on the left.
5 The company achieved its productivity target by offering incentives to the work-force.
6 You can go to sightsee in London from the top of a double-decker bus.
7 In addition to lose all my money, I realised my credit card had been stolen.
8 I can't stand him coughing and sneezing all over us. He should stay at home if he's got a cold.
9 It's no use to tell me all your problems. You'll have to see the student counsellor.
10 She burst out crying as soon as she saw our shocked faces.
11 Most cats enjoy be stroked.
12 I'm afraid I just can't face to go into the witness box and tell all those people what happened.

The infinitive has several forms.

to do: • *They hope to visit you.*
to be doing (for a continuous action):
• *It's nice to be leading such an exciting life.*
to have done (for a completed or past action):
• *We were sorry to have missed you.*
to have been doing (to stress the frequency or length of the action):
• *He appears to have been making phone calls from the office every day.*

For passive infinitives see **Unit 9**.

The infinitive is used with **to** after certain verbs, including **ought**, **have**, **used**, and **be able**. See **Section 4** of the Appendix.
Notice the position of **not** before **to**:
• *Try not to worry.* • *He's determined not to give in.*

The infinitive is used without **to** after most modal verbs, **would rather**, **had better**, **let**, ***make**, ***see**, ***hear**, ***feel**, **watch**, **notice**, ***help** (informally).
***If these verbs are used in the passive, the infinitive with **to** is used. Compare:
• *I saw her take the money.*
• *The champion was seen to shake hands with his opponent.*

Notice the very common **It is + adjective + to + infinitive**:
• *It is difficult to understand what you mean.* • *It was nice to see you.*

Also notice the construction **object + to + infinitive** after certain verbs:
• *I want you to enjoy yourselves.* • *She begged him not to go.*

The idea of purpose is usually expressed by **to + infinitive**, **in order to + infinitive** or **so as to + infinitive**:
• *He tiptoed upstairs so as not to wake the children.*

Notice: • *I have work to do.* • *Nobody is to blame.* • *The house is to let.*

B Correct the sentences if necessary. Tick any which are already correct.

1 They didn't ask that I leave early.

2 The army made him to complete his training course.

3 I hope to drop in on you next time I'm in the area.

4 Try to don't keep interrupting the speaker this time.

5 It's easier to learn a language in the country where it's spoken.

6 The doctor seems to have left a prescription here for you.

7 I was delighted to receive your most appreciative letter the other day.

8 In my view parents should not let their children to watch too much television.

9 He enrolled at a language school in Pisa for learn basic Italian.

10 It seems strange to be standing here, looking out at Sydney Harbour.

11 She didn't want that you go to all this trouble for her.

12 No wonder he was sacked! He seems to have been fiddling the accounts for years.

The following verbs can be used with either **the gerund or the infinitive**, depending on the meaning required:

a **remember**, **forget**, **stop**, **go on**, **regret**
b **interested in**, **interested to**
c **try**
d **need**
e **used**, **be/get used to**
f **like**, **enjoy**, **love**, **hate**, **prefer**
g **allow**, **advise**, **forbid**, **permit**
h **mean**.

The differences in meaning are explained in **Section 5** of the Appendix, but try to work them out for yourself before doing the next exercise.

C Complete the sentences with the gerund or the infinitive of the verbs in brackets.

1 Humility means (be) able to admit you're sometimes wrong.

2 You will not be permitted (enter) the building without the Chief Fire Officer's permission.

3 I'd be interested (know) if the chair in astrophysics is still vacant.

4 I'll never forget (see) the factory chimney collapse in a cloud of smoke and rubble.

5 Bankers advised the owners of the ailing theme park (reduce) entry charges in a bid to attract more visitors.

6 All the report's recommendations need (review) in the light of the committee's statements to the press.

7 The politician was accused of trying (stir up) trouble in his constituency as a ploy to divert attention from his own affairs.

8 I don't think my uncle will ever get used to (be) at home all day instead of (go) out to work.

D Match the first half of each sentence with the correct ending.

1 He objected
2 We'd rather not
3 She's looking forward
4 I insist on
5 Kindly allow me
6 I think you need
7 Everyone should be able
8 You'd better
9 I'm afraid it means
10 I always enjoy
11 He was made
12 She always used
13 His father wants him

A to write a polite letter.
B write a polite letter.
C to writing a polite letter.
D writing a polite letter.

Conditionals, wishes and regrets

The main linking words for conditional clauses are **if** and **unless**, but **even if**, **as/so long as**, **supposing**, **whether ... or**, **however** (+ adjective/determiner), **whoever**, **wherever**, **whenever**, etc., **providing/provided (that)**, **no matter who/how/when** etc. can also be used:

- *If they're short of money, they don't eat out.* (**zero conditional**)
- *You'll have a tussle with the management if you go ahead with that plan.* (**first conditional**, possible future action) Note that *if you should go ahead...* or *should you go ahead...* are more formal.

- *If they had a bigger garden, they could grow their own vegetables.* (**second conditional**, hypothetical but possible)
Similarly:
- *If you were to join the committee, we'd be very pleased.* Note that *Were you to join...* is more formal.
- *If you hadn't been late, you would have understood the lecture.* (**third conditional**, referring to a past situation)

There are also **mixed conditionals**:
- *If you hadn't been late, you'd know what we're talking about now.*

and a more formal version of the **third conditional**:
- *Had you arrived on time, you would have understood the lecture.*

A Complete the sentences with the correct tense of the verbs in brackets.

1 If you (make) a run for it, you'll catch the train.
2 If Laura (not eat) so much, she wouldn't have put on weight.
3 If they (have) their car serviced regularly, it never lets them down.
4 The earthquake would have caused less damage if the houses (be) of stronger construction.
5 If there (be) a good breeze on Sunday, we'll go hang-gliding.
6 You can get there more quickly if you (take) the short cut across the playing field.
7 If you (leave) the milk out of the fridge in this weather, it'll go off.
8 Would you contribute to the fund if I (ask) you?
9 If I (drop) Eve's vase, she'd have been furious.
10 If you (be) really my friend, you'd lend me the money.
11 Had the councillors been re-elected, your proposal (be) accepted.
12 Productivity will improve if manufacturing procedures (be) streamlined.
13 (Be) you to take out the relevant insurance policy, you would be completely covered.
14 No matter what (happen), I'll always stand by him!
15 Supposing the computer (break down), what would you do?
16 You can invite whoever you (like) to the barbecue.

B Complete the second sentence so that it means the same as the first one, using the word given. You must use between **three** and **eight** words, including the word given. (Contractions count as two words.)

1 Should you persist in your defiance of instructions, disciplinary action will be taken.

go

If you _____ disciplinary action.

2 If you changed your mind, you'd be welcome to join our staff.

change

Were you _____ delighted to have you on the staff.

3 If I find that what you've told me is true, I'll resign my post.

out

Should your information _____ in my resignation.

4 If he fails the final examination, he won't be able to graduate.

be

Unless he _____ unable to graduate.

5 Sally's dog wasn't muzzled, and so it bit the postman.

have

If Sally's dog _____ the postman.

6 Because the evidence was withheld, the prisoner was found guilty.

presented

Had the evidence _____ acquitted.

I wish/If only + past simple are used to express a wish or regret about a current situation, by imagining its opposite:
- *I wish (that) Mark knew about it.* • *If only Mark knew about it!*
  (Sadly, Mark doesn't know about it.)
Notice also:
- *I would rather Mark knew about it.* (a preference rather than a wish)
- *It's time (that) Mark knew about it.* (In my opinion he should.)

I wish/If only + would are used for a future wish – something we would like to happen:
- *If only Mark would come back!* (I'm afraid he won't.)
- *I wish you'd stop doing that.* (You're annoying me.)

I wish/If only + past perfect are used for a past wish or regret:
- *I wish someone had told Mark about it.*

Note that we use **could** instead of **would** with **wish** when the subject pronouns are the same:
- *I wish I could see him.* (NOT *I wish I would see him.*)

Were is often used instead of **was** after **wish** and **If only**:
- *I wish Luke were here.*

As if/as though are often used in similar hypothetical situations:
- *Don't treat me as if I were a child.*
- *He spoke as though he had been insulted.*

C Match the correct wish or regret on the left with the situation on the right.

1 If only he would tell her!
2 I wish he had stayed.
3 If only we knew what to do!
4 I wish he had told her.
5 I wish we'd known what to do.
6 It's time he stopped smoking.
7 I'd rather he stayed.
8 If only he'd stopped smoking!

A It's a pity he didn't tell her.
B We have no idea what to do.
C We didn't know what to do.
D I'd like him to tell her.
E It's a pity he didn't stay.
F I'd like him to stay, if possible.
G I think he should stop smoking.
H He should have stopped smoking.

D Complete the sentences, using the correct tense of the verb in brackets.

1 No matter how many people (come) tonight, we'll have a great time!
2 He looked at me as if I (just land) from the moon.
3 Supposing she (not agree), what would you do next?
4 However late you (be), there'll be a warm welcome for you.
5 Wherever they (end up), I'm sure they'll be happy.
6 It seemed as though nobody (spot) the obvious flaw in the plan.
7 We'll go along with the deal, provided we (receive) our fair share of the profits.
8 I wish the firm (not go) bankrupt, but the shares would still have been worthless.
9 Supposing the police (not come), what would you have done?
10 I'd be on your side even if you (not be) my friend.
11 He stared at me. It was as if he (not hear) a word I'd said.
12 However difficult you (find) the test, just try to complete it.

E Make a new sentence for each situation, starting with *I wish*.

1 What a pity he's so boring!
2 It was a mistake of mine, accepting that job.
3 How unfortunate that they all heard about it!
4 It'd be useful to have shares in the company, but I haven't any.
5 I'd like him to contribute his opinions more tactfully.
6 I should have gone to the conference.
7 I simply can't remember Myra's address.
8 Is it ever going to stop snowing?

UNIT 9

Passives

Passives are used whenever an action is more important than the agent – for example, in reporting the news or scientific experiments:
- *A woman has been arrested for the abduction of baby Emily Smith.*

The object of the active verb becomes the subject of the passive sentence, and the verb **be** is used in the correct tense with the past participle of the relevant verb. **By** + the **agent** is used only if it contributes important information:
- *Coastal buildings have been damaged by gales.*

Intransitive verbs, e.g. **arrive**, cannot become passive, because they have no object. Certain other verbs, e.g. **let**, **fit**, **lack**, **resemble**, **suit**, cannot normally become passive.

After modal verbs, **passive infinitives** are used (see **Unit 7**):
- *He ought to be arrested.*   • *You might have been killed.*

Passive -ing forms are possible:
- *She likes being driven to work.*   • *Having been fed, the dog went to sleep.*

A Complete the text with the correct passive form of the verbs in brackets.

An ingenious device like a bed of nails, which 1) _____ (originally use) by the great Carthaginian general Hannibal to restrain his elephants, is currently 2) _____ (put) to a similar use in the USA and parts of Britain. It 3) _____ (know) as the Stinger, and recently it 4) _____ (successfully deploy) in Greater Manchester and the Midlands. When a joyrider in a stolen vehicle 5) _____ (involve) in a police chase, the Stinger can 6) _____ (lay out) on the road in front of the speeding driver, bringing the car to an abrupt halt. Last week a car chase in Bolton, which had lasted 90 minutes, 7) _____ (end) in 30 seconds, when the fugitive's tyres 8) _____ (puncture) by the Stinger. It 9) _____ (establish) that this device saves police time and enables more joyriders to 10) _____ (catch), as well as reducing the length of dangerous high-speed chases.

B Follow the same instructions as for Exercise A.

In the mid-1990s the classical music world was rocked by what seemed a truly sensational discovery – six long-lost Haydn piano sonatas 1) _____ (find) in Germany. Apparently the sonatas 2) _____ (discover) by a music teacher called Winfried Michel at an elderly lady's home. Unfortunately, the manuscripts, which 3) _____ (pronounce) absolutely genuine by several eminent musicologists, 4) _____ (only make) available as photocopies, so no scientific tests could 5) _____ (carry out) in order to verify their authenticity. Music professionals 6) _____ (nevertheless throw) into a state of great excitement.

A prestigious recording of the sonatas 7) _____ (arrange) and authoritative articles on them 8) _____ (publish). It soon came to light, however, that the sonatas 9) _____ (compose) by none other than Winfried Michel himself. It is unclear whether they should 10) _____ (regard) as homage to a great composer or simply a forgery, albeit a very clever one.

Many verbs, like **give**, **award**, **lend**, can have two objects. When putting these verbs into the passive, it is more usual to make the 'person object', rather than the 'thing object', the subject of the passive verb:
• *I was given back my change.*   (NOT *My change was given back to me*).

C Improve the sentences if necessary by putting the 'person object' first. Tick any which are already correct.

1 I was promised a review of my case in due course.
2 The news was told to the whole community.
3 The survivors are being lent warm clothing.
4 She will be sent a free gift with her mail order catalogue.
5 A lucky mascot has been given to me, to use in my exams.
6 A postgraduate diploma will be awarded to her as soon as she has completed her practical assignments.
7 A chance to participate in the Olympic Games is being refused him, on the grounds of his unreliability.
8 However, he has been offered a place in the national team for the forthcoming international matches.
9 You will be shown your living quarters for the duration of your stay in the camp.
10 A bribe seems to have been offered to the officials in charge of the institution at the time.

Passive constructions are often used with verbs like **say**, **believe**, and **know**.

It + passive + that-clause:
• *It is said that three people died in the accident.*
• *It was once believed that the earth was completely flat.*

Subject + passive + to + infinitive:
• *Three people are said to have died in the accident.*
• *The earth was once believed to be completely flat.*

Sometimes there are two passive constructions in the same sentence:
• *It is known that York was invaded by the Vikings.*
• *York is known to have been invaded by the Vikings.*

Other verbs which are used in this way include: **consider**, **think**, **understand**, **report**, **allege**, **expect**, **fear**, **claim** and **deny**. The verb **be rumoured** only exists in the passive form.

See **Unit 7** for a list of infinitive forms.

D Complete the second sentence so that it means the same as the first one, using the word given. You must use between **three** and **six** words, including the word given. (Contractions count as two words.)

1 It is expected that tax increases will be announced in tomorrow's budget statement.

to

Tax increases _____ in tomorrow's budget statement.

2 We understand that inner-city crime rates are going up in most areas.

be

Inner-city crime rates _____ in most areas.

3 They say the rock star's wife has had at least two facelifts.

have

The rock star's wife _____ at least two facelifts.

4 We fear that nine crew members were lost overboard in the storm.

are

Nine crew members _____ overboard in the storm.

5 It was considered that Ralph's speech was one of the best.

to

Ralph's speech _____ one of the best.

6 We can't deny having made mistakes in the early stages.

that

It _____ made in the early stages.

7 Police reported that a man had been helping them with their inquiries.

was

A man _____ police with their inquiries.

8 The accused was alleged to have committed fraud.

had

It _____ committed fraud.

If **phrasal verbs or verbs with prepositions** become part of a passive sentence, they must not lose their particle:

• *The child was extremely well looked after.*

E Complete the sentences if necessary, by choosing the correct particle from the box. Tick any which are already correct.

up	down
in	away
out	off

1 What a mess! Sam's toys haven't been put.

2 He wasn't here last night. His bed hasn't been slept.

3 The situation is serious, but it'll have to be faced, I'm afraid.

4 This is the third time our meeting's been put.

5 All cigarettes must be extinguished before you enter the building.

6 The girls were brought on a farm near the Welsh border.

7 Cheques should be made to Wellingtons plc.

8 I must warn you that if you have anything to say, it'll be taken and may be used in evidence against you.

UNIT 10

Recycling

A Choose the correct word or phrase to complete each sentence. Write the letter in the space.

1 We regret _____ you that you have exceeded your overdraft facility.

   a) to inform   b) informing   c) to tell to   d) telling

2 Why don't you try _____ the key anti-clockwise?

   a) to turn   b) on turning   c) turning   d) turn

3 The company's apology _____ regarded as an exercise in damage limitation.

   a) were   b) was   c) would   d) had

4 We don't allow _____ in the classrooms.

   a) that people smoke   b) smoke   c) people to smoke
   d) to smoking

5 The accused denied _____ in the vicinity of the murder scene.

   a) to have ever been   b) have ever been   c) having been ever
   d) ever having been

6 Why don't you do what you're told, instead of _____ such a song and dance about it?

   a) to make   b) making   c) made   d) make

7 The children _____ to stay up late.

   a) don't allow   b) aren't let   c) aren't allowed   d) would rather

8 I rashly posted the parcel without _____ it.

   a) weighing   b) weigh   c) weighed   d) to weigh

9 I suppose you just went to the disco _____ improve your conversational skills!

   a) so as   b) for   c) in order to   d) too

10 He wasn't responsible. He wasn't _____.

   a) blame   b) to blame   c) blaming   d) for blame

11 What a dangerous thing to do! You _____ have been killed!

   a) may   b) can   c) must   d) might

12 For the rest of his life he lived in fear of _____ tracked down.

   a) having   b) be   c) being   d) been

13 All that rubbish will have to be _____ at once.

   a) get rid of   b) got rid of   c) got rid   d) getting rid of

14 You'll get a free month's subscription, _____ you renew your membership by the end of January.

   a) unless   b) however   c) were   d) provided

15 By the time I applied, all the holiday vouchers _____ used up.

   a) had been   b) have been   c) was   d) are

16 I felt as if I _____ a confidence.

   a) have betrayed   b) would betray   c) had betrayed
   d) am betraying

17 I wish I _____ more about the logistics of the expedition.

    a) would know   b) knew   c) know   d) can know

18 _____ bread is regarded by some as a therapeutic activity.

    a) To make   b) Made   c) Making   d) Having made

19 It's time she _____ promotion, in my view.

    a) get   b) got   c) will get   d) have got

20 The candidate _____ to have withdrawn her application.

    a) claimed   b) said   c) denied   d) reported

21 There's nothing I like more than _____ for a brisk walk along the seashore.

    a) go   b) out   c) walking   d) going

22 How can you waste all that money on _____?

    a) gamble   b) to gamble   c) gambling   d) the gamble

B Think of **one** word only which can be used appropriately in all three sentences in each group.

1 Can you please _____ that the children are in bed by seven.

I was very sorry I wasn't able to _____ Luke off at the airport.

The solution was obvious to me, but Jade just couldn't _____ it.

2 So long as you bring a group with you, you're allowed a _____ ticket.

When there's a _____ cubicle, I'll pop in and change, and then see you in the pool.

For a man with a large overdraft, he's surprisingly _____ with his money.

3 You'd better take a vote if you can't _____ a consensus.

The effects of environmental pollution will _____ right across the planet.

We've been trying to _____ Graham all day, but he's not answering his phone.

4 The Stinger device may help the police to _____ more joyriders.

If your body's resistance is low, you're more likely to _____ a cold.

Sorry, I didn't quite _____ what you said just then.

5 The manuscripts of the piano sonatas are not available in their original _____ .

A fine is a _____ of punishment for a minor offence.

Now Heather's moved to the local state school, she's in the same _____ as her cousin.

6 The theft of their savings _____ the Dodgson family into a panic.

At the second fence the horse reared up and _____ its rider.

Rushing to the controls, Will _____ a switch, and the engine juddered to a halt.

C Complete the text by putting **one** word in each space.

A central feature of 1) _____ 12th and 13th centuries in Europe was the concern of the great aristocratic families to ensure that their landed estates 2) _____ handed down intact to future generations. In 3) _____ to prevent their inheritance from 4) _____ divided, it 5) _____ traditional to insist that their younger sons 6) _____ remain unmarried. It was usual for the eldest son 7) _____ have his bride chosen for him, probably from another related noble family, and if the wife 8) _____ not 9) _____ in producing the male heir needed to carry on the line, she 10) _____ be discarded, and another bride would be chosen. 11) _____ potentially anarchic situation subsequently arose, 12) _____ loveless marriages on 13) _____ side, and rebellious bachelor knights on the other. 14) _____ social problem was brilliantly 15) _____ by the invention of courtly love, in which an unmarried knight 16) _____ swear eternal love, respect and obedience to a married lady. The energies of younger sons 17) _____ thus cleverly channelled into adventurous exploits and chivalrous deeds, all 18) _____ the sake of their noble lady. 19) _____ in all, courtly love went a long way 20) _____ palliating the internal contradictions of mediaeval aristocratic society.

D Complete the text by making a new word from each word given in capitals.

A LUCKY ESCAPE

Sergeant Bob Mann was one of the few 1) _____ of an ill-fated expedition to the wilds of Borneo. He has a SURVIVE

2) _____ tale to tell of his time there, and of the FASCINATE
medical 3) _____ he was given in a remote jungle TREAT
village. When a wound on his hand became

4) _____ infected, a local witch doctor plunged it DANGER
into a jar containing snake flesh and herbs. Although

this 5) _____ remedy may seem a little NATURE

6) _____ , it probably saved Bob from an unpleasant SCIENCE
death from gangrene. 7) _____ Bob made his way EVENT

out of the jungle, and since then he has made a full

8) _____ . Needless to say, he is extremely RECOVER

9) _____ of the help he received. However, it seems APPRECIATE
unlikely that snake flesh will be available on

10) _____ from pharmacies any time soon! PRESCRIBE

UNIT 11

Reported speech

When direct speech is changed into **reported speech**, with a reporting verb in the past, the verb tense, the pronouns and the time-phrase may all have to be changed to indicate the time shift to the past:

• *'We'll be getting married this year,'* he said. (direct speech)
  He says (that) they'll be getting married this year.
  (reported speech with a present reporting verb)
  He said (that) they would be getting married that year.
  (reported speech with a past reporting verb)

It is usually better style to use more precise **reporting verbs** than **say** or **tell** when turning (usually informal) direct statements into (usually more formal) reported ones. Examples are: **advise**, **apologise**, **congratulate**, **promise**, **remind**.

See **Section 6** of the Appendix for a complete list of these verbs and their different grammatical patterns.

A Match the direct speech on the left with the most appropriate reporting verb on the right.

B Now put the direct statements in Exercise A into reported speech, using the verbs you have chosen, and starting each sentence with *She*.

1	'I've had better marks than anyone else all term!'	A threaten
2	'You did it! I saw you! You stole my watch!'	B accuse
3	'If you don't give me your money, I'll hit you!'	C suggest
4	'I'm very sorry I didn't get round to writing earlier.'	D boast
5	'Why don't we all go for a drive in the country?'	E insist
6	'I must, I simply must see the manager at once!'	F estimate
7	'Please, please, don't tell anyone you've seen me!'	G beg
8	'That's right. Your flight's taking off at midnight.'	H apologise
9	'Don't forget to bring the binoculars, will you?'	I confirm
10	'I imagine Mexico City has about 20 million inhabitants by now, but I could be wrong.'	J remind

C Follow the instructions for Exercise A.

D Now follow the instructions for Exercise B, starting each sentence with *He*.

1	'It's five o'clock already, you know.'	A assure
2	'Yes, that's fine. I'll be able to help.'	B blame
3	'Don't worry, there'll be no difficulty, believe me.'	C deny
4	'How kind of you to bring me the flowers!'	D warn
5	'If I were you, I'd keep it under my hat.'	E admit
6	'.... and another thing, there'll be a 2% surcharge.'	F refuse
7	'I didn't do it! I didn't rob the old lady!'	G congratulate
8	'No, I'm afraid I'm not prepared to make a speech.'	H add
9	'Be careful when you cross the road, won't you?'	I point out
10	'Well done! You've passed the test first time!'	J advise
11	'I'm sure it was Charlotte who let us down.'	K thank
12	'Yes, it was my fault. I caused the accident.'	L agree

The modals **should**, **would**, **could**, **ought** and **might** do not change tense in reported speech, and neither do the **second** and **third conditionals**. With a reported second or third conditional, **that** is needed, and a comma is necessary to separate the two clauses if the **if** clause comes first:

* *He pointed out that if she had bought him a ticket, he could have seen the play too.*

E Turn the sentences into reported speech.

1 'If I had known, I'd have come earlier,' she said.
2 He said, 'Unless John tells the truth, somebody'll get hurt.'
3 'I really think you should join the tennis club this summer,' she said.
4 'If you practised more, you might be able to make a career out of music,' her teacher said.
5 'I wouldn't have had the accident if the brakes had been repaired properly,' he said.
6 'He'll be sent to prison if he commits a further offence,' said the magistrate.
7 'You can stay here as long as you like,' he said.
8 'I wish Bob would buy himself a new suit,' said Maggie.

Notice how **reported questions** are formed from the two types of direct question in English.

a questions starting with a question-word:
* *'When will you next be in Paris?'*
  He asked when she would next be in Paris. (NOT ... *when would she next be in Paris*)
* *'When does your plane take off?'*
  She asked when his plane took off.
Notice that no *do/did* auxiliaries are needed in reported speech, and that the word order is the same as in a statement.

b questions starting with a verb:
* *'Can you come tomorrow?'*
  She asked if/whether I could go the next day/the day after/the following day.
If/whether connect the reporting verb and this type of question.
If has no connection here with conditional **if**. **Whether** must be used before an infinitive: • *He was not sure whether to believe them.*
* *I didn't know whether to laugh or cry.*

F Correct the reported questions if necessary. Tick any which are already correct.

1 I asked how far was it to the station.
2 They wondered how many people lived in Tokyo.
3 She asked me unless I could do the shopping for her.
4 Her father asked her was what she had told him true.
5 The committee enquired whether she might accept the job.
6 The traffic warden asked why had I parked there.
7 I asked the old man what was his recipe for long life.

8 We wondered how did our neighbours manage to keep their garden so neat.

9 The officials asked him what did he want.

10 I only wanted to know where he had been for so long.

> **Reported requests or commands** usually involve the use of the **infinitive** with **to:**
> - *'Take that away!'*   *He told me to take it away.*
> - *'Please don't talk.'*   *She asked us not to talk.*
>
> Use **ask** for a polite request, **beg** for an earnest request, **instruct** or **tell** for a command, and **order** for an authoritative command:
> - *She ordered the children to sit down and be quiet.*

G Match the direct request or imperative on the left with its reported version on the right.

1	'Kindly stand back, would you!'	A	She asked us to stand back.
2	'Please don't cry!'	B	She ordered us to stand back.
3	'Leave the room now!'	C	He begged me not to cry.
4	'Would you mind opening the door?'	D	He told me not to cry.
5	'Stand back!'	E	He told me to leave the room immediately.
6	'You mustn't cry!'	F	He asked me to leave the room.
7	'Would you leave the room, please?'	G	She ordered me to open the door.
8	'Open the door!'	H	She asked me to open the door.

H Complete the second sentence so that it means the same as the first one, using the word given. You must use between **three** and **six** words, including the word given. (Contractions count as two words.)

1 'You've passed the exam? Oh, well done!' my aunt said to me.

on

My aunt _____ the exam.

2 'I'm sorry I forgot to set the security alarm,' said the receptionist.

for

The receptionist _____ set the security alarm.

3 'Why don't you postpone your trip till the autumn, Jim?' suggested Sarah.

off

Sarah suggested _____ trip till the autumn.

4 'Don't forget to enclose a cheque, will you?' the clerk said to me.

in

The clerk reminded _____ the envelope.

5 'It's a good idea to rehearse your speech in front of a mirror,' George told me.

run

George advised _____ in front of a mirror.

Linking words and discourse markers

The main linking words expressing **concession and contrast** are **despite, in spite of, however, although, even though, much as, as/though** (after adjectives), **but, yet, all the same, even so, nevertheless**.

Despite and **in spite of** can only be followed by a noun or gerund:
• *In spite of having a fax machine, he couldn't send the documents.*
The alternative construction is **in spite of/despite the fact that**:
• *She married him, in spite of the fact that he treated her badly.*
All the other conjunctions and connectors are followed by a verb clause.

Note how **as** and **though** are used after adjectives:
• *Intelligent though she is, I don't think she'll win the competition.*
• *Brave as he was, the soldier dreaded the onset of battle.*

Although, **even though** and **much as** can come at the beginning of the sentence or introduce the second or additional clause:
• *Much as I enjoy his company, I don't want him here the whole time.*

But and **yet** normally introduce the second or additional clause:
• *She's charming, yet there's something a little odd about her.*

All the same, **even so**, **nevertheless** and **however** all need a comma or commas to separate them from the rest of the sentence:
• *He decided to go, all the same.*   • *All the same, he decided to go.*

However is a more formal alternative to **but**. It is rarely used in spoken English:
• *Klaus was a loyal friend. However, she found him irritating at times.*

A Correct the sentences if necessary. Tick any which are already correct.

1 In spite of he revised hard for his exams, he didn't pass.
2 Much as I approve of her enthusiasm, I'm worried she'll overdo her weight training.
3 He doesn't all the same know what he's talking about.
4 She would love the opportunity, although it seems unlikely at the moment.
5 There are no grants available. Nevertheless, you may be awarded a scholarship.
6 My first reaction was one of distaste, yet there was an element of humour in the situation.
7 Despite his extended illness, he managed to complete his doctoral dissertation.
8 Quiet this spot seems now though, you ought to see it when the tourists are here in August!
9 'Try a bit harder!' 'However I don't want to!'
10 I can't accept, but it's very kind of you to offer, all the same.

11 Even though your lack of agreement, you must admit it's a strong case.

12 Even so his creditors are baying for satisfaction, he has just bought a BMW!

The main linking words expressing **cause** are **as**, **since**, **because**, **participles** (see **Unit 18**) and **adjectives** like *aware*, *distraught*, *horrified* which express feelings that would cause certain behaviour:

- *As I hadn't had time for lunch, I bought a sandwich.*
- *Realising that no one would help him, he abandoned the idea.*
- *Suddenly aware of the pain, she keeled over on the ground.*
- *Distraught that Susan had rejected him, Toby rushed wildly out of the room.*

Notice that **as**, **since**, and **because** are followed by a verb clause, **participles** by a verb clause with **that**, and **adjectives** either by a preposition + noun or by a verb clause with **that**.

For is a more formal alternative to **but**. It is not normally used in spoken English, and cannot be used to begin a sentence.

On account of, **due to**, **owing to** and **because of** are followed by a noun or gerund:

- *Stevenson moved to the South Seas because of the climate.*

B Use these words to complete the sentences. Do not use any word more than once.

disgusted	because	for	horrified	deprived	told
surprised	embarrassed	sad	alone	due	aware

1 Gillian blushed, _____ that she might have embarrassed him.

2 _____ of sweets in his childhood, Antonio had fortunately never acquired a sweet tooth.

3 _____ again in her tiny room, Lucy couldn't help crying a little.

4 _____ it could publish any late news in its evening edition, the local paper had an advantage over its competitors.

5 _____ at the thought of missing the party, Sandra tried to cheer herself up by watching a video.

6 The toddler was crying bitterly, _____ he'd lost his mother.

7 _____ to hear the unexpected news, Peggy phoned her mother and told her immediately.

8 _____ to wait until he was needed, the boy sat down and watched the rest of his team play.

9 _____ at the catastrophe, the onlookers panicked and fled.

10 _____ to serious problems with the track, trains to Manchester Victoria will not be running until further notice.

11 _____ by the attention they were receiving, the boys tried to creep out of the room.

12 _____ by the mess, the residents set to work to clear it up before it became a health hazard.

The main linking words expressing **result** are **therefore, consequently, as a result, (and) so, so that, so ... that, such ... that, enough,** and **too ... (for someone) to** + infinitive. **As a result of** comes before a noun or gerund.

Such can be used with a noun, or an adjective + noun:
- *It was such a nice day/such nice weather that we went out.*
- *It was such a surprise for Percy!*

So ... that is used with an adjective or adverb, and also with **much, little, many, few** + noun:
- *He talks so fast that you can't understand him.*
- *We had so little time that we didn't manage to see everyone.*

Enough comes before a noun but after an adjective or adverb:
- *There wasn't enough time to see him.* • *He isn't old enough to join the navy.*

C Rewrite the sentences, using *too* or *enough*.

1 The matter is so important that you should deal with it yourself.
2 She didn't study much, so she didn't pass the end-of-term test.
3 The door was so narrow that we couldn't squeeze through.
4 She had so little energy that she couldn't keep going all day.
5 The leisure centre is so inaccessible that hardly any tourists find it.

D Rewrite the sentences using *so* or *such ... that.*

1 They had very little money, and couldn't afford to run a car.
2 There was a lot of food. We could have fed ten hungry men with it!
3 You're a really experienced worker, so you should know what to do.
4 He hasn't had much acting experience, so we can't give him the part.
5 I draw very badly, so I can't do a very good sketch map.

In case is used to explain precautions or things done in advance. It is followed by a present or past tense, or (less often) by **should** (see **Unit 3**):
- *I'll take an umbrella in case it rains.*
- *I took an umbrella in case it rained/should rain.*

DO NOT use **will** or **would** after **in case**.

E Complete the sentences with the correct tense of the verb in brackets.

1 I went on a first aid course, in case I ever (need) to know about it.
2 Take your money with you in case you (see) any good souvenirs to buy.
3 I always pack my shorts in case the weather (be) fine.
4 I've been looking for her everywhere, in case she (get lost).
5 I think I'll lock my briefcase in the boot in case someone (spot) it and (try) to break into the car.
6 He was planning to work out every day, in case he (be select) for the match.
7 I'm looking for other jobs, in case I (not get) this one.

Discourse markers are words or phrases which play an important part in the structure of a spoken or written text by signposting the logical progression of ideas. They may do this by:

a referring the listener or reader back to previous events or statements:
- *following the incident, in such circumstances, at that time, hitherto, be that as it may, accordingly, in those days*

b introducing new topics:
- *With regard to finance, Financially speaking, In terms of finance, As for finance, in financial terms, As far as finance is concerned, Regarding finance*

c clarifying the chronology of events or ideas:
- *The first point is, In the first place, Firstly, A further point is, Moreover, Similarly, One final thought is, Last but not least, In conclusion, To sum up*

d making specific references to people, facts or events:
- *the aforementioned, the following terms, the former, the latter, the undersigned, respectively, the facts are as follows, the above address*

e indicating the speaker's or writer's views:
- *as I see it, in my view, frankly, I suppose*

F Complete this letter with the most appropriate discourse markers from the study box. Then answer the questions, using the clues provided by the discourse markers.

Dear Sir,

We, 1) _____ , are writing to you to complain about the proposed closure of the Midwest Bank in the village of Little Stopping. The facts 2) _____ . Since both Gourlays and Boyds closed their branches in the nearby villages of Hopwell and Stopton 3) _____ , local people have been left with no option but to travel the eleven miles to Merryford or the twenty miles to Worchester. 4) _____ , although nearer and therefore more accessible by public transport, only offers banking facilities three days a week. 5) _____ , while providing a good choice of banks, is regarded by most people as too far away to be of much use.

6) _____ of public relations, the 7) _____ closure of your branch in Little Stopping would be a disaster, in blatant disregard of the wishes of many of your 8) _____ loyal customers.

We urge you to reconsider your decision. Kindly send any comments you have on this issue to us at 9) _____ .

Yours faithfully,

Joan Morris   Jamie Rogers   Edward Patching   Liz Fowler

10 How many times is the closure of the Midwest Bank mentioned?
11 Which bank had a branch in Hopwell?
12 Which town only offers banking facilities three days a week?
13 What are the two main points made in the letter?
14 In your opinion, which discourse markers from the text should only be used in a very formal style, as in this letter?

Relative clauses

Relative pronouns connect a relative clause to a main clause. They are **who**, **whom**, **which**, **that**, **whose**, **where**, **why**, **when** and **what**.

Who/whom refer to people. **Which/that** refer to animals or things, although people who love animals often use **who** when speaking of them. **Whom** is very unusual, especially in informal English, and is generally omitted or replaced with **who**:
* *We'll take Timmy to the specialist (who) we've heard so much about.*

Whose is possessive, for people or things:
* *She works for a company whose chief executive has been arrested for fraud.*

Where is used after nouns referring to place, **when** after nouns referring to time, and **why** after the word **reason**. **Where/when** can often replace **in/on/at which**:
* *I think that's the church where/in which my grandparents were married.*
* *It was a day when everything seemed to go wrong.*
* *Is there any reason why he can't come?*

What means 'the thing that':
* *I'll explain what he said.*
* *What I like for breakfast is hot buttered toast.*
* *She'll give you just what you want.*

A Correct the sentences if necessary. Tick any which are already correct.

1 There's the woman who she sold me the oranges.
2 This is my brother, who's wife's French.
3 Did you ever meet the model who's married Jeff's cousin?
4 I don't like people which talk too loudly.
5 That's the car whose brakes are being repaired.
6 I know a little taverna at where you can get a wonderful meal.
7 Do you understand what he said?
8 I suppose that's the house where we'll have to stay in.
9 Could we arrange a time when we'll both be free?
10 I'm afraid I haven't sent exactly what he asked for.
11 That I can't stand is queuing in the rain.
12 Have you any idea to whom I'll be speaking to?
13 Is that the school which you studied?
14 Deirdre will show the new students which to do.
15 You'd better tell me the reason for he didn't turn up.
16 That's the old chap whom you met at the bus stop last week, isn't it?
17 That was the day when I mislaid my passport.
18 What he told you is hopelessly inaccurate.

Defining relative clauses give us the necessary information to know which person or thing is referred to:
• *I did the work (that/which) he asked me to do.*
In this type of clause there is no comma. **That** or **which** can be used, or the pronoun can be omitted if it is the object.

Which and **that** are often interchangeable. In defining clauses, however, **that** is commonly used instead of **which** after **superlatives**, **every(thing)**, **all**, **only**, **some(thing)**, **any(thing)**, **no(thing)**, **none**, **little**, **few** and **much**:
• *It was the strangest case that had ever come to Dr Martin's notice. No disorder that he had read about had such bizarre symptoms.*

Which is used

a to refer to a whole previous sentence, and needs a comma before it:
   • *Nicholas never offers to pay, which always annoys me.* (NOT *what always annoys me)
b with a preposition/particle:
   • *This is the room in which Wagner died.* (formal).
   • *This is the room (which) Wagner died in.* (informal)
c in **non-defining clauses**, which give information that is not really necessary:
   • *I did the work, which was well paid.*
   A comma is used to separate the relative clause from the main clause. **That** cannot be used to introduce this type of clause.

B Explain the difference in meaning between each pair of sentences.

1 a) She decided to take the first train that stopped in Strasbourg.
  b) She decided to take the first train, which stopped in Strasbourg.
2 a) The people, who hadn't seen the weather forecast, were caught unawares by the hurricane.
  b) The people who hadn't seen the weather forecast were caught unawares by the hurricane.
3 a) We couldn't eat the food, which was bad.
  b) We couldn't eat the food that was bad.
4 a) I was hoping to visit my cousin, who lives in New Zealand.
  b) I was hoping to visit my cousin who lives in New Zealand.
5 a) They picked all the fruit that had ripened.
  b) They picked all the fruit, which had ripened.

If **who**, **which** or **that** is the **object** of the relative clause, not the subject, the pronoun can be, and often is, omitted:
• *I received the order you despatched last week.* (*which/that* = object)
• *I've received the goods, which are in my office now.* (*which* = subject)

Notice that we do not use a possessive adjective in the following type of sentence:
• *It's the bike Dad gave me.* (NOT *It's my bike Dad gave me.)

C Combine the sentences to make one new sentence, including a defining relative clause. Make any necessary changes, and omit the relative pronoun if possible.

1 The bus goes up Edward Avenue. It doesn't stop at the railway station.
2 The debate went on all night. The backbenchers had demanded it.
3 The escaped convicts stashed away the gold bars. They had stolen the gold in an earlier bank raid.
4 It was her dream cottage! She had always wanted one like that.
5 They booked into the hotel. They had stayed there on their honeymoon.
6 The bodyguards were flanking the King. They had revolvers concealed inside their jackets.
7 It wasn't their dog. No, I was taking care of their cat.
8 The tree had died. They cut it down.
9 That's the cruise. I've always wanted to go on that one.
10 I think it was the manager. I was speaking to him.

D Correct or improve the sentences if necessary. Tick any which are already correct.

1 It's the tallest building which I've ever seen.
2 Everything she had told us turned out to be true.
3 He was arrested for speeding, which unfortunately was reported in the local newspaper.
4 There is very little that escapes the senior partner's eagle eye.
5 He'll be playing with the same racquet, with which he always plays.
6 Next Tuesday I'll have to visit the dentist again which I detest.

> In non-defining clauses, determiners like **some**, **all**, **neither**, **none**, **(a) few**, **(a) little**, **both**, **most**, **much** and **several**, superlatives and expressions of quantity can be used with **of whom** (for people) and **of which** (for things):
> - *They'll introduce you to a lot of people, most of whom you'll forget immediately.*
> - *I was offered lamb or chicken, neither of which I like.*

E Combine the sentences to make one new sentence, including a relative clause.

1 She had invited a hundred guests. I didn't know any of them.
2 Growling in the corner were two big dogs. They both looked extremely dangerous.
3 The manager called in my new colleagues. I had met one or two of them already.
4 There were several large holes in the road. Three of them had to be repaired urgently.
5 There were some vegetables left over. I was able to use a few of them in some soup for supper.
6 The talk was attended by over two hundred delegates. Most of them took notes.
7 The researchers reported back on the questionnaires. The most interesting ones showed a marked change in leisure habits among older people.
8 He comes from a large family. All of them now live in Australia.

Adverbs

Adverbs can modify verbs, adjectives, other adverbs, prepositions and whole clauses or sentences:
• *He kicked the ball well past the goalie. Unfortunately, that never happened again.*
Adverbs of **frequency**, **time**, **manner** and **place** are the most common.

Most adverbs are formed by adding **-ly** to an adjective or **-ally** after **-ic**:
• *slow~slowly* • *spasmodic~spasmodically*
If the adjective ends in **-le**, the **-e** is replaced with **-y**: • *reliable~reliably*
If the adjective already ends in **-ll**, only add **-y**: • *full~fully*

Most adjectives ending in **-y** change like this: • *angry~angrily, happy~happily*
Some adjectives ending in **-ly**, e.g. *likely, lovely, lonely, ugly, deadly*, are usually used as adverbs like this: • *friendly~in a friendly way*
Others ending in **-ly**, e.g. *early, daily, weekly, monthly*, can be used as adjectives or adverbs with no change.

Some adverbs have the same form as adjectives. For example:
• *hard, fast, far, near, early, late, direct, straight*
Notice also: • *good~well*

A Write the correct form of the adverb for these adjectives.

1 graceful	6 hard	11 inevitable
2 good	7 heavy	12 fast
3 important	8 cruel	13 noisy
4 full	9 timid	14 jolly
5 straight	10 illegal	15 increasing

Avoid putting an adverb between the verb and its object:
• *I like riding very much/I very much like riding.* (NOT *I like very much riding.*)

Time adverbs normally go right at the beginning or end of the clause:
• *Tomorrow I'm going there/I'm going there tomorrow.*

Frequency adverbs, e.g. **always**, **never**, **sometimes**, usually go between the subject and verb: • *I always drink coffee.*
or between two parts of the verb: • *She's never been late.*

Many **adverbs of manner** can be used in different positions in a clause, although the end position is most typical:
• *He tore the letter up slowly.* • *She quickly left the room.*
Front position gives the adverb more emphasis: • *Suddenly the door flew open.*

Long adverbs and **adverbial phrases** usually go at the end of the clause:
• *She read it aloud monotonously.* • *He crossed the road without looking.*

B Correct the sentences if necessary. Tick any which are already correct.

1 Tomorrow is the boss having a day off.
2 She likes very much watching videos at home.
3 She turned to him with a contemptuous smile.
4 I went to the principal's office immediately.
5 They yesterday mowed their lawn.
6 I've always enjoyed reading, travelling and playing music very much.
7 He slammed suddenly the book down on the table.
8 Alma stamped out angrily of the office.
9 I always make sure I do every day my homework.
10 We go frequently for a picnic in the forest.
11 Always the foreman gives the workmen a ticking off.
12 The nurse suddenly rushed out of the operating theatre.

> Some common adverbial phrases are **with hindsight/in retrospect, in the wake of, by no means, by ...%, in monthly instalments, without more/ further ado, with reference to, at the expense of**.

C Complete the sentences with the phrases from the study box above.

1 _____, he realised he should not have resigned.
2 The army was sent to the province, _____ popular unrest there.
3 The news sent the stock market plummeting _____.
4 They are paying for their new car _____.
5 _____, he put on his coat and left the room.
6 He was an extremely prolific writer, but his huge output was achieved _____ his health.
7 _____ your letter of 15th February, please note that I shall be consulting my legal advisors forthwith.
8 No, I'm afraid he's _____ the sort of friend I would have chosen for you.

D Choose the correct word or phrase from the pair in brackets to complete each sentence.

1 I simply can't remember what happens _____ of the book.
(in the end/at the end)
2 We waited and waited, and _____ our turn came.
(eventually/at the end)
3 There's a marvellous shot _____ of the film, with the heroine running along a deserted sandy beach.
(in the beginning/at the beginning)
4 I'm sorry I won't be able to help you with the decorating. I'm _____ very busy myself.   (presently/actually)
5 They climbed steeply for a hour and a half, and _____ they reached the summit.   (at last/lastly)
6 He had to jump-start the car, but he _____ got it going.
(in the end/finally)

There are many **confusing pairs** like **dead/deadly**, which do not follow normal adjective/adverb rules.

Deadly is an adjective, meaning *lethal*, while **dead** can be used as an adjective meaning *not alive*, or as an adverb meaning *completely*:

* *You're dead right.* (informal)

E Choose the correct word from the pair in brackets to complete each sentence. Refer to Section 7 of the Appendix for a brief definition of the words if necessary.

1 The vicar lives _____ to the church. (close/closely)

2 Take it _____! I didn't mean to be rude! (easy/easily)

3 Make sure the onions are _____ chopped. (fine/finely)

4 He's a _____ good golfer, so I think he'll beat you. (pretty/prettily)

5 They'll be moving to Leeds _____. (short/shortly)

6 Hold _____! Here comes a speed hump! (tight/tightly)

7 I can ——- recommend that restaurant. (high/highly)

8 The villagers campaigned _____ for the bypass to be re-routed. (hard/hardly)

9 It's _____ known that he's the best in his field. (wide/widely)

10 Be there at nine o'clock _____, or you'll miss all the bargains. (sharp/sharply)

11 You can get in _____ with this voucher. (free/freely)

12 I feel very hard done by. He just isn't playing _____. (fair/fairly)

13 I couldn't believe it when they turned me down _____! (flat/flatly)

14 They drove _____ from Milan to Paris without stopping. (direct/directly)

15 They turned up very _____ for the celebrations. (late/lately)

16 They _____ refused to consider my proposition. (flat/flatly)

17 Don't make a noise. The baby's _____ asleep. (sound/soundly)

18 He cut her _____ with a wave of the hand. (short/shortly)

19 I _____ forgot my passport. I only remembered it at the last minute. (near/nearly)

20 She hit the target _____ in the centre. (right/rightly)

See **Unit 16** for the use of **negative adverbs** at the beginning of a sentence.

Recycling

A Choose the correct word or phrase to complete each sentence. Write the letter in the space.

1 They'll explain _____ you need to know to complete your report.
   a) what   b) that   c) which   d) how

2 The TV company _____ contract is up for renewal is losing money.
   a) which   b) whose   c) the   d) who's

3 In _____, it was obviously the wrong thing to do.
   a) hindsight   b) the wake   c) retrospect   d) the whole

4 I'll have to do overtime tonight, _____ is very tiresome.
   a) which   b) what   c) that   d) so

5 There were _____ few tickets sold that the concert was cancelled.
   a) a   b) very   c) so   d) such

6 The piano was _____ heavy for us to carry from the removal van.
   a) far   b) much   c) so   d) too

7 I'm afraid that's the best _____ can do for you.
   a) which   b) I   c) that   d) what

8 He _____ that he had three Rolls-Royces at home.
   a) threatened   b) reminded   c) boasted   d) informed

9 You've got to be _____ certain before you decide.
   a) deadly   b) deathly   c) dead   d) dearly

10 She burst into tears when he spoke to her _____.
   a) sharp   b) sharpish   c) sharper   d) sharply

11 Her cousin is _____ related to the Hapsburg family.
   a) nearly   b) close   c) closely   d) near

12 We accused him _____ a blatant lie.
   a) to telling   b) to tell   c) in telling   d) of telling

13 You _____ assumed that we'd be starting at 8.00.
   a) right   b) rightly   c) fairly   d) fair

14 The witness _____ ever having seen the prisoner.
   a) denied   b) admitted   c) insisted   d) objected

15 Police are reported _____ found illegal drugs in a secret hiding place in the star's home.
   a) they have   b) having   c) to have   d) have had

16 No, he _____ ever jogs round the park these days.
   a) doesn't   b) occasionally   c) hardly   d) almost

17 It's by _____ means the best book I've ever read.
   a) no   b) all   c) far   d) some

18 She waited for twenty minutes and _____ arrived at the head of the queue.
   a) lastly   b) finally   c) at the end   d) eventual

B Read this jumbled memo from an employer to members of staff, and put the sentences in the correct order, using the discourse markers to help you.

To: All staff
From: Chief Executive
Date: 22.08.01
Re: Break-in incident

a Be that as it may, the police have always advised against this type of direct action, if intruders are spotted on the premises. Therefore the company would like all staff to maintain a low profile if such a situation recurs.

b Last but not least, please remember that the company is ultimately responsible for the safety of its employees while on the premises, and it is our policy to encourage you to safeguard yourselves from harm at all times.

c Following the recent incident during the lunch break, when an attempt was made by opportunistic thieves to steal computers from the main office, I want to remind staff of company policy on intruders.

d Accordingly, do NOT follow Don's and Neil's example. Instead, restrict yourself to challenging a possible intruder verbally. On no account should you resort to physical restraint or violence.

e Firstly, however, I must thank two members of staff, Don and Neil, for their bravery and presence of mind. As no doubt you all know by now, they confronted and succeeded in capturing the intruders.

C Complete the second sentence so that it means the same as the first one, using the word given. You must use between **three** and **eight** words, including the word given. (Contractions count as two words.)

1 At the moment people think the accident is Nick's fault.
   blamed
   Nick is currently _____ the accident.

2 'I didn't harm anybody!' cried the accused.
   to
   The accused denied _____ anybody.

3   Even though the invaders were short of ammunition, they won the battle.
   a
   Despite _____ by the invaders.

4 Your scheme is brilliant, but it won't succeed.
   doomed
   Brilliant though _____ failure.

5 Although it's fun being with her, I think she talks too much.
   company
   Much as I _____ too talkative.

6 There is a rumour that the principal is planning to retire early.
   rumoured
   The principal _____ early retirement.

7 There was no further delay in awarding the prizes.
   more
   The prizes _____ ado.

8 I was in the middle of my speech when Pippa interrupted me.
   cut
   Pippa _____ through my speech.

D Complete the text by putting **one** word in each space. The main focus of this task is on grammar rather than vocabulary.

A substance produced 1) _____ disease-transmitting insects 2) _____ provide the key to fighting these same diseases. Mosquitoes and blackflies transmit malaria and river blindness respectively, both of 3) _____ cause a large number of deaths every year. However, scientists 4) _____ now discovered, in some of these insects, a substance called a peptide 5) _____ kills the viruses and parasites 6) _____ carry. 7) _____ introduced techniques have allowed researchers 8) _____ study these minute insects in 9) _____ to find out more about the peptides.

Professor John Wells said yesterday that if his team 10) _____ identify the genes responsible for 11) _____ the peptides, they 12) _____ introduce into the world genetically altered mosquitoes 13) _____ were incapable of 14) _____ the disease. In the 15) _____ of these exciting developments, it 16) _____ hoped that science 17) _____ be able to eradicate some major tropical diseases sooner rather than later.

E Choose the correct linking word or relative pronoun to fill each gap.

THE JARGON JUNGLE

According to a recent survey, one in five office workers in Britain no longer understands 1) _____ their colleagues are talking about. They complain of being left floundering at meetings, 2) _____ corporate buzz words are rife these days. Secretarial recruitment firm Office Angels administered the survey to over 1000 office staff, 65 per cent of 3) _____ said they were having to cope with complicated management jargon derived from corporate gurus, American slang and the internet.
4) _____ some employees thought this type of language was simply distracting and irritating, others went so far as to dismiss the speakers 5) _____ used this language as pretentious and even untrustworthy. 6) _____ that puzzled listeners can find the courage to seek clarification, they may discover the speaker's meaning. Most do not ask, 7) _____ , for fear of revealing their ignorance.

A spokesperson for Office Angels said that, 8) _____ companies and organisations develop their own jargon, it can either help to bring individuals together 9) _____ it can exclude and confuse people, as 10) _____ as masking inexperience and lack of expertise.

Verb inversion

In formal English the subject and verb are occasionally inverted, to give emphasis or literary or dramatic effect. This should be avoided in spoken or informal English.

Inversion may take place in

a   adverb clauses beginning with **Scarcely/Hardly... when/before, No sooner... than**:
  • *Hardly had he raised the alarm(,) when the fire engine arrived.*
  • *No sooner had she told him her address than she regretted it.*

b   negative adverb clauses beginning with **Under no circumstances, On no account, In vain, At no time, In no way, Never/Not for one moment, Seldom, Rarely, Never**:
  • *In vain did they try to persuade him.*

c   conditional clauses in which **if** is replaced by **had, had... but, had... only, should**:
  • *Should the rope break, the dinghy will float away.*
  • *Had Colin but informed the police, he would be safe now.*

d   clauses with **so + adjective** (or **little, few, much, many**) or **such + noun**:
  • *So little did he know about her(,) that he was not even sure of her name.*
  • *Such was my annoyance(,) that I tore up the letter.*

A Rewrite the sentences, putting the words in italics at the beginning, and making any other necessary changes.

1 They had *seldom* participated in such a fascinating ceremony.
2 I pleaded with him *in vain*. He was adamant.
3 Miss Weaver will not be offered the job *under* any *circumstances*.
4 If the film *should* be a box-office success, there may be a sequel.
5 He was *so surprised* to be addressed by the Queen that he didn't answer at once.
6 If only they *had* confirmed by phone, the airline could have warned them.
7 He had *hardly* entered the house when the police arrested him.
8 I *never* for one moment thought the consequences would be so far-reaching.
9 She has *rarely* travelled more than fifty miles from her village.
10 You must *on no account* lift heavy weights like that again.
11 I had *scarcely* put down the phone when it rang again.
12 The defendant did not express his misgivings *in any way*.
13 The task was *so* difficult that expert assistance was required.
14 If they *had* accepted our offer, we would have moved house by now.

B Match the two halves of the sentences correctly.

1 No sooner had Karen parked her car

2 Such was her fury that

3 Scarcely had the plane landed

4 Should you need any help,

5 Nowhere else in the world

A I'll be available all afternoon.

B when it was surrounded by photographers.

C than a lorry crashed into it.

D can you find palaces as fine as these.

E she threw the book across the room.

Inversion also takes place

a after **only** and **as**:
 • *Only yesterday did I hear the news.*
 • *They live in Hollywood, as do most of the other stars.*
 Also note the use of **Not only... but also**:
 • *Not only did we get wet, but we also lost our passports.*

b in clauses with ***here** and ***there**, and other adverbial expressions of place.
 Note that **do/did** are not used: • *Here are the answers.*
 • *Up jumped the cat.* • *In the corner sat a large pig.*
 Note also that continuous tenses are rare:
 • *There goes the bus!* NOT ***There is going the bus!***
 In this case inversion does not take place if the subject is a pronoun:
 • *Here you are!* • *Down it jumped.* • *Round the corner she ran.*

 *****Inversion after these words is normal, not just a formal use.

c in short answers with **neither**, **nor** and **so**, formally and informally:
 • *Neither do I.* • *Nor is he.* • *So are you.*

C Correct the sentences if necessary, beginning with the same word. Tick any which are already correct.

1 Over fell I, and broke my leg.

2 'I'd rather have a walk in the morning.' 'So I would.'

3 Not only she twisted her ankle, but she also dropped her purse.

4 Down in the valley lay a fertile-looking vineyard.

5 Only recently did scientists discover a cure for certain types of leukaemia.

6 Charlotte Brontë died of tuberculosis, as did all her sisters.

7 Up the stairs did the plump old housekeeper puff.

8 Look, there go the children on their way to school.

9 Right through the underwater tunnel swam she.

10 Only if you pay cash will you get the car.

11 Into the valley of death rode the six hundred.

12 There is the famous statue of Admiral Lord Nelson standing.

13 Only last week found I the information I'd been looking for.

14 Here the police come! Someone must have called them.

D Complete the second sentence so that it means the same as the first one, using the word given. You must use between **three** and **eight** words, including the word given. Be careful, because inversion may not be required in every sentence.

1 It isn't worth considering his suggestion for a moment.

giving

Not for one moment _____ consideration.

2 He was so disgusted at the way she behaved that he refused to speak to her.

her

Such _____ he refused to speak to her.

3 Adele tries hard, but she doesn't get anywhere.

hard

However _____ nowhere.

4 The volunteers' efforts to avert the catastrophe were unsuccessful.

attempt

In vain _____ avert the catastrophe.

5 I was never shown how to operate the machine.

ever

At no time _____ the machine work.

6 The firm had never celebrated anything so lavishly before.

such

Never _____ laid on by the firm.

7 It wasn't until last week that the minister admitted he was wrong.

error

Only last week _____ of judgement.

8 Tick the box if you wish to take advantage of the offer.

accept

Should _____ tick in the box.

9 We may have to reject applications in a few cases.

be

In a few cases, applications _____ down.

10 Invitations were sent out as soon as the date was chosen.

been

Hardly _____ invitations were sent out.

11 In order to stay open, the charity shop needs at least four helpers.

enable

No fewer _____ the charity shop to stay open.

12 If his father hadn't advised him against it, he might have become a record producer.

for

Had it not _____ a record producer now.

13 The employees insisted on being given a full bonus.

satisfy

Nothing but _____ the employees.

14 This computer data is strictly confidential.

revealed

Under no circumstances _____ to anyone.

UNIT 17

Comparison and similarity

As is used in three main ways to express **similarity**.

a as a preposition, when it describes a function:
   - *He was disguised as a security guard.*
   - *I used the encyclopedia as a doorstop.*

b as a conjunction with a verb clause or prepositional phrase:
   - *He stayed at the Raffles Hotel, as he had done the previous time.*
   - *In Greece, as in Spain, people are hospitable to strangers.*

c in expressions such as **as you know**, **as you like**, **as you suggested**.
   (See **Unit 16** for inversion after **as** in formal English.)

Like is a preposition, followed by a noun or pronoun, used for **similarity or comparison**:
   - *I'm a teacher, like my father.*   • *Like her friends, she loves rock concerts.*

Like can be used as an alternative to **such as**, when offering an example:
   - *The great French Impressionists, such as/like Monet, ...*

Note that **like** is sometimes used instead of **as** with a verb clause:
   - *They ignored the ban on smoking, like they did last time.*
   However, this is not generally considered correct.

A Complete the sentences, by inserting *as* or *like*.

1 You don't look anything _____ your mother.

2 _____ we expected, the singer didn't arrive on time.

3 _____ your teacher, I advise you to read more in order to widen your vocabulary.

4 He dug a snow hole and waited for help, _____ he had been instructed to do.

5 Her father was a great sportsman, just _____ her grandfather.

6 Her father was a great sportsman, just _____ her grandfather used to be.

7 We don't need the box, but we can use it _____ firewood.

8 She went to the party dressed up _____ Cleopatra.

9 Several state museums, _____ in other countries, are imposing admission charges.

10 _____ you say, we shouldn't argue about it.

11 She worked _____ a bilingual secretary for two years.

12 The local council, _____ others in the area, is taking a strong line on parking offences.

13 _____ his colleagues, Yves has a postgraduate qualification.

14 The twentieth century produced a number of female political leaders, _____ Indira Gandhi and Margaret Thatcher.

15 _____ you, Colette experienced considerable difficulty in adapting to an alien environment.

As...as is used with adjectives or adverbs. **As much/many...as** is used with nouns or verbs:
- *The road's as straight as a ruler.*
- *Exercise as much as you can.*
- *Take as many oranges as you want.*

Negative comparisons are made with **not as/so + adjective/adverb + as**:
- *The proposal isn't as attractive as it seemed at first.*

Twice, **three times**, **half** etc. can precede comparisons, and they can be modified with **(not) nearly**, **just**, **nothing like**, **almost**, **every bit**, **exactly**:
- *He's twice as old as you are.*   • *It wasn't half so difficult as I thought.*
- *My cake's every bit as nice as yours.*

B Correct the sentences if necessary. Tick any which are already correct.

1 She's nothing like so good at tennis like her friend.
2 Mine cost three times as much as yours.
3 Have as many potatoes that you like.
4 His hand is so steady as a rock.
5 The cottage isn't as well-built as we thought.
6 She works just as hard as you do.
7 Eat as much as you can, now you're feeling better.
8 Last night's current affairs programme was almost as interesting as last week's.
9 The dictionary wasn't nearly as helpful than I had hoped.
10 Their population is twice as large as ours.
11 Laurie drank half as much beer like Hugo.
12 Their offer is every bit as acceptable than yours.

The same...as is used before a noun, pronoun, verb clause or prepositional phrase:
- *Her name's the same as her cousin's.*

The same...that can also be used before a verb clause, and **that** may be omitted if it is the object:
- *He's living in the same house (that) he used to live in.*
- *It's the same dog that's been hanging around all week.*

C Correct the sentences if necessary. Tick any which are already correct.

1 That's same formula you told me last week.
2 They're the same people we went to the theatre with.
3 I borrowed the same book as I'd taken out the week before.
4 That's same man that we saw in the bank robbery!
5 The medicine will have the same effect as last time.
6 The rules are same same in my country.
7 The traffic's probably the same on the bypass as in the town centre.
8 Did you pay the same than I did?

The **comparative** of most two-syllable adjectives is formed by adding **-er**. With adjectives ending in **-y**, the **-y** is replaced with **-ier**. With most other adjectives, **more/less** are used:
- *a smaller dog* • *a prettier flower* • *a less interesting book*

Than is always used in a comparison: • *Yours is better than mine.*

Comparatives can be modified with **a bit, a little, even, much, a lot, far, a great deal**:
- *Today's puzzles are far more difficult to do than yesterday's. They're a great deal more complicated.*

Double comparatives convey the idea of change:
- *She's getting thinner and thinner.*
- *He's becoming more and more cantankerous.*

When two changes happen together, we sometimes use **The..., the...**:
- *The older you get, the more you learn.*

The superlative of most short adjectives and adverbs is formed with **the + -est**. Longer words take **the most/least**. Note these irregular superlatives:
- *best* • *worst* • *furthest/farthest*

Superlatives can be modified with **by far** for emphasis:
- *She's by far the most talented musician in the group.*

D Correct the sentences if necessary. Tick any which are already correct.

1 More you work, more money you earn.
2 The more it is difficult, more harder he tries.
3 He's been working longer that you.
4 This meat's tougher as yesterday's.
5 I found myself becoming more and more terrified.
6 You're the more infuriating person I've ever met.
7 He's a great deal the best boxer in the world.
8 The patient looked worse a week ago than yesterday.
9 My cousin is very taller than me.
10 We all live a long way away, but Jim lives the furthest.
11 I think the driver is a bit the tireder than me.
12 At the moment he's less neurotic than I've ever seen him.
13 The more, the merry.
14 Our plans are getting more and more out of hand.
15 It was the dreariest hotel I'd never had the misfortune to stay in.
16 That one's the slowliest train.
17 The view from the penthouse suite is by far the best.
18 Your work's more impressive then anyone else's.
19 The greater your input, the more satisfaction you get out of a project.
20 I suppose you've chosen the least unpleasant option.

Participles

> **Present participles** (e.g. *going, breaking, starting*), and **past participles** (e.g. *gone, broken, started*) are used with auxiliary verbs to form continuous, perfect and passive forms, or as adjectives:
> - *He's just dashing after her.*   • *It'll be done as soon as possible.*
> - *It's an exhausting job.*   • *She's got a broken arm.*
>
> Note the difference between **adjectives ending in -ing** and **-ed**. The present participle (e.g. *exciting, interesting, boring*) describes the person or thing that is initiating the action. The past participle (e.g. *excited, interested, bored*) describes someone's reactions to something:
> - *I thought the race was very exciting.*   • *We weren't very interested in the film.*
>
> Participles can be used to give a **reason** for doing something, or to show a **time connection** between clauses/phrases:
> - *Realising she was wrong, she apologised.*   • *Having paid the bill, he left the hotel.*
>
> The subject of the participle clause should be the same as in the main clause, but note the following exceptions to this rule: **generally/broadly speaking, taking everything into consideration/account, supposing, providing, considering, judging by/from**:
> - *Generally speaking, these plants grow better in chalky soil.*
> - *Providing no one objects, I'll reschedule the meeting.*

A Complete the sentences by filling the gaps with a suitable participle.

1 _____ delivered the message, the boy went home.

2 We were awfully _____ by the company's decision, which seemed quite wrong to us.

3 He was thrilled by the film and thought it very _____.

4 The burglar must have got in through the _____ window.

5 _____ you had no money, what would you do?

6 _____ rather exhausted, she decided to give the meeting a miss.

7 The departmental head spoke to his assistant, _____ why he was being so uncooperative.

8 _____ packed our cases, we took a taxi to the airport.

9 _____ everything into consideration, I think you're right.

10 How can we motivate the children? They always look so _____ when we talk to them.

11 Claudia entered the room, _____ a tray of soft drinks.

12 _____ unable to concentrate, I fell asleep.

13 _____ unexpectedly into the room, she took the intruder by surprise.

14 _____ by his appearance, Timothy doesn't spend much on his clothes.

15 He was sitting in his usual corner, _____ miserable and _____ his pipe.

Present participles can be used after certain verbs and their objects, e.g. **see**, **hear**, **feel**, **smell**, **notice**, **watch**:
• *I heard a warbler singing in the woods.*
• *Did you notice the man sitting in the corner?*
This suggests that we heard/noticed an action which continued, whereas if an **infinitive without to** is used instead, it suggests that we heard/noticed the whole of the action, including its completion. Compare:
• *I saw her plant the tree.* (I saw her finish the planting.) with
• *I saw her planting the tree.* (I saw her in the middle of planting.)

B Decide whether to use a present participle or an infinitive (without *to*) in these sentences.

1 We watched her (close) the door.   (The door is shut now.)
2 I saw him (repair) the fence.   (I didn't see him finish it.)
3 Can you smell the chicken (cook)?   (It isn't ready to eat yet.)
4 She heard a door (bang).   (just once)
5 I didn't notice them (stand) there.   (I didn't see them leave.)
6 I felt anger (well) up inside me.   (a brief feeling of anger which soon passed)
7 He saw a man (throw) something that glinted in the sun.   (It was a quick action that is now over.)
8 He watched the customs official (open) his case and (take) out his clothes garment by garment.

After, **on**, **until**, **as**, **once**, **when**, **while**, **whenever**, **before** and **since** can all be followed by participle clauses:
• *Once correctly installed, the system will give years of trouble-free use.*
• *On being accused, the young man immediately confessed.*
• *After buying the flowers, he took them to the hospital.*
• *Whenever sunbathing, make sure you use a sunscreen.*

Remember that the subject of the main clause should also be the subject of the participle clause, apart from certain exceptions (see study box on **page 60**).
So the following sentence is wrong:
*Once correctly installed, you will have no trouble with the system.

C Complete the sentences with one of these words: *as, since, when, after, once, on.* Use each word only once.

1 _____ taken out of the oven, the cake should be left to cool on a wire rack.
2 She's been bedridden _____ undergoing her last operation.
3 _____ making the arrangements for the wedding, don't forget to order the flowers.
4 _____ having concluded the interviews, they spent some time discussing the respective merits of the candidates.
5 _____ being welcomed to the town, Lady Higginbottom gave an eloquent speech in reply.
6 He struck me _____ being rather eccentric.

Some **past participles used as adjectives** change their meaning according to their position.

Concerned after a noun means *relevant* or *affected*, but before a noun it means *worried*:
• *The grant will be given to the family concerned.*
• *Concerned parents have expressed their anxiety.*

Adopted after a noun means *chosen*, but before a noun it usually refers to a child who officially becomes part of someone else's family:
• *There was uproar over the policies adopted.*
• *The adopted child will never discover the identity of his parents.*

Involved after a noun means *relevant* or *affected*, but before a noun it means *complicated*:
• *I'll have a word with the people involved.*
• *He gave us a long and involved explanation.*

D Correct the sentences if necessary. Tick any which are already correct.

1 When booking a room for myself and my wife the other day, the receptionist was rather rude to me.

2 Looking at my diary, there were several double-booked appointments.

3 Remember to use unleaded petrol whenever filling the tank.

4 I hope you've mentioned this to the concerned people in the matter.

5 Not having written about the required topic, the teacher gave my presentation a low mark.

6 It was an extremely involved story. I couldn't make head or tail of it.

7 While working in California, my house was damaged by an earthquake.

8 Being such a sunny day, I got up early and went for a swim.

9 Judging from his expression, you're about to be disciplined!

10 Do you know anyone having been to the Canary Islands?

11 The employees involved will have their pay docked.

12 The club approved of the solution adopted by the sub-committee.

13 Whenever leaving the premises, please ensure that the security system is switched on.

14 Once ensconced in his comfortable armchair, the television didn't bother him at all.

Adjectives

> **Adjectives** are used to modify nouns or as complements to verbs like **be** and **seem**:
> - *a romantic novel*   • *Martin seems happy, and Tracy is cheerful.*
>
> Notice these similar adjectives: **asleep/sleeping, afloat/floating, afraid/frightened, ajar/open, awake/waking, ablaze/blazing, alone/lone, alight/burning, alive/live**. The first one of each pair cannot be used before a noun, and is normally used with the verb **be**:
> - *He is awake.*   • *The ship was afloat.*   • *The house was ablaze.*

A Complete each sentence with the correct adjective from the pair in brackets.

1 All the guests are fast _____. (asleep/sleeping)

2 Her mother hated living all _____. (alone/lone)

3 The firemen had to carry the _____ children to safety. (afraid/frightened)

4 The salvage teams watched the_____ wreck from the shore. (ablaze/blazing)

5 They can't get to sleep. They're wide _____. (awake/waking)

6 I think I can smell a(n) _____ cigarette in the room. (alight/burning)

7 It's a (n) _____ concert, coming to you via satellite from Rome. (alive/live)

8 Flies buzzed in through the _____ door. (ajar/open)

9 As soon as we're _____, we'll set sail for France. (afloat/floating)

> With certain verbs, like **be, seem, sound, *look, *appear, *taste, *feel** and ***smell**, adjectives, not adverbs, are used:
> - *This dish tastes delicious.*   • *The house looks dirty.*
>
> *These verbs can be used with an adverb when they refer to an action rather than a state:
> - *She tasted the dessert appreciatively.*   • *He looked seriously at me.*
>
> Certain other verbs, e.g. **sit, lie, stand, fall, become, go, get** and **turn**, can also be followed by adjectives, when the adjective describes the subject:
> - *I went red with embarrassment.*   • *She fell ill and died.*
> - *The mountain stood powerful and threatening ahead of me.*

B Correct the sentences if necessary. Tick any which are already correct.

1 She turned palely with fear.

2 I felt the bird's wing gently.

3 The boy stood motionless in the corner.

4 This trick seems easy to do, but it isn't.

5 I'm feeling more enthusiastic now you've explained it all to me.

6 He became angrily when he saw what had happened.

7 This pasta tastes garlicky.

8 Don't look at me so resentfully. It wasn't my fault.

9 Your friend Carrie sounds charming.

10 The patient was lying unconsciously on the bed.

Adjectives can be used in certain expressions with **the**, when we are generalising, to indicate a whole group of people: • *the rich, the poor, the old, the disabled, the dead, the unemployed, the blind, the deaf*
Some adjectives of nationality can also be used like this, including all nationality adjectives ending in **-sh** or **-ch**: • *the British, the Spanish, the French*

Plural nouns with numbers become singular when they are used as adjectives: • *a ten-mile walk, a three-hour journey*

C Correct the sentences if necessary. Tick any which are already correct.

1 The new toilets in town are for the disabled people.

2 It will probably be a two-hours lecture.

3 Dominic works at a special school for blind.

4 The eleven-year-old girl won first prize.

5 In many societies it is true that the rich get richer, and the poor get poorer.

6 French negotiated with Spanish over the return of the wanted fugitives.

The order of adjectives is important where there is more than one adjective in front of a noun. The following order should generally be observed:
opinion, size, age, shape, colour, origin/nationality, material/purpose, NOUN.

However, some adjectives and nouns are used so often together that the above rule does not apply:
• *We drank some delicious Spanish white wine.* NOT *white Spanish wine*

D Unscramble the following sentences.

1 saw a I silk sweet green little scarf

2 was huge castle a there mediaeval stone hill the on

3 beautiful ship at quay moored white a sailing was the

4 battered is table leather a there old suitcase the on

5 live ancient cottage the sea by they fisherman's in an

6 was her striped bag shopping carrying she canvas a heavy arm full vegetables of on

7 introduced a handsome executive she to young was remarkably

8 wearing smart business a a jazzy suit grey waistcoat he was with

9 cakes butter the Danish unsalted makes with she only best

10 an oriental extremely carpet exotic he bought just has

E Match the adjectives, connected with people's emotions or character, with their approximate opposites.

1	unperturbed	A	sensitive
2	lazy	B	cheerful
3	gloomy	C	forgiving
4	strict	D	garrulous
5	thick-skinned	E	slapdash
6	reserved	F	sceptical
7	defensive	G	integrated
8	gullible	H	apprehensive
9	indecisive	I	unreliable
10	methodical	J	easy-going
11	alienated	K	aggressive
12	sincere	L	purposeful
13	carefree	M	devious
14	vindictive	N	anxious
15	dependable	O	energetic

F Complete the sentences with the correct adjective from the box. Use each word only once.

> sworn   dire   gruelling   blatant   mere   burgeoning
> insatiable   first-hand   innovative   primary   abortive
> contemporary   fierce   lucrative   heinous

1 He committed the offence in _____ disregard of the rules.
2 The children have a(n) _____ appetite for sweets.
3 The company made a(n) _____ effort to improve productivity, but finally had to call in the receivers.
4 Her father's always been a(n) _____ critic of modern art.
5 You can't expect him to know any better – he's a(n) _____ child.
6 Overwork and a(n) _____ reading tour of the USA contributed largely to Charles Dickens' death.
7 Howard Barker is hailed by some as one of our most _____ playwrights.
8 Police consider the murder one of the most _____ crimes in recent years.
9 The island was quite content with its _____ prosperity.
10 From the moment the boys saw each other, they were _____ enemies.
11 The company is in _____ need of financial assistance.
12 You need to find a(n) _____ market for your products.
13 It is hard for _____ authors to achieve the status of earlier writers who have become household names.
14 Unemployment is the _____ focus of concern in many people's minds.
15 Josephine's actually worked in the diplomatic service, so she has _____ experience.

Recycling

A Choose the correct word or phrase to complete each sentence. Write the letter in the space.

1 He'll believe anything. He's so _____.

  a) garrulous   b) gullible   c) credible   d) believable

2 At _____ time did I ever promise you a pay rise.

  a) any   b) no   c) all   d) some

3 He's got plenty of _____ experience as he's worked in that field already.

  a) second-hand   b) first-hand   c) primary   d) tertiary

4 The feuding families have been _____ enemies for years.

  a) sworn   b) promised   c) cursed   d) blood

5 Not only was there no tea, _____ there was no food either.

  a) and   b) nor   c) but   d) so

6 The girl felt _____ with hunger.

  a) faintly   b) fainting   c) fainted   d) faint

7 Here is an example of an ancient _____ Chinese vase.

  a) beautiful   b) tiny   c) patterned   d) exotic

8 People in this village have got an _____ appetite for news.

  a) inexorable   b) inevitable   c) insatiable   d) inedible

9 Hardly had he sat down _____ he was sent for again.

  a) when   b) than   c) after   d) that

10 Even the other convicts considered it a _____ crime.

  a) guilty   b) hard-bitten   c) heinous   d) hell-bent

11 Nothing was arranged – it was all very _____.

  a) take away   b) worn out   c) slapdash   d) slap up

12 She gave me the same advice _____ you did.

  a) like   b) than   c) as   d) who

13 _____ you are, the more you laugh.

  a) The happier   b) More happy   c) The happy   d) Happier

14 She's _____ about her nursing exams, but I'm sure she'll do well.

  a) alienated   b) keen   c) stressed   d) apprehensive

15 All the way along the winding street _____.

  a) he came   b) came he   c) did he come   d) comes he

16 Don't worry about making a noise. The children are wide _____.

  a) waking   b) awake   c) woken   d) awoke

17 She's always been one of your _____ critics.

  a) fiercest   b) most violent   c) wildest   d) hardest

18 _____ has such a stunning achievement been recorded.

  a) Always   b) Seldom   c) Today   d) Recently

19 When _____ money into the slot, be sure to use undamaged coins.

  a) on inserting   b) having inserted   c) to insert   d) inserting

20 The mother sat by her _____ child's bedside all night.

  a) asleep   b) sleep   c) sleeping   d) overslept

B Read the text and decide which word (A, B, C or D) best fits each space.

GETTING TO SLEEP

If you suffer from insomnia, there are 1) _____ natural remedies which won't make you feel terrible the next day. Start with essential oils, which 2) _____ either via skin absorption or by diffusion in the lungs when you inhale them. A combination of lavender and geranium oils, for example, is 3) _____ recommended to get you to sleep 4) _____ travelling.

If you have an aversion to aromatherapy, why not try 5) _____ to soothing sounds? The right kind of sound can help 6) _____ drop off by slowing your bodily processes down to a sleep-ready state. Playing relaxing music or sounds from 7) _____ natural world can make the transition from alert, wakeful state to sleep mode much 8) _____ .

Another solution is to sleep with a hop pillow under your head. The hop plant, 9) _____ better known for its use in making beer, provides the stuffing for an aromatic pillow, 10) _____ calming qualities have been known about for centuries.

Perhaps the 11) _____ popular sleep therapy at the moment is the use of flower essences. It 12) _____ native Australians who originally discovered the different healing properties of certain flowers, and nowadays many people combat sleeplessness by using blends of flower essences.

	A	B	C	D
1	plenty	lots	other	several
2	march	run	work	do
3	deeply	highly	very	extremely
4	from	after	on	in
5	listening	hearing	focusing	concentrating
6	to	we	you	with
7	another	a	only	the
8	easier	easy	easiest	ease
9	also	although	even	as
10	these	those	which	whose
11	greatest	more	most	mainly
12	was	were	is	concerns

C Complete the text by putting **one** word in each space. (Do not use contractions – they count as two words.)

Education was not formally integrated into the European Union policy portfolio 1) _____ the 1993 Maastricht Treaty, although the first Community legislation with an impact on the education sector was adopted as long ago as the 1960s. These early 2) _____ dealt with mutual recognition of qualifications. Achieving recognition by one member state of a qualification obtained in 3) _____ was an important pre-condition for implementing the free movement of workers.

Citizens of EU countries 4) _____ are students now enjoy the same rights of access to higher education in all member states 5) _____ they do in their home country, 6) _____ that they have the relevant qualifications for entry. Growing numbers of student exchange activities 7) _____ been developed, of 8) _____ the oldest and most famous is the Erasmus programme. 9) _____ recognising course credits, Erasmus allows university students to study for one year in a different member state. A separate programme, Leonardo da Vinci, gives young school leavers, students and graduates the 10) _____ to receive vocational training.

Few EU initiatives enjoy 11) _____ wholehearted and widespread political support as these higher education programmes. The key issue for future initiatives is to build on this success 12) _____ being over-ambitious. Unfortunately, these programmes are becoming 13) _____ expensive, and this is now the primary 14) _____ of concern.

D Complete the text by making a new word from each word given in capitals.

THE VILLAGE SHOP

For some years now I've had 1) _____ experience of | HAND

running a small shop, and, I must say, it's not always easy. There are the under-age youngsters who try to

buy cigarettes, in blatant 2) _____ of the law and | REGARD

their own health. They probably make the 3) _____ | ASSUME

that I can't tell how old they are! It's also hard

keeping an adequate range of 4) _____ products and | HOUSE

food in stock – there'd be 5) _____ in the village if I | ROAR

ran out of milk or eggs! I have to decide on the

6) _____ merits of, say, washing powder or flour, as | RESPECT

I haven't got room to stock both. Some customers can be

quite rude, although they often 7) _____ later. And | APOLOGY

I don't enjoy 8) _____, relaxing weekends like most | CARE

of my regulars – I have to stay open. But at least I don't

suffer stress from 9) _____, because I really like my | WORK

job, 10) _____ all its difficulties. | SPITE

UNIT 21

Prepositions

> **Prepositions** are words or groups of words, normally used before a noun or pronoun to express a relationship between one person/event etc. and another:
> • *She walked into the operating theatre.* • *He seemed strangely out of breath.*
>
> Prepositions may relate to space, time, cause, origin, purpose, source, agent, instrument, possession, topic or abstract ideas:
> • *They arrived at midnight.* • *He's done it for his own reasons.*
> • *The shirt is made of cotton.* • *We live in hope.*
>
> Refer to **Section 8** of the Appendix for a list of expressions with **above**, **over**, **beneath**, **below**, **under**, **at**, **by**, **between**, **among**, **in**, **on**, **out of**.

A Use an expression with *above*, *over*, *under*, *below* or *beneath* to complete each sentence.

1 He's too young to be allowed in this bar. He's _____.

2 Nobody would ever suspect her. She's _____.

3 There'll be no trouble about repairing the television if it goes wrong. It's _____.

4 Don't let those children get too wild! Keep them _____.

5 He's taller than most people. He's of _____.

6 The main thing is, don't hurt him. _____, keep him safe.

7 That's rather unfair. You're hitting _____.

8 I'm afraid I can't work for anyone else. You see, I'm _____ to my present employers for two years.

9 He whispered the answer. 'Yes,' he said, _____.

10 Someone who robs an old lady of all her savings is _____, and deserves to be punished.

11 Use one of the _____ prepositions to complete these sentences.

12 It's very frosty this morning. The temperature must have dropped _____.

13 Shall we discuss the problem after lunch, _____?

14 He's a freelance film director, and travels all _____ making his films.

15 The village is well _____, and at risk of being flooded if the sea wall is breached by a particularly high tide.

16 Doctors think heart attacks are sometimes brought on by being _____ at home or at work.

17 You'll have to tell me the truth. Stop trying to pull the wool _____!

18 If you don't bargain with the market traders, you'll be paying _____ for their goods.

B Match each expression with *at* on the left with its approximate paraphrase.

1	at a loss	A	unoccupied, with no purpose
2	at short notice	B	going very fast
3	at any rate	C	deep down inside (a person)
4	at present	D	no matter what it takes
5	at a loose end	E	without much advance warning
6	at once	F	fighting another country
7	at heart	G	immediately
8	at hand	H	unsure what to do
9	at first sight	I	taking the most hopeful view
10	at times	J	near, ready, available
11	at war	K	sailing, on a ship
12	at all costs	L	in danger
13	at sea	M	the first time (I) saw (her)
14	at best	N	anyway
15	at risk	O	occasionally
16	at high speed	P	now

C Complete the sentences with the correct preposition, choosing from *between*, *among*, *out of* and *over*.

1 Bob's been _____ work for six months now.

2 _____ you and me, Smith hasn't got much of a future in the firm.

3 That book's too high up on the shelf. It's just _____ my reach.

4 She's _____ jobs at the moment, so she's struggling to make ends meet.

5 Unfortunately the catering committee can never agree _____ themselves.

6 I went on waving until the car was _____ sight.

7 We'll discuss the affair _____ a cup of tea.

8 It's no good trying that snack machine – it's _____ order.

9 The boys were hiding _____ the bushes in the garden.

10 There's a footpath _____ the canal and the main road.

11 No, I certainly won't give permission. It's _____ the question!

12 I can only admire his conscientiousness. It's _____ and above the call of duty.

13 I'm afraid those sandals are _____ stock at the moment, madam.

14 General Gibson settled in quite happily _____ the Polynesian natives.

15 I'm hoping to be reimbursed for my travelling expenses, otherwise I'll be rather _____ pocket.

16 The lift wasn't working, so she was _____ breath by the time she reached the top floor.

17 A prize was awarded to Fawzia, _____ others.

18 Children, put your coats on if you want to play _____ doors.

19 The photo's _____ focus, unfortunately, but you can still make out the figure in the doorway.

20 This information is rather _____ date, so we can't use it in our new brochure.

D Complete each sentence with the correct preposition from the pair in brackets.

1 _____ second thoughts, I'll have the lentil soup after all. (In/On)

2 Giles was mortified to discover that he had sent Cordelia a photograph of his ex-girlfriend _____ mistake. (by/at)

3 The results will be published _____ due course. (in/on)

4 'Could I possibly use your phone?' 'Oh, _____ all means.' (by/in)

5 The intrepid women explored the remotest part of the sierra _____ horseback. (by/on)

6 _____ all likelihood, we will never know the real reason. (In/On)

7 Kindly sign the contracts in triplicate and send back to head office _____ return. (by/on)

8 Nobody helped him. He managed it all _____ his own. (by/on)

9 The company is keeping its head above water this year, but it will have to become more efficient _____ the long run. (in/on)

10 The proposal looks good _____ paper, but there may be snags in its practical application. (in/on)

11 The victims of the industrial accident should, _____ rights, be compensated by the factory owners. (at/by)

E Complete the text by putting a suitable preposition in each space.

1) _____ the whole, Flora was content with her life. 2) _____ day she was a librarian in a large city library, but 3) _____ her spare time she lived in a world of dreams. Her secret, all-devouring passion was reading – novels 4) _____ particular – and she had read almost all the classics that the library had 5) _____ stock. She read voraciously, 6) _____ her lunch hour, her tea break, and the long evenings 7) _____ home. She would even read 8) _____ her way home, walking slowly 9) _____ her book open.

The small flat where she lived 10) _____ herself was piled high 11) _____ books. She knew her favourites 12) _____ heart, empathising with the characters and thinking 13) _____ them as real people. 14) _____ short, she had found that books fulfilled her emotional needs better than people did, and 15) _____ any case, she had now completely forgotten how to relate to people other than characters in novels.

Difficult verbs

Make usually conveys the idea of creating or producing something new:
• *make a speech, a fuss, a noise, the beds, a (new) thing, (someone) ill/well/better, a mistake, a change*

Do is used with work, obligations or general activities:
• *do homework, housework, military service, your duty, a favour, (someone) good, with/without*

A Complete the sentences with the correct form of *make* or *do*.

1 If you agreed, you'd be _____ me a great favour.

2 It's no good playing with Victoria. She _____ such a fuss if she doesn't win.

3 The visiting foreign dignitaries were invited to _____ speeches at the ceremonial opening of parliament.

4 What on earth have you _____ with the paper I was reading just now?

5 If you _____ any noise, they'll hear us and call the police.

6 A complete rest would _____ you an awful lot of good.

7 Well, there just isn't any coffee. You'll have to _____ without.

8 The housekeeper always _____ the beds straight after breakfast.

9 He's having a new suit _____, as he can't find one in his size.

10 What do you feel like _____ this weekend? Walking? Eating out? Going for a swim?

11 Now that he's over eighteen, he'll have to _____ his military service.

12 Doctor, is this treatment really going to _____ me better?

13 Try to avoid _____ so many mistakes in the final version.

14 I didn't manage to _____ my homework, as I was at a rehearsal last night.

15 I expect the new manager will be _____ a few changes in some departments.

16 He always _____ the hoovering, but not without a bit of grumbling!

17 John, have you got a moment? I could _____ with some help.

18 I don't see what the problem is, Jess. You're _____ a mountain out of a molehill.

19 Shall I _____ a beef casserole for dinner?

20 I'm afraid I can't make it to the meeting tonight. I've got too much to _____.

Say is used for direct or reported speech, with no personal direct object:
- *He just stood there and said nothing.*

Tell is followed by a direct object:
- *tell the truth, a lie, fortunes, a story, someone something*

Speak is often used for a single utterance or for knowledge of languages:
- *Can you speak French?*
Note: • *He stopped speaking to me after our argument.*

Talk is less formal, more conversational than **speak**, and refers to a longer activity: • *The trouble with Marian is she talks too much.*
- *Can the baby talk yet?*
Note: • *talk something over, talk about* (discuss)

B Complete the sentences with *say, tell, speak* or *talk*, in the correct form.

1 She was _____ to go home.
2 They _____ quietly to each other for a long time.
3 'Come in,' he _____.
4 The postman didn't _____ me he had delivered a parcel.
5 How many languages do you _____?
6 _____ me! I must know! What did he _____ to you?
7 Don't believe him. He always _____ lies.
8 Now, stop _____, everybody, and listen to me.
9 You must be silent while the judge is _____.
10 There is nothing more to be _____ on the subject.
11 You can always _____ the supervisor if you don't feel well.
12 I've just got one thing to _____, so listen carefully.
13 They will have to be _____ to pull their socks up.
14 Everything will be all right if you _____ the truth.
15 I was so surprised I couldn't _____ a word.
16 Every time he tries to _____, he stutters.

Arise/arose/arisen means to occur (of a problem, difficulty or need) or to stand up (formal or poetic):
- *Should any problems arise, let me know.*

Rise/rose/risen means to move upwards or stand up, and cannot take a direct object:
- *He rose to his feet.*

Raise/raised/raised means to move something upwards, or cause something to grow or appear, and takes a direct object:
- *He raised his eyes from his work.*
Note: • *raise a smile/laugh, an army, a family, a protest, doubts, fears, suspicions*

C Correct the sentences if necessary. Tick any that are already correct.

1 I watched the sun, a great red ball, raise slowly over the horizon.

2 Please raise your hand if you need the invigilator's help.

3 Wait until the dough has rose before kneading it again.

4 The actress rose from her sofa and swept out of the room.

5 The comedian just about managed to raise a laugh from his listeners.

6 Arise, Sir Galahad! Henceforth, you will serve your queen as her knight.

7 As the curtain was slowly raised, there were gasps of admiration from the audience.

8 If any more difficulties should rise, just let me know.

9 Taxes will probably raise next year.

10 Inflation is rising steeply in some countries, and more gradually in others.

Lie/lay/lain means to be flat or horizontal: • *She's lying on the beach.*

Lie/lied/lied means not to tell the truth: • *He's lying, I tell you!*

Lay/laid/laid means to put something down: • *Lay the book on the table.*
• *The hen's laying an egg.*
Note: • *lay the table, lay the blame on someone or something, lay bare (reveal), lay hold of someone/something*

D Complete the sentences with the correct form of *lie* or *lay*.

1 Yesterday the mayor _____ the foundation stone of the new leisure centre.

2 How long do you think those fossils have _____ there?

3 All the blame was _____ on the hospital management.

4 Would you mind _____ the table for supper, please?

5 How long have you been _____ to your friends? Why don't you tell the truth for a change?

6 I'm afraid Mrs Worth won't be coming tonight. She's _____ down at the moment, with a migraine.

7 In some cases, both birds take their turn at sitting on the eggs that the hen bird has _____.

8 Despite the sweltering heat outside, Sharon _____ down on her bed and tried to sleep.

9 The international mediators are hoping that both sides will _____ down their weapons and sit down at the negotiating table.

10 'Don't speak!' he said, _____ a finger on his lips.

11 You may not like the photo, but remember, the camera never _____.

12 We're having the new carpet _____ tomorrow.

13 Take your time. The ultimate decision _____ with you.

14 The city of Paris _____ on the River Seine.

Key word sentences

> **Key word** exercises require you to rewrite sentences using a key word and
> keeping approximately the same meaning. There are two areas to focus on:
>
> **a grammatical**
> You need to be familiar with all the main structures, such as passives, conditionals,
> wishes, regrets, reported speech, inversion of the verb, gerund and infinitive. (See
> relevant units for practice of these points.)
>
> **b lexical**
> You need to have a good knowledge of advanced vocabulary, including idioms and
> phrasal verbs.
>
> Key word items may be grammatical, lexical or 'lexico-grammatical'
> (a combination of both). See **Units 8**, **9**, **11**, **15**, **16** and **25** for exam-type
> key word sentences.

A Match the phrase or clause on the left with its approximate paraphrase on the right.

1	get a word in edgeways	A	be extremely busy
2	bark up the wrong tree	B	find a solution to
3	be made redundant	C	bears no resemblance to
4	give their verdict	D	make them angry
5	have their hands full	E	manage to interrupt
6	resolve the problem of	F	evade the issue
7	incur their wrath	G	take the full force of
8	there's no similarity between	H	say what they have decided
9	bear the brunt of	I	be mistaken
10	beg the question	J	lose your job

B For each sentence, write a new sentence which is as similar as possible in meaning. Use the word given, but do not alter it in any way.

1 The prisoner answered the question honestly.

   honest

2 It is said that he was born in Segovia.

   reputed

3 We had nearly finished when Isabel arrived.

   about

4 They've been behaving very strangely recently.

   recent

5 His medical treatment appears to have had a serious effect on his mental state.

   affected

6 The star was surrounded by screaming fans as soon as he arrived at the stage door.

arrival

7 The staff have always esteemed the headmaster very highly.

esteem

8 The electrician advised me to have the wiring checked.

advice

9 The guided tour takes place every hour.

intervals

10 She herself admits to being rather selfish.

admission

C Follow the instructions for Exercise A.

1 except for
2 I infer from what you say
3 there's no difference of opinion between them
4 instead of
5 voice their disapproval of
6 it's none of my business
7 take everything into account
8 be no match for an opponent
9 have misgivings about
10 brace themselves for

A as an alternative to
B it doesn't concern me
C consider all the facts
D say they are against
E have no chance of winning
F apart from
G prepare themselves for
H be worried or doubtful about
I they agree
J I understand from what you imply

D Follow the instructions for Exercise B.

1 She is certainly not a good cook.

means

2 I had no idea it was a breach of protocol.

unaware

3 The store should definitely give you your money back.

refund

4 The tourists were most impressed with the castle.

impact

5 Building societies will have to guard against their rivals.

laurels

6 They're faced with the choice of two alternatives.

horns

7 Taxpayers had to pay the cost of the privatisation plan.

foot

8 I did all I could to expedite the matter.

utmost

9 Juliet simply couldn't wait for his return.

long

10 By the time we all sat down to dinner, the Morrises still hadn't arrived.

sign

11 I think you've misunderstood the situation.

stick

12 The firm didn't go bankrupt, because they took Gerry's advice.

thanks

13 You'd feel much healthier if you had a relaxing break.

do

14 When the assembly line was introduced, five hundred workers were dismissed.

advent

15 His colleagues were shocked to hear of Ahmed's illness.

came

16 Alan complains all the time.

nothing

17 She'll probably win first prize.

stands

18 The policeman pointed out the speed limit sign to us.

drew

E Fill in the boxes to complete the missing words.

1 You can only get this product here. It's _____ to this store.

E ☐☐☐☐☐☐☐

2 She became a _____ name, after hosting her own TV chat show.

H ☐☐☐☐☐☐

3 What the crowd _____ in numbers, it made up for in enthusiasm.

L ☐☐☐☐

4 I really didn't know what to do. I was in a _____.

Q ☐☐☐☐☐☐

5 It's stalemate. Both sides refuse to negotiate. How can we break the _____?

D ☐☐☐☐☐☐

6 I hate throwing food away. It goes against the _____ to waste anything.

G ☐☐☐☐

7 There's no need to _____ tears over his problems. He can cope.

S ☐☐☐

8 No review can do _____ to Steven Spielberg's amazing new film.

J ☐☐☐☐☐

9 Be more _____ with electricity. Switch the lights off when you go out.

E ☐☐☐☐☐☐☐☐

10 Reggie has a _____ to get irritable when he's tired. He's often cross with the children then.

T ☐☐☐☐☐☐☐

UNIT 24

Dependent prepositions

Many **adjectives and nouns** are followed by a particular preposition:
- *They have every confidence in his judgement.*
- *Margarine is a substitute for butter.*

See **Section 9** of the Appendix for a list of common adjectives and nouns with their **dependent prepositions**.

Note that if adjectives or nouns have similar or opposite meanings, they often take the same preposition:
- *be ready/prepared for school*
- *be married/engaged/ related to someone*
- *be furious/angry/irritated with someone*
- *be frightened/scared/terrified of snakes*
- *be happy/sad about something*

A Complete the sentences with the correct prepositions.

1 I understand you will be eligible _____ promotion soon.

2 We regret the delay _____ despatching your order.

3 She was very conscious _____ her lack of experience on her first day at work.

4 He's come up with a new solution _____ the problem.

5 At least here you'll be safe _____ unwarranted intrusion.

6 There's no doubt _____ his feelings for you.

7 She's always been lacking _____ tact.

8 I would like to take this opportunity _____ thanking my hosts.

9 I have complete confidence _____ his ability to handle the situation.

10 Be very patient _____ Ryan. He's suffered a lot, you know.

11 It's a strange smell, isn't it? It's peculiar _____ this type of plant.

12 How very typical _____ her! Nothing is ever her fault!

13 Is there any chance _____ our meeting in the near future?

14 Despite her age, she takes pleasure _____ pitting her wits against all comers.

15 The island is rich _____ minerals and other natural resources.

16 It's obvious he's incapable _____ holding down a job.

17 I really don't see any point _____ continuing this correspondence any longer.

18 Without the certificate, you won't be sufficiently qualified _____ the job.

19 There's no question _____ your leaving us so soon.

20 Would you kindly inform me who is responsible _____ the travel arrangements?

21 We had great difficulty _____ hearing the station announcements.

22 She's convinced _____ the justice of her case.

23 I must point out that I'm not in the habit _____ walking around in my pyjamas.

24 He's always been rather envious _____ his older brother.

25 He takes pride _____ showing off his prize cucumbers.

Many **verbs** are followed by a particular preposition:
- *I've been puzzling over the problem for hours.*

See **Section 10** of the Appendix for a list of common verbs with their **dependent prepositions**.

Remember that verbs of similar or opposite meanings often take the same preposition: • *apply/send/ask for information*
- *care/worry about someone* • *agree/disagree with someone*

B Complete each space in the conversation between two business colleagues with the missing verb or preposition.

'Come in, Harold!'

'I must 1) _____ for arriving so late. The traffic, you know.'

'Oh, don't 2) _____ about that. The meeting's been put off anyway. Come in and help yourself 3) _____ coffee. Let me be the first to congratulate you 4) _____ your promotion.'

'Oh thanks, Paul. Yes, I'm delighted. But it hasn't been announced officially yet. Could you possibly 5) _____ it to yourself for a bit?'

'Well, of course, Harold. When do you think you'll be taking up the new post, then?'

'I'm not sure. It all 6) _____ on the contract, which I haven't seen yet. They're sending it to me this week. I was determined to 7) _____ on a pretty big salary increase, I can tell you.'

'Quite right too. It's a lot more responsibility.'

'Yes, and my outgoings are considerable these days. I still have to provide 8) _____ Julie and the kids, of course, even though we split up over two years ago. What about you, Paul? Any jobs *you've* 9) _____ for lately?'

'Not a thing. You're the only one here who's moving on. But don't worry, we won't 10) _____ it against you!'

'Good. Of course there's no need 11) _____ us to lose touch. I value your judgement, you know.'

'Well, thanks, Harold. I'm always happy to advise a friend.'

'I've been thinking, Paul. I may have difficulty 12) _____ adjusting to living in Munich – I must confess 13) _____ a slight feeling of apprehension.'

'Oh, I have every confidence 14) _____ you, Harold. You'll be a huge success 15) _____ our German colleagues, just wait and see!'

C Match the two halves of the sentences correctly.

1 You should insure property
2 The local restaurants are well supplied
3 The coach was blamed
4 The charity is devoted
5 The accused pleaded guilty
6 Jonathan struggled
7 After the row, Jane was seething
8 The sales assistant is attending
9 The intruder was mistaken
10 She's always fishing

A to a customer at the moment.
B with the youth who had attacked him.
C with resentment.
D for compliments.
E for a doctor.
F to the charge of arson.
G against fire and theft.
H with organically grown vegetables.
I to raising money for the disabled.
J for his team's poor performance.

D Complete the text with the correct verb, noun or preposition.

Scientists are still curious 1) _____ the effects of the oceanographic phenomenon called El Niño, which occurs in the south-west Pacific Ocean. There is no 2) _____, however, about the reason 3) _____ its occurrence. Every few years, a rise 4) _____ surface temperatures due to a temporary decrease in trade winds makes sea levels rise, and waves head north-east up the coast of South America. El Niño is noted 5) _____ its effect on local climates, but recent research has shown that it is also 6) _____ for wider atmospheric changes, resulting, for example, 7) _____ temporary drought in the Sahel or failure of the maize harvest in Zimbabwe.

Now scientists involved 8) _____ oceanographic research are 9) _____ on a new theory, that El Niño can produce changes 10) _____ ocean patterns that may last for decades. Computers at the Naval Research Laboratory in Mississippi, fed 11) _____ the latest satellite information on sea temperatures and wave heights, show that the giant waves that roll across the Pacific may be the result 12) _____ a previous El Niño, which will continue to affect the circulation of the North Pacific for years to come.

The 1982 El Niño, the strongest of the 20th century, is 13) _____ of causing the flooding of the Mississippi basin in 1993, with the loss of life and serious 14) _____ to crops and property that resulted.

Recycling

A Choose the correct word or phrase to complete each sentence. Write the letter in the space.

1 Your car's very _____. It hardly seems to use any petrol at all.

   a) economical   b) economic   c) ecumenical   d) ecological

2 I'm in a terrible _____. I just don't know what to do.

   a) problem   b) quandary   c) loss   d) trouble

3 _____ to the bank manager's loan, Gerald's struggling company managed to stay solvent.

   a) With thanks   b) Thank you   c) Thanks   d) Gratefully

4 We have every confidence _____ his powers of diplomacy and organisation.

   a) on   b) in   c) with   d) by

5 Is there any chance _____ the machinery repaired?

   a) to have   b) of having   c) for having   d) of being

6 By appearing on the soap powder commercials, she became a _____ name.

   a) housewife   b) housekeeper   c) house   d) household

7 Now that John has decided he doesn't want to stand, we'll have to find a substitute _____ the post.

   a) to   b) as   c) for   d) in

8 It's hard to do _____ to such a masterpiece.

   a) judgement   b) justice   c) fair play   d) fairness

9 It's crucial that he _____ attend the ceremony.

   a) should   b) must   c) will   d) ought

10 At the moment the ruling party is on the _____ of a dilemma.

   a) hooves   b) points   c) feet   d) horns

11 How you invest your money is none of my _____.

   a) affair   b) business   c) matter   d) care

12 I'm afraid you've got the wrong end of the _____.

   a) loaf   b) pot   c) leg   d) stick

13 I'm _____ a complete loss to understand why you reacted so violently.

   a) at   b) in   c) on   d) by

14 _____ you cut down your carbohydrate intake, you'd have lost weight by now.

   a) Did   b) Were   c) If   d) Had

15 If the level of VAT is _____ this year, small businesses will be affected.

   a) raised   b) risen   c) arisen   d) raising

16 Don't _____ anything to him if you can help it.

   a) speak   b) say   c) talk   d) tell

17 I couldn't hear what he said, because he was muttering _____ his breath.

    a) out of   b) under   c) in   d) on

18 I object _____ to do all the work myself.

    a) to being asked   b) to asking   c) being asked   d) on being asked

19 The stones have _____ buried in the sand for a thousand years.

    a) lied   b) lying   c) laid   d) lain

20 I want _____ clear up the mess you've made!

    a) that you   b) you to   c) you do   d) you should

21 We shall review the salary arrangements _____ due course.

    a) in   b) on   c) by   d with

22 The magistrate _____ his disapproval of the young man's behaviour.

    a) said   b) told   c) voiced   d) spoke

23 Nobody would question the PM's integrity. He is above _____.

    a) contempt   b) suspicion   c) average   d) all

24 I'll _____ you just one more story before you go to sleep.

    a) tell   b) speak   c) say   d) talk

25 If only I _____ lost my temper in the meeting!

    a) wouldn't have   b) wouldn't   c) hadn't   d) didn't

B Complete the second sentence so that it means the same as the first one, using the word given. You must use between **three** and **eight** words, including the word given. (Contractions count as two words.)

1 The villagers, though few in number, were incredibly friendly.

lacked

What the villagers _____ in friendliness.

2 My business partner and I are in complete agreement.

difference

There is _____ my business partner and me.

3 In the end they left me to settle up with the restaurant.

foot

In the end I _____ the restaurant bill.

4 He himself admits to having wasted a lot of money.

admission

By his _____ wasted a lot of money.

5 Getting upset over Michael's departure is pointless.

tears

There's no _____ over Michael's departure.

6 The effects of the gale were felt mainly along the south coast.

brunt

The south coast _____ the gale.

7 All she does is sit in the office drinking coffee.

but

She does _____ drinking coffee.

C Complete the text by putting **one** word in each space. (Do not use contractions – they count as two words.)

The Great Pyramid of Giza is probably the most famous 1) _____ the seven wonders of the ancient world. It 2) _____ built by King Khufu (known as Cheops to 3) _____ Greeks) around 2450 BC, and its neighbour, 4) _____ is a little smaller, was constructed later 5) _____ his son Khefren. By the time of the beautiful Queen Cleopatra, they 6) _____ already stood against the desert skyline through the reigns of more 7) _____ a hundred kings or pharaohs. 8) _____ centuries archaeologists have puzzled 9) _____ the reasons for their construction. Now a new solution 10) _____ the mystery 11) _____ been proposed, according to 12) _____ the Great Pyramid was intended 13) _____ a focus for 14) _____ pharaoh's complicated funeral ceremony. Astronomers think 15) _____ narrow passages 16) _____ from the royal burial chambers 17) _____ aligned with certain stars in the 26,000-year cycle of the constellations, 18) _____ that the dead king's soul could 19) _____ launched to the stars. The latest discovery is a hitherto unopened door in the depths of the Pyramid. Who can imagine what 20) _____ behind it?

D Complete the text by making a new word from each word given in capitals.

Hi Kevin

How's work going since your colleague's 1) _____?　　RESIGN

It's very sad, really, that he's had a nervous 2) _____,　　BREAK

but I think you should put in an 3) _____ for his job.　　APPLY

You'd have a good chance of getting it, I'm sure. I'll do my

4) _____ to persuade you, anyway!　　MOST

Things are hectic here at the office – we're under

5) _____ as usual, so there's far too much to do. And　　STRONG

our team leader's 6) _____, which doesn't help.　　DECIDE

It's quite an 7) _____ for him to come to any　　ACHIEVE

8) _____ at all, so he simply fails to get things　　CONCLUDE

organised. There's a 9) _____ feeling that he isn't　　SPREAD

going to be with us for long! There's also a bit of

muttering about the new staff contracts, but I feel they're

making a mountain out of a 10) _____ about all that.　　HILL

Well, see you at the hockey this Saturday maybe?

All the best

Lee

Phrasal verbs with *down*

blow   break   bring   calm   chop   close   come   crack
cut   fall   flag   get   go   hand   jot   let   lie   mark
narrow   note   pelt   play   pour   pull   put   run
sit   slam   slow   squat   tear   tie   tone   track
tumble   turn   wind

Down often has the meaning of a downward movement, or a decrease, or of stopping an activity.

A Rewrite the sentences, using a phrasal verb with **down**, to produce the opposite meaning of the words in italics. Choose from the verbs in the box above.

1 We all *stood up* when the managing director walked in.
2 The building society has *set up* a branch in Warmsley.
3 Inflation has been *rising* steadily since January.
4 When Caroline heard the terrible news, she *remained calm*.
5 Rain was *gently falling*.
6 The teacher *quietly put the book* on the table.
7 The company will probably want to *publicise* the results.
8 The old lady was adamant that her cat should be *kept alive*.
9 After three days of continuous bombardment, the White Tower *remained standing*.
10 Having Bruce to stay has really *cheered me up*.
11 He *got very excited* after his meeting with the trade union officials.
12 The secretary *carefully put the notice up on* the board.

B Use verbs from the box above to complete the sentences.

1 You'll have to ⬚⬚⬚⬚ down when you come to the crossroads.
2 The town council decided to ⬚⬚⬚⬚ down the building, as it was unsafe.
3 The small boy ⬚⬚⬚⬚⬚⬚⬚ down on the ground and examined the insect.
4 The force of the gale ⬚⬚⬚⬚ down hundreds of trees.
5 I know you're angry, but you should ⬚⬚⬚⬚ down the language you're using. It's too aggressive.
6 From the time of his arrival in prison, Jones was ⬚⬚⬚⬚⬚⬚ down as a troublemaker.
7 It's a difficult choice, but at least we've ⬚⬚⬚⬚⬚⬚⬚ it down to five out of the hundred applicants.
8 The escaped convict was finally ⬚⬚⬚⬚⬚⬚ down to a hiding place in the Far East.

9 The aim of the popular uprising was to ☐☐☐☐☐ down the government.

10 As fewer orders came in, the firm began to ☐☐☐ down its sales force.

11 If there is any more subsidence, that cottage will ☐☐☐☐☐☐ down into the sea.

12 The reporter ☐☐☐☐☐ down the details of the court case for inclusion in his article.

C Complete each sentence with a phrase from box A followed by a phrase from box B. Do not use any phrase more than once.

A	B
flagged down	they offered me.
I turned down the job	on fraud everywhere.
I felt badly let down	at the moment.
wind down	a taxi.
and jotted down	chopping down the tree.
rather tied down	the professor's points.
running down	properly.
have been handed down	his wife's achievements.
will prevent them from	by him.
cracking down	through the centuries.

1 Family traditions _____

2 Jeremy is forever _____

3 The man in a business suit _____

4 With two small children, she's _____

5 The preservation order _____

6 I listened to the lecture _____

7 The authorities are _____

8 After the interview _____

9 When Steve wouldn't help, _____

10 The holiday gave us a chance to _____

Phrasal verbs with *after*, *back* and *about*

after
go   look   take

back
bring   call   cut   fall   get   give   go   hold   keep   pay
put   ring   set   take   talk   turn

about
bring   go   put   set

Back often has the meaning of returning something (to someone) or of remembering the past.

A Match each phrasal verb with the correct definition. (There may be other possible definitions.)

1	bring about	A	pursue
2	ring back	B	return something to its correct place
3	take after	C	take care of
4	answer back	D	cause
5	go about	E	be like an older relative
6	turn back	F	delay or hinder the progress of something
7	cut back	G	not tell the whole truth
8	put (it) about	H	reduce
9	put back	I	reply rudely or defiantly to someone in authority
10	set back	J	return someone's phone call
11	go after	K	retreat
12	look after	L	recover something that had been taken away
13	fall back	M	approach or tackle (a problem)
14	keep (something) back	N	make someone return the way they have come
15	get back	O	spread (a rumour)

B Complete each sentence with the correct form of a phrasal verb from the box above.

1 The gangsters lay in wait for their victim, and _____ him with their fists.

2 The salesman has left us a brochure to look at. He said he'd _____ soon, to see if we want to place an order.

3 I can lend you some money for a sandwich. You can always _____ me _____ tomorrow.

4 Legends about the Green Man _____ right _____ to the Middle Ages.

5 Especially when you're tired and under stress, it's important to _____ yourself and your health.

6 Alex _____ mending the clock, but he soon had to admit defeat.

7 We were halfway across the bay when two of the boys felt seasick, so we thought we'd better _____ and put them ashore.

8 Everyone _____ their daily tasks as if nothing had happened.

9 I was just leaving the office when the receptionist _____ me _____. She'd forgotten to give me a message.

10 Police had difficulty in _____ the demonstrators, who were threatening to break through the security cordon.

11 You've been to Austria recently, haven't you? When did you _____?

12 If we don't get any applications for the job, we'll just have to _____ on part-time staff as a temporary measure.

C Complete each sentence with a phrase from box A followed by a phrase from box B. Do not use any phrase more than once.

A
held back
bring back
ring you back
set my roses back
bring about
go about
went after
take back

B
memories of a person or place.
raising the money?
his anger.
a change in the law.
the pickpocket.
what you said about him.
when I get home.
by several weeks.

1 We are campaigning to _____

2 You'll have to _____

3 A passer-by _____

4 I'll _____

5 How are you going to _____

6 A severe frost could _____

7 Sometimes a certain smell can _____

8 For the children's sake he _____

Phrasal verbs with *off*

be   break   call   clear   come   cordon   cut   doze   drop   fight
get   give   go   keep   laugh   lay   let   live   pay   pick   pull   put
ring   rip   round   scare   scrape   see   send   set   shake   shave
show   switch   take   tell   throw   turn   wear   work   write

Off often has the meaning of a movement away, or of separating people or things.

A Decide whether the definitions are true (T) or false (F). Give the correct definition(s) if necessary.

1	pick off	collect a person from a place
2	live off	survive
3	round off	complete, give the finishing touch to
4	be off	separate someone from another person
5	scare off	frighten someone away
6	switch off	stop concentrating
7	show off	make someone feel embarrassed by behaving badly
8	set off	cause to explode
9	see off	be present at someone's departure
10	rip off	steal from or cheat someone

B Complete each sentence with the correct form of a verb from the box above.

1 When Roger saw the restaurant kitchen, it completely _____ him off eating there.

2 If milk smells bad, you can be certain it has _____ off.

3 He always leaves his room in a mess. I'm forever _____ him off about it.

4 The mixture in the saucepan was beginning to _____ off a very unpleasant odour.

5 The police had to _____ off the embassy to protect staff from the demonstrators.

6 Detectives cannot interview the victim until the operation is over and the effects of the anaesthetic have _____ off.

7 Maria's car was so badly damaged that her insurance company _____ it off.

8 Just fill in the application form, and _____ it off.

9 I've been trying to _____ off this cold for the last week.

10 Surely you don't mean that! _____ off it!

11 I must _____ off soon. I've got to collect Louise from school.

12 With a bit more planning, his idea might have worked, but I'm afraid it didn't really _____ off.

C Add **it** where necessary to the following sentences, and say what **it** means or might mean.

1 The party's been cancelled. She called off last week.

2 I have great confidence in the PM. I'm sure he'll pull off.

3 I went for a long walk to work off the effects of the huge meal.

4 You don't need the light on in here. Turn off, please.

5 Eva suddenly rang off in the middle of our conversation.

6 I'll drop off at your house on my way to work tomorrow.

7 How on earth are you ever going to scrape all off?

8 His father dozed off while watching the news.

9 I knew they disapproved of me, but I just laughed off.

10 I suppose Noel will shave off one day!

11 Jane decided the moment had come to break off.

12 Don't you know this is private property? Clear off, will you!

D Complete each sentence with a phrase from box A followed by a phrase from box B. Do not use any phrase more than once.

A	B
will be laying off	without a penny.
put off	in two hours' time.
set off	all too quickly.
will pay off	as he is hoping.
let off	by what people say.
wore off	before first light.
kept off	500 workers until after the summer.
will be taking off	very lightly in the accident.
got off	fireworks in their garden.
cut her off	during the cricket match.

1 The plane _____

2 Fortunately Zoë _____

3 The factory _____

4 I don't think his gamble _____

5 Her family _____

6 The boys _____

7 The rain _____

8 James refuses to be _____

9 The effects of our holiday _____

10 We'll have to _____

UNIT 29

Phrasal verbs with *through*, *for* and *by*

through
break   check   fall   get   go   look   pull   put   run   see
sleep   think

for
account   apply   ask   call   care   fall   fish   go   look   make
mistake   pay   send   stand

by
get   go   put   stand   tick

Through often has the meaning of doing something completely or thoroughly.

A Match each phrasal verb with the correct definition. (There may be other possible definitions.)

1 mistake for	A	not wake up during an emergency, alarm etc.
2 stand for	B	arrange for someone to come
3 check through	C	provide the necessary money for
4 see through	D	be connected (on the phone)
5 get by	E	go in the direction of
6 apply for	F	look through to see if everything is correct
7 make for	G	not be deceived by, see the truth behind
8 sleep through	H	pass (of time)
9 go for	I	confuse with
10 get through	J	have just enough (usually money) to manage
11 call for	K	ask for (a job)
12 send for	L	attack
13 think through	M	collect someone (from their home, office etc.)
14 pay for	N	consider all the aspects
15 tick by	O	represent

B Complete the crossword with verbs from the box above, using the clues provided.

Across:

1 I hope I'll be able to stay on in the job long enough to _____ the project through.

4 You shouldn't _____ compliments like that! (4, 3)

7 Although he's in a critical state after the accident, the doctors think he'll _____ through.

8 Could you just _____ through these accounts and see if they're correct?

10 A good friend will always stand _____ you.

11 It's hard to _____ for the old lady's disappearance.

12 Do you think Ellen and Roy will be able to _____ by on one salary?

13 When he moves to Edinburgh, he'll have to _____ for a flat.

Down:

2 If you need anything, just _____ me for it.

3 I was enjoying myself so much that I hardly noticed the time _____ by.

4 Her plan cannot possibly succeed. I'm sure it'll _____ . (4, 7)

5 She's so beautiful, he'll _____ for her as soon as he sees her.

6 Can we _____ through the instructions again, please?

7 Luckily, I had some money _____ by for a rainy day.

9 When her mother died, Agatha had to _____ for her invalid sister single-handedly.

10 Journalists are hoping to _____ through the secrecy surrounding the royal family's decision.

Recycling

A Choose the correct word or phrase to complete each sentence. Write the letter in the space.

1 The road was closed, so we had to _____ and find an alternative route.

a) put down   b) turn back   c) go about   d) go off

2 They _____ for Paris at midnight.

a) set off   b) made for   c) went off   d) got down

3 I knew your family would stand _____ you.

a) for   b) off   c) by   d) about

4 How could you have _____ him for your brother?

a) confused   b) considered   c) thought   d) mistaken

5 It is vital that we _____ a change in people's attitudes.

a) bring down   b) bring back   c) bring about   d) look after

6 Giuseppe's secretary _____ a call to the office in Milan.

a) put through   b) applied for   c) put by   d) set about

7 We'll have to _____ down the options before coming to a decision.

a) slow   b) narrow   c) bring   d) wind

8 Rosa certainly _____ her mother in her devil-may-care approach to life.

a) looks after   b) calms down   c) cares for   d) takes after

9 Ingrid broke _____ in tears when we told her about the accident.

a) off   b) through   c) down   d) for

10 I'm so tired I think I'll probably _____ off in the cinema.

a) doze   b) sleep   c) turn   d) fall

11 If a bus doesn't come, you can always flag _____ a taxi.

a) after   b) for   c) down   d) off

12 Look, I _____ it all back. I should never have spoken like that.

a) take   b) put   c) call   d) give

13 I think a couple of coffees will _____ off the meal nicely.

a) go   b) send   c) round   d) wear

14 The official _____ quickly through my file, and then handed it back to me.

a) saw   b) looked   c) got   d) turned

15 If you're interested in *Mastermind,* you can send _____ free tickets and be part of the studio audience next time they record it.

a) off   b) by   c) about   d) for

16 You shouldn't have sent Sebastian that Valentine's card. I think you've scared him _____!

a) back   b) down   c) off   d) through

17 The rain was simply _____ down on the deserted street.

a) pelting   b) spraying   c) showering   d) dripping

18 She talks so fast, it's difficult getting a word in _____!

a) sideways   b) halfway   c) edgeways   d) any way

B Read the text and underline the **ten** phrasal verbs. Give a definition for each one, according to its meaning in the text.

When Laura was a university student, she found it very difficult to get by on her grant, so she decided to look for a part-time job. When she spotted an advertisement in the local paper for snack bar staff, she sat down to apply for the job. She wasn't sure how best to go about presenting herself on paper, so she just jotted down the details of her background and experience, and sent the application off immediately.

The owner of the snack bar, a Mr Edwards, rang a couple of days later to ask her to come for an interview the following Saturday. When she arrived at Tasty Bites, she was very nervous because she felt sure he could see through her claims to have worked as a waitress before, and would turn her down as a matter of course. But finally the interview was over, and when he shook hands with her and said 'See you next week, then!', she realised she had pulled it off.

C Match the first half of each sentence with the correct ending.

1 How do you account for
2 I'm not sure you've
3 If your car's out of action,
4 Surely he didn't sleep through
5 She's putting it about
6 I can't stand the way
7 Have they cordoned off

A thought this through sufficiently.
B he's always showing off.
C that his wife has left him.
D all that noise!
E the discrepancies in your reports?
F the scene of the crime?
G I'll call for you tonight.

D Complete the text by putting **one** word in each space. (Do not use contractions – they count as two words.)

THE CUCKOO ROLLER OF MADAGASCAR

This bird is about the same size 1) _____ the European roller, and has many features in common 2) _____ its near relatives.

3) _____ the European family, however, the cuckoo roller can reverse its outer toes, 4) _____ it to perch 5) _____ gripping a branch with two toes forward and two back. Its eating habits are also quite different. 6) _____ nearly all other rollers take food on the wing or pluck reptiles or large insects from the ground, the cuckoo roller stays high up in the forest canopy, 7) _____ on caterpillars, stick insects and, 8) _____ important of all, chameleons.

Subtly blending its colours to the forest backcloth, and 9) _____ leaving the safety of the branches except to cross from one tree to 10) _____, the chameleon is an elusive prey. 11) _____ on open ground, 12) _____ myriad dangers it normally avoids, the chameleon's slow, swaying walk 13) _____ it difficult to see against the leaves. 14) _____ good is its camouflage that the cuckoo roller has to 15) _____ up with long periods of watching and waiting, 16) _____ a tell-tale movement betrays its victim's presence. At 17) _____, experts assume this is 18) _____ happens, because 19) _____ the fact that this bird is widespread throughout Madagascar, 20) _____ observer has yet seen it in the process of catching its prey.

Phrasal verbs with *up*

blow	bottle	break	bring	build	call	catch	cheer
clear	crop	cut	draw	dress	eat	end	fill	fix
flare	get	give	go	grow	hang	hurry	hold	keep
liven	look	make	own	pick	pull	put	seal	settle
shoot	show	shut	speak	split	stay	stir	sum	take
tie	turn						

Up often has the meaning of an upward movement, or of approaching, completing or increasing.

A Match each phrasal verb with the correct definition. (There may be other possible definitions.)

1	stir up	A	confess, admit
2	sum up	B	come to a stop (of a vehicle)
3	own up	C	summon for military service, conscript
4	draw up	D	put on smart clothes
5	hang up	E	try to cause (trouble)
6	call up	F	raise your voice
7	liven up	G	not go to bed early
8	dress up	H	summarise
9	settle up	I	make more lively
10	speak up	J	suddenly become angry
11	stay up	K	pay all that is owed
12	flare up	L	finish a phone call

B Rewrite the sentences, using a phrasal verb with **up**, to produce the opposite meaning of the words in italics. Choose from the verbs in the box above.

1 His visit certainly *depressed me*.
2 Have you *let the dog loose?*
3 The child *left her food untouched*.
4 Jeremy tends to *express his emotions openly*.
5 When did Ramon and Anna *start their relationship?*
6 He was determined to *continue* smoking.
7 My uncle usually *goes to bed* at 9 o'clock.
8 The officer *emptied* his wine glass.
9 The lawyer *opened* the envelope with a flourish.
10 As soon as controls were lifted, prices *came down*.
11 Ted *stopped* playing tennis when he was sixty.
12 I'll *drop you off* at seven o'clock.

C Use verbs from the box on page 94 to complete the sentences.

1 She quickly ⬜⬜⬜⬜⬜ up the basics of the language.

2 You'll have to ⬜⬜⬜⬜⬜ up your strength by eating properly.

3 Be quiet! Just ⬜⬜⬜⬜ up!

4 How long can you ⬜⬜⬜⬜ up this pretence?

5 I'll ⬜⬜⬜ you up with a room. Leave it to me.

6 The carpet was ⬜⬜⬜ up into three smaller pieces.

7 An accident ⬜⬜⬜⬜ up the flow of traffic in the town centre.

8 Guy Fawkes and his fellow-conspirators did not succeed in ⬜⬜⬜⬜⬜⬜⬜ up the Houses of Parliament.

9 The Brontë sisters all ⬜⬜⬜⬜ up in Yorkshire.

10 First Sam worked in Canada, then Florida, but he finally ⬜⬜⬜⬜⬜ up in France.

11 Come on! ⬜⬜⬜⬜⬜ up, or we'll be late!

12 I waited for ages, but my cousin never ⬜⬜⬜⬜⬜⬜ up.

D Complete each sentence with a phrase from box A followed by a phrase from box B. Do not use any phrase more than once.

A	B
clear up	last month.
put you up	if you need to stay overnight.
made up,	if you ask me.
crop up	his room before doing his homework.
pulled up	on her farm in Cornwall.
look Lorenzo up	in front of the hotel.
brought him up	if we pass through Rome.
shot up	at the meeting.

1 We should _____

_____

2 The taxi _____

_____

3 The boy was told to _____

_____

4 Tom's grandmother _____

_____

5 Prices simply _____

_____

6 I didn't expect that topic to _____

_____

7 I can easily _____

_____

8 The story was obviously _____

_____

Phrasal verbs with *out*

branch	break	carry	check	come	cross	cry	drop	eat
find	get	give	hand	keep	lay	leave	let	lock	look
make	measure	pass	pick	point	pull	put	rub	rule
set	share	slip	sort	stick	storm	take	think	throw
try	turn	wash	wear	work				

A Decide whether the definitions are true (T) or false (F). Give the correct definition(s) if necessary.

1	slip out	leave quietly and unobtrusively
2	wear out	disappear
3	carry out	perform (an operation, an experiment or a duty)
4	cross out	delete
5	sort out	distribute
6	break out	make an escape
7	leave out	omit
8	storm out	leave angrily
9	work out	calculate
10	make out	manage to see
11	rule out	erase
12	find out	study
13	set out	begin (a journey)
14	keep out	prevent from entering
15	pick out	pluck or scratch
16	branch out	split

B Complete each sentence with the correct form of a verb from the box above.

1 I really don't feel like cooking. Couldn't we _____ out?

2 We're _____ my mother out for the day on Sunday.

3 Jason never completed his university course. He _____ out halfway through.

4 In the end it _____ out that the police had suspected Ferguson all along.

5 Her clothes were all neatly _____ out on the bed, ready for packing.

6 I happened to _____ myself out of the house last week.

7 We'll have to _____ out to him that he simply can't throw his weight around like that.

8 Liz has always been squeamish about the sight of blood. Last week she actually _____ out when she cut her finger.

9 The driver picked up speed and _____ out into the main stream of traffic.

10 Volunteers are going to _____ out soup and bread to the homeless.

11 He hasn't been _____ out yet, has he? Surely he hasn't served his sentence yet?

12 It's no good covering up for him. The truth will have to _____ out in the end.

13 It's rude to _____ your tongue out at people, Marian.

14 You're not going to _____ those bottles out, are you? We could take them to the bottle bank.

C Add **it** where necessary to the following sentences, and say what **it** means or might mean.

1 I want to try out before agreeing to buy.

2 There'll be enough for all of us. I'll measure out.

3 I think the diary's stuck behind the radiator. Can you get out?

4 The girl cried out in pain as the doctor dressed her wound.

5 Do you think this ink stain will wash out?

6 Look, you've spelt my name wrong! Rub out!

7 Are you sure you've really thought out?

8 If there's a lot of work to do, we can share out.

9 I wonder if Jamal has got it right. Could you check out?

10 You want the file on the Kingman family? I'll look out for you when I have time.

D Complete each sentence with the correct verb from the pair in brackets.

1 I'm afraid the authorities have already _____ out the bypass option. (ruled/rubbed)

2 As glass, paper and plastic are all disposed of separately now, we have to _____ out our rubbish before it's collected. (share/sort)

3 I'm not sure Jenny's coming with us. She said she might have to _____ out at the last minute. (get/drop)

4 If I were you, I'd _____ out the recipe before the dinner party. (measure/try)

5 The cleaners _____ out all the lights, then set the burglar alarm and left the building. (put/took)

6 The ex-President's memoirs, currently being serialised in a leading newspaper, are _____ out next week. (coming/getting)

7 The bank clerk called the police when he saw what looked like a gun _____ out of the man's jacket pocket. (pulling/sticking)

8 Civil Service mandarins have designed a complicated and lengthy interview procedure, whose purpose is to _____ out candidates of the highest calibre. (work/pick)

9 To implement the Common Agricultural Policy, farming subsidies have been _____ out on a massive scale by the EU. (handed/laid)

10 When his car hire business showed signs of imminent collapse, Ibrahim decided to _____ out into another, potentially more lucrative, field – the property market. (slip/branch)

Phrasal verbs with *over*, *apart* and *with*

over
blow   boil   bowl   check   cloud   get   go   hand   look   pull
run   stop   take   think   turn

apart
come   take   tell

with
confuse   deal   do   fight   go   identify   part   reason   side   toy

A Match each phrasal verb with the correct definition. (There may be other possible definitions.)

1	get over	A	see the difference between
2	deal with	B	match
3	take apart	C	consider
4	check over	D	recover from
5	reason with	E	make sure something is in good condition
6	hand over	F	transfer, surrender
7	tell apart	G	support someone holding a particular view
8	stop over	H	handle, do
9	go with	I	move to one side when driving
10	side with	J	cease (of a storm)
11	think over	K	break a journey (especially for a night)
12	confuse with	L	try to persuade
13	blow over	M	dismantle
14	pull over	N	mistake for

B Complete each sentence with the correct form of a phrasal verb from the box above.

1 Sadly, the old lady will have to _____ her beloved budgie when she moves into the old people's home. They don't allow pets there.

2 I opened the back of the watch to put a new battery in, and the whole thing suddenly _____ in my hands! I hope I can get it repaired.

3 Could you please _____ those instructions again? Kate wasn't listening the first time.

4 There was a terrible smell in the kitchen. The soup had _____ and put the gas out.

5 You simply can't _____ the twins _____ if they're wearing identical outfits.

6 No wonder Ryan often comes home from school with a black eye. He's always _____ the other boys!

7 I always get Madeleine to _____ my reports before I hand them in to the boss. He's a stickler for spelling and punctuation, and she's got a good eye for that sort of thing.

8 The company's personnel department need good management systems to _____ their workload effectively.

C Complete each sentence with a phrase from box A followed by a phrase from box B. Do not use any phrase more than once.

A
got over
will cloud over
toy with
has always identified with
could do with
was quite bowled over
finally turned over
took over

B
later on today.
the feminist cause.
the small private company.
her tragic loss.
by the success of the plan.
the fourth time I tried it.
some financial assistance.
the food on her plate.

1 The engine _____

2 The state airline _____

3 My sister _____

4 Everyone _____

5 I expect it _____

6 The newly-weds _____

7 Sally could only _____

8 It was a long time before she _____

D Complete the text with phrasal verbs from the box on page 98, in the correct form.

It all started when the milk 1) _____ over, on the little stove in the workshop. Tony was supposed to be keeping an eye on it. Bill didn't even notice. He never made the coffee – he was always much too busy 2) _____ apart the old radios that came to be repaired. However, it was the last straw for Roger.

'Can't I trust you to do anything right?' he shouted.

Tony turned, surprised. He tried to 3) _____ with his brother. 'Well, Rog, you're the one who wants hot milk in your coffee.'

Bill looked up and 4) _____ with Tony. 'Tony's right. Why don't *you* keep an eye on it in future?' he said gruffly.

Roger looked at his brothers in despair. There had to be a better way of 5) _____ with the constant friction between them, but he hadn't found it yet. 'Sorry, Tony, I'm a bit irritable at the moment, I know. I could 6) _____ with a holiday, that's what it is,' he said.

'So could I,' said Tony, turning back to his work and 7) _____ idly with his pen. 'So could we all,' said Bill grumpily.

There was silence in the workshop again. The row had 8) _____ over for the time being.

Phrasal verbs with *on*

add	bring	call	carry	catch	count	get	go	hang	have
hold	keep	let	live	look	move	pass	pick	put	ramble
send	soldier	switch	take	touch	try	turn			

On often has the meaning of attaching or continuing.

A Match each phrasal verb with the correct definition. (There may be other possible definitions.)

1	look on	A	ask someone for help
2	get on	B	continue
3	take on	C	continue bravely despite difficulties
4	count on	D	employ
5	bring on	E	become popular
6	let on	F	be a spectator
7	soldier on	G	induce or cause
8	call on	H	rely on, have confidence in
9	catch on	I	make progress
10	keep on	J	reveal information

B Rewrite the sentences, using a phrasal verb with **on**, to produce the opposite meaning of the words in italics. Choose from the verbs in the box above.

1 Toby *took off* his three-piece suit.
2 You'll have to *let go* when I tell you to!
3 The little girl *stopped* talking when the teacher came in.
4 Remember to *switch off* the electricity at the mains.
5 He *spoke briefly and to the point* about the arrangements.
6 Are you going to *keep to yourself* what happened?
7 The tax was *deducted* before the bill was paid.
8 Are you *being serious with me*?

C Use verbs from the box above to complete the sentences.

1 The fashion editor wondered if the trend would ☐☐☐☐☐☐ on.
2 Would you like to ☐☐☐ that suit on, sir?
3 Tonight, ladies and gentlemen, I'd just like to ☐☐☐☐☐ briefly on one or two topics of general interest.
4 The old man only has his state pension to ☐☐☐☐ on.
5 If I'm in trouble, I can always ☐☐☐☐☐ on Rosemary to help me.
6 ☐☐☐☐ on a minute! Wait for me.
7 My grandmother is ☐☐☐☐☐☐☐ on a bit now. She's over eighty.

8 They ⬚⬚⬚⬚⬚ on to the next item on the agenda without answering his question.

9 If the boss asks you, don't ⬚⬚⬚ on that I've told you. Keep it to yourself.

10 A chain letter is a letter which is ⬚⬚⬚⬚⬚ on from one person to another, until someone breaks the chain.

11 Perhaps we should ⬚⬚⬚⬚ on Gabriela when we pass through London.

12 It'll be a muddy walk, so we'd better ⬚⬚⬚ our boots on.

D Complete each sentence with a phrase from box A followed by a phrase from box B. Do not use any phrase more than once.

A	B
was brought on	his unsuspecting assistant.
is being sent on	by overwork.
is getting on well	somewhere in the street.
have carried on	without a pay rise.
soldier on	in her new job.
was picked on	until we find someone suitable.
turned on	to the new address.
take on	to clean the whiteboard.
keep on advertising	too much extra work.
going on	their business for 100 years now.

1 For no apparent reason, the professor _____

_____

2 The workers decided to _____

_____

3 Philippa _____

_____

4 The new boy _____

_____

5 Car manufacturers _____

_____

6 Dave's nervous breakdown _____

_____

7 Her mail _____

_____

8 Be careful not to _____

_____

9 We'll have to _____

_____

10 There was a loud party _____

_____

Recycling

A Choose the correct word or phrase to complete each sentence. Write the letter in the space.

1 Don't _____! I haven't finished explaining yet!

   a) hang up   b) hold on   c) hang on   d) call up

2 The motorist must have run _____ the fox without noticing.

   a) out   b) on   c) over   d) up

3 It _____ out that the mayor had bribed several councillors to vote for him.

   a) resulted   b) pointed   c) broke   d) turned

4 I expect the new trend will soon _____ here.

   a) catch up   b) catch on   c) take up   d) identify with

5 It's difficult to tell identical twins _____.

   a) on   b) out   c) apart   d) over

6 Paloma will have to _____ her antiques, because she needs the money.

   a) part with   b) take out   c) move on   d) clear up

7 I'll use my credit card to _____ up before we check out.

   a) take   b) sum   c) bottle   d) settle

8 Scientists _____ a carefully controlled experiment on the mystery virus.

   a) carried over   b) measured out   c) carried out   d) put up

9 As darkness fell, there was nothing for it but to _____ for the nearest village.

   a) call   b) go   c) make   d) stand

10 There is no time to do anything but _____ briefly on the most important points.

   a) touch   b) run   c) go   d) pick

11 Owning an animal can really tie you _____.

   a) out   b) down   c) back   d) off

12 The terrorist headquarters was blown _____ in the army attack.

   a) down   b) up   c) out   d) over

13 Don't worry if you make a mistake. Just _____ it out.

   a) rule   b) slip   c) leave   d) cross

14 It's no good trying to _____ with Eddie. You'll never change his mind.

   a) deal   b) discuss   c) reason   d) side

15 Thank goodness you'll be there. I'm _____ on your support.

   a) holding   b) calling   c) hanging   d) counting

16 The lecture hall gradually emptied as Professor Jackson _____ on.

   a) kept   b) passed   c) rambled   d) touched

B Read the text and underline the **eleven** phrasal verbs. Give a definition for each one, according to its meaning in the text.

For her first evening's work at Tasty Bites, Laura dressed up in a black skirt and white blouse, as she had been told to look smart. However, when she turned up, she found out that the proprietor had been less than honest with her about the job. Not only did she have to serve the customers, but she also had to work in the kitchen. When she pointed this out to Mr Edwards, he was not at all apologetic. Still, she decided to go on working at the snack bar for the time being. After all, she was getting on well in the job. 'And I can really do with the money!' she told herself.

Three months later, she saw an advertisement in the paper for a Saturday sales assistant at a department store. She thought it over carefully, and decided to apply for it. 'But I won't let on to Mr Edwards until I'm sure I've got the new job!' she thought. The prospect of doing something different cheered her up considerably.

C Complete each sentence with a phrase from box A followed by a phrase from box B. Do not use any phrase more than once.

A	B
picked out	to the disco.
set out,	of the station.
took her out	the best display.
keep foxes out	I bought another one just like it.
make out	from under his school cap.
ruled out	of the chicken shed.
laid out	there was a clap of thunder.
pulled slowly out	the banquet in the palace.
wore out,	the possibility of a cure.
stuck out	Marcella's handwriting.

1 We haven't entirely _____

2 The competition judges _____

3 The little boy's ears _____

4 Tracy's boyfriend _____

5 The steam train _____

6 The royal servants _____

7 The farmer found it hard to _____

8 I can't quite _____

9 When my favourite sweater _____

10 Just as we _____

Phrasal verbs with *away*, *across* and *around*

---

away
back   blaze   break   call   clear   die   fade   gamble   give
get   go   pass   pull   put   scare   send   stow   take   throw

across
come   get

around
crowd   fool   get   hang   look   shop

Away often has the meaning of movement away from the speaker.

A Decide whether the definitions are true (T) or false (F). Give the correct definition(s) if necessary.

1	put away	return something to its correct place
2	give away	lend or borrow something
3	call away	summon someone (often on business)
4	back away	go backwards in fear or dislike
5	go away	continue
6	get across	convey (a message)
7	get around	be (socially) active
8	shop around	consider a number of possibilities before buying something
9	scare away	make someone leave by frightening them
10	pass away	walk past
11	fool around	cause damage
12	fade away	gradually disappear

B Complete the crossword with verbs from the box above, using the clues provided.

Across:

1 Be careful you don't _____ away all your savings at the casino.

4 I'm afraid the doctors say his cousin is about to _____ away.

6 I'm in no hurry. I'll _____ around here until you're ready.

8 I can't stand cats! _____ it away!

10 We heard the last few notes of the concerto _____ away in the evening air.

11 If you don't need that plastic bag, just _____ it away.

14 The driver just managed to _____ away as the traffic warden approached.

15 The film's message didn't _____ across very clearly.

16 The shop hasn't got the batteries in stock. They'll have to _____ away for them.

17 You needn't rush. I'll _____ around the museum while I'm waiting.

18 Two famous players have decided to _____ away from the International Chess Association.

Down:

1 Jack Hobbs, the millionaire, wants to _____ away all his money to the poor.

2 The gunners began to _____ away at the target, the moment the signal was given.

3 Could you _____ away the dirty plates, please?

5 How did the boy get to New York? Did he _____ away on a plane?

7 I'm not sure I managed to _____ across the urgency of the situation.

9 She's fainted! Don't _____ around! Give her air!

12 If you talk loudly in the woods, you'll _____ away the wild animals.

13 I can't understand how the police let the robbers _____ away.

14 All the toys must be _____ away at once.

16 We're going to _____ around and compare prices before we decide.

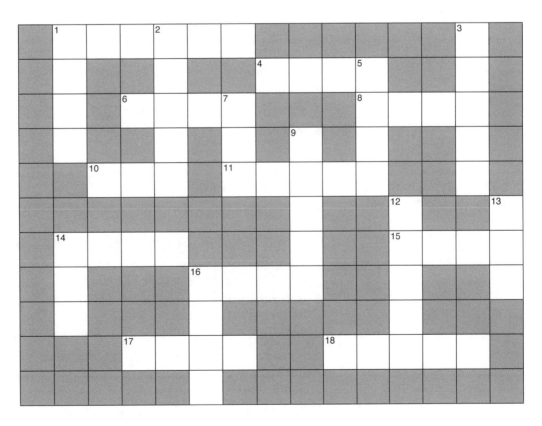

Phrasal verbs with *in* and *into*

---

in
barge   break   burst   butt   call   check   drop   fill
fit   get   give   hand   join   move   pay   phase   plug   pop
pull   send   settle   show   sink   stay   take   tune

into
break   bump   burst   come   dig   fool   look   run   rush
talk   turn

In/Into often have the meaning of including, or of an inward movement.

A Match each phrasal verb with the correct definition. (There may be other possible definitions.)

1	take in	A	meet accidentally
2	butt in	B	pay an unexpected visit
3	bump into	C	persuade to do
4	look into	D	start to occupy a house, office, etc.
5	drop in	E	deposit (money)
6	talk into	F	introduce (a system) in easy stages
7	turn into	G	complete (a form)
8	pay in	H	interrupt rudely
9	phase in	I	change into, become
10	fill in	J	investigate
11	move in	K	participate
12	join in	L	deceive

B Complete each sentence with the correct form of a phrasal verb from the box above.

1 By an amazing coincidence, George _____ into his long-lost brother in Berlin.

2 It was some time before the enormity of what had happened _____ in.

3 No wonder you can't get Jazz FM. The radio's not properly _____ in.

4 Completed application forms should be _____ in by Friday.

5 Katarina can _____ her father into anything. She twists him round her little finger!

6 We were completely _____ in by his hard-luck story.

7 If you have time, do _____ in for coffee.

8 We'll give the newcomers a chance to _____ in, then invite them round to meet the neighbours.

9 That young tomboy has _____ into a most attractive woman.

10 Lucy will have to _____ into her savings to pay for the operation.

11 Don't just _____ in like that, without knocking!

12 The manager asked his secretary to _____ the visitors in.

13 The local authorities have decided to _____ in the new taxes over a five-year period.

14 If you give us your bank details, your salary will be _____ in on the 28th of every month.

C Add **it** where necessary to the following sentences, and say what **it** means or might mean.

1 Here's the hairdryer. You can plug in over there.

2 The door was flung open and Gloria burst in.

3 I'll probably stay in tonight, as I've got a cold.

4 Have you finished the report? Hand in tomorrow, please.

5 Rolf pulled in for petrol at the motorway services.

6 The new clerk needs to be the right sort of person to fit in here.

7 I don't think poor Mrs Gates can take all in.

8 Well, I give in! I'll do whatever you like!

9 That horse is completely wild. You'll have to break in.

10 If you'd like a lift, get in.

11 If you feel energetic enough, why not join in? The dance steps are quite easy.

12 When you receive the application form, you must fill in and return to our central office immediately.

D Complete each sentence with a phrase from box A followed by a phrase from box B. Do not use any phrase more than once.

A
moving in
came into
have broken into
rush into
fool me into
burst into tears
check in

B
the isolated house.
as she waved goodbye.
anything.
before we have dinner?
soon?
believing you!
a fortune.

1 On her aunt's death Karin _____

_____

2 Burglars _____

_____

3 Daisy _____

_____

4 It's no good. You can't _____

_____

5 Don't you think we should _____

_____

6 Is your sister _____

_____

7 Think about it. Don't _____

_____

Three-part phrasal verbs

carry on with	face up to	get up to	look down on
catch up with	feel up to	go ahead with	look up to
come down with	get along with	go along with	miss out on
come in for	get away with	go on with	put up with
come out in	get down to	go through with	run out of
come up against	get on with	grow out of	send away/off for
come up with	get out of	hold on to	settle up with
cut down on	get rid of	keep up with	walk out on
do away with	get round to	live up to	write away/off for

A Decide whether the definitions are true (T) or false (F). Give the correct definition(s) if necessary.

1 put up with — tolerate
2 get away with — avoid punishment
3 come in for — receive, be the object of
4 do away with — restore, decorate
5 come up with — produce (an idea, solution etc)
6 get round to — appear on stage
7 look down on — consider another person superior
8 grow out of — move upwards
9 face up to — confront, tackle (a problem, etc)
10 get along with — have a good relationship with
11 go through with — accompany
12 run out of — use up completely

B Rewrite the sentences, using a phrasal verb from the box above, to produce the opposite meaning of the words in italics.

1 Bernadette *is very contemptuous of* certain groups of people.
2 The company decided to *stop work on* the project.
3 I would find it very difficult to *oppose* the committee's proposals.
4 The doctor advised Luciano to *eat more* carbohydrates for the sake of his health.

5 During his holiday he *lost touch with* current events.

6 Trevor has *volunteered to do* the work.

7 The guests *didn't pay their hotel bill* before leaving.

8 After their many arguments, Bryan *stayed with* his wife.

9 I wish we'd *kept* those old mirrors when we moved house.

10 Jacqui makes a point of *ignoring* the latest fashions.

C Complete each sentence with the correct form of a phrasal verb from the box opposite.

1 I don't think I can _____ with his behaviour any longer.

2 If you're interested, why don't you _____ for details of the job?

3 Carolina has always _____ very well with her colleagues.

4 Are you sure you _____ to coming out tonight?

5 I'm sorry I didn't _____ to replying earlier.

6 On last year's expedition the team _____ against terrible difficulties.

7 Anna won't be at work today. She's _____ with flu.

8 I think I'd better _____ to some work now.

9 Sadly, the boy couldn't _____ to his father's expectations.

10 I wonder what mischief the children are _____ to this morning?

11 I'm afraid we've _____ of coffee, so would you like tea?

12 Most problems in life just have to be _____ to.

D Complete each sentence with a phrase from box A followed by a phrase from box B. Do not use any phrase more than once.

A	B
do away with	those stamps. They're valuable.
go through with	the monarchy.
hang on to	the wedding.
get away with	spots yesterday.
missing out on	a great deal of criticism lately.
came out in	such a good opportunity.
come in for	murder!

1 Sarah was disappointed at _____

_____

2 The boss always lets Fred _____

_____

3 The President has _____

_____

4 Many people would like to _____

_____

5 The baby's ill: she _____

_____

6 You should _____

_____

7 Rachel decided she couldn't _____

_____

Phrasal verbs as nouns

breakdown	dropout	hold-up	onlooker	stand-in
break-in	getaway	knockout	onset	stopover
breakthrough	get-together	lay-by	outbreak	stowaway
breakup	go-ahead	lay-off	outburst	take-off
castaway	goings-on	layout	outlook	takeover
check-in	grown-up	let-down	sell-out	turnout
comedown	handout	let-up	setback	upbringing
cutback	hangover	lookout	standby	

A Complete each sentence with the correct noun from the box above.

1 Tony's been demoted to Assistant Manager. What a _____ for him!

2 Customs officers were on the _____ for illegal drugs.

3 The tourist office has a free _____ on cheap accommodation in London.

4 Patricia suffered a nervous _____ when she lost her job.

5 Miguel's devotion to the company contributed to the _____ of his marriage.

6 If you were a _____ on a desert island, how would you cope?

7 Scientists have made an important _____ in the field of genetic engineering.

8 The planning authorities gave the school the _____ for an extension.

9 At South London University, there were several _____ from the Computer Science course this year.

10 Tommy, ask a _____ to help you next time you want to do some painting.

11 Keith has always had a rather narrow _____ on life. I put it down to his strict _____.

12 It poured down all day without any _____.

13 The whole room was stunned into silence by Gordon's angry _____.

14 The robbers made an incredibly quick _____ in a waiting car.

15 The _____s in the building trade are a direct result of the _____s in government spending.

16 The advantage of flying Air Canada is that the fare includes a free _____ in Vancouver.

17 Whenever Mrs Khan chairs the meeting, we get a much better _____.

18 To the delight of the _____s, the Princess posed on the steps for photographs.

B Complete the crossword with words from the box opposite, using the clues provided.

Across:

3 Can be relied on in an emergency

5 The act of assuming power

7 A commercial success (e.g. a concert)

10 See 1 Down

11 See 17 Down

12 A person who hides aboard a ship or plane to gain free passage

13 & 9 Down   An armed robbery

14 Arrangement of written material on a page

19 A sudden occurrence (of disease or war)

20 A hindrance to a plan

21 See 18 Down

23 Delayed after-effects of drinking too much alcohol

Down:

1 & 10 Across A person substituting for an actor

2 A disappointment

4 & 10 Across The illegal entering of a building

6 A blow rendering an opponent unconscious

8 A place for drivers to stop, off the main road

9 See 13 Across

15 The beginning (of something bad)

16 & 22 To register (at a hotel)

17 & 11 Across Happenings, events

18 & 21 Across Informal meeting or social gathering

22 See 16 Down

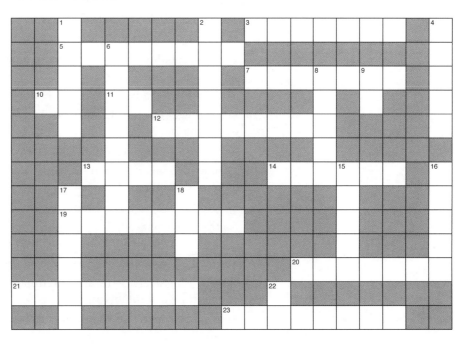

UNIT 40

Recycling

A Choose the correct word or phrase to complete each sentence. Write the letter in the space.

1 The speaker failed to get his message _____ to his audience.

  a) around   b) in   c) across   d) out

2 The reporter announced solemnly that the President had _____ in his sleep.

  a) passed away   b) died away   c) passed out   d) dropped off

3 He's been to the USA, Australia and India this year. He certainly gets _____!

  a) on   b) around   c) out   d) away

4 Look, I'm sorry to _____ in, but I think I can help you.

  a) move   b) plug   c) butt   d) pop

5 The elaborate bridal costumes of the coastal Indians are _____ from mother to daughter.

  a) taken after   b) put by   c) parted with   d) handed down

6 Politicians frequently _____ a lot of criticism.

  a) come out in   b) catch up with   c) come in for   d) get up to

7 I was disappointed when I saw the film. It was a real _____.

  a) let-down   b) breakdown   c) turnout   d) dropout

8 You'll lose marks if you don't _____ in all the gaps.

  a) send   b) fill   c) fit   d) join

9 He gambled _____ his life's savings before starting on his wife's.

  a) across   b) around   c) out   d) away

10 Did you notice Bob trying to _____ doing the washing-up?

  a) get up to   b) break out of   c) get out of   d) get along with

11 To beat the holiday traffic, we'll have to _____ out at dawn.

  a) set   b) go   c) move   d) drive

12 I could probably _____ out the answer if I had a pencil, some paper and a calculator.

  a) think   b) study   c) hand   d) work

13 Delilah wasn't at all hungry, and could only _____ with the food on her plate.

  a) finger   b) toy   c) snack   d) side

14 I know it's a pretty boring routine, but you'll just have to _____ on for the moment, I'm afraid.

  a) count   b) live   c) soldier   d) move

15 As the years passed, Joe's memories of his terrible experience _____ away, and he began to lead a normal life again.

  a) faded   b) backed   c) passed   d) got

16 This is a big decision to make. Think it _____ before you give me your final word tomorrow.

  a) over   b) upon   c) carefully   d) on

B Read the text, and underline the **twelve** phrasal verbs. Give a definition for each one, according to its meaning in the text.

Unfortunately, the department store ruled Laura out, as she had no relevant experience. So she went on waitressing part-time at Tasty Bites, until the day she arrived at work to find that the place had been closed down by the authorities for reasons of hygiene.

When she had got over her initial surprise, she decided to look around for another, more secure job. Eventually she was taken on at the local airport, where she worked at the checkout in the duty-free shop. The hours were long and the other staff rather unfriendly, but Laura was determined to put up with the job. At least she was able to spend her breaks watching the planes take off and land, and join in the general feeling of excitement that pervades a bustling international airport. But her university studies were beginning to suffer and so, when she was laid off at the end of the busy summer season, she gave up any further ideas of trying to earn money, and went back to her books.

C Complete each sentence with a phrase from box A followed by a phrase from box B. Do not use any phrase more than once.

A
are the result of
made their getaway
was blamed on
allows them a stopover
the goings-on
an impressive turnout
your seat belts

B
at the student hostel.
his upbringing.
in a stolen car.
ready for take-off.
government cutbacks.
in Hong Kong.
for the by-election.

1 There was _____
2 Police investigated _____
3 The culprits _____
4 Please fasten _____
5 The hospital closures _____
6 Their ticket to Sydney _____
7 The accused's antisocial behaviour _____

D Follow the instructions for Exercise C.

A
came across
owned up
talk him into
will get around
blazed away,
hung around

B
completely out of control.
pretty fast.
to having started the rumour.
giving up golf.
outside the star's home.
a rare coin among her loose change.

1 The plain-clothes policeman _____
2 Josephine _____
3 The fire _____
4 Eventually he _____
5 News of their affair _____
6 She'll never _____

Email and the internet

A Choose the correct word(s) from the pair in brackets to complete these sentences about using the internet and your computer.

1 Once you are online, you can find out information by using a (search engine/reference file), see what people are discussing by accessing the messages in (an outbox/a newsgroup), join a (cybercafé/chat room) for a real-time conversation, or interact with your friends on a (social networking/blogging) site.

2 If you receive an email from someone you don't know which has an (attachment/application), the standard advice is not to open it, in case it contains a (file/virus); in fact, it is probably wise to (save/delete) it at once.

3 These days computers don't (crash/download) as often as they used to, but it's still good practice to (back up/cut and paste) at regular intervals.

4 To open a folder or document, just move your (cursor/finger) on to its (toolbar/icon) and (double-click/single-switch).

B Read the text, then decide which word from A, B, C or D is most appropriate for each space.

PENICILLIN BEFORE PENTIUMS FOR THE POOR

One of the hottest topics on the international development agenda is how to harness the power of 1) _____ for the benefit of developing countries. What is sometimes called 'the death of distance', brought about by the 2) _____, allows professional services such as 3) _____, education and training to be provided easily and quickly to 4) _____ areas. Some of the gains can be seen in countries as diverse as India and Morocco, where innovations range from 5) _____ government announcements to local craftsmen selling their wares to a 6) _____ market. But already a huge and expanding 7) _____ divide is opening up between developed and developing nations. The major task facing world leaders at present is to 8) _____ everybody on the planet with clean water, basic education and the drugs needed to fight preventable diseases. Installing a 9) _____ in every classroom and linking us all to 10) _____ must be a lesser 11) _____, for the time being at least.

	A	B	C	D
1	ISP	ICT	IMF	IOU
2	computer	telephone	modem	internet
3	stationery	software	hardware	equipment
4	far	uninhabited	remote	secluded
5	online	broadcast	recorded	programmed
6	global	technical	village	shrinking
7	physical	digital	electrical	economical
8	supply	give	donate	administer
9	plug	video	mobile phone	modem
10	the real world	cyberspace	virtual reality	outer space
11	priority	advantage	importance	criteria

C Complete the text with these words. There is one more than you need.

data	mouse	computers	cable
exchange	satellite	smartphone	

What is broadband?

Broadband is essentially a method of connecting 1) _____ to the internet so that 2) _____ can be transmitted and received over high-speed networks. You can be connected to broadband by Digital Subscriber Line (DSL) in areas where the local telephone 3) _____ has been enabled, by 4) _____, which is mostly laid underground, by 5) _____, or by using a 6) _____, which operates through mobile phone networks.

D Do the same in this task. There is one more word than you need.

ISP	web	cables	organisers	desktop
e-readers	package	printer	router	

What is wi-fi?

Wi-fi stands for Wireless Fidelity, and is all about freedom from wires. Any number of 1) _____ or laptop computers, electronic 2) _____, smartphones or 3) _____ can be connected to the internet without the need for any 4) _____ or installing extra phone lines. It means you can access the 5) _____ anywhere in the house on any computer. You can get a complete wi-fi 6) _____ by contacting your 7) _____, who will be happy to send you a 8) _____, pre-configured and ready to plug in.

E Do the same in this task. There is one more word than you need.

online	website	password	public
transfers	log-in	customers	fraud

What is internet banking?

Internet banking allows 1) _____ to conduct financial transactions on a secure 2) _____ operated by their bank. Transactions such as payments, 3) _____ and checking account balances are performed via the internet. People are advised not to use a computer in a 4) _____ place for their internet banking. In addition, protection against 5) _____ through the authentication of a memorable 6) _____, as in most internet shopping sites, is not considered secure enough for personal 7) _____ banking in most countries, so more complex systems are used.

F Answer these questions as fully as you can, in conversation or in writing.

1 What are the advantages and disadvantages of email over traditional letter writing?

2 Do you feel the internet performs a useful function in connecting people with each other? Do you feel it enriches our existence? Or do you think it is a waste of time, and merely encourages us to make virtual relationships instead of real ones?

The media and the arts

A Complete the text with these words and phrases. There is one more than you need.

press	jingles	subliminal	commercials
disseminate	slogans	hoardings	advertising agency
	pressure groups	posters	brand

Advertising on television is big business. Advertising 1) _____ and 2) _____, if they are catchy enough, often become part of our culture. However little attention we pay to 3) _____, we cannot avoid being influenced by the constant repetition of a 4) _____ name or image. The message we receive may even be 5) _____, so that we are not aware of it. Not all advertisements are purely financially motivated, however. Political parties and 6) _____ aim to 7) _____ their views more widely by putting up 8) _____ on street 9) _____ and by buying space in the 10) _____ and time on the small screen.

B Match the words on the left, connected with newspapers, with the correct definitions.

1	obituary	A	critical assessment of a book, film etc.
2	leader	B	leading editorial article
3	horoscope	C	regular article about celebrities
4	review	D	announcement of a death, with a short biography
5	gossip column	E	phrase or title at the top of an article
6	headline	F	humorous or satirical drawing
7	deadline	G	time limit for reporting news
8	cartoon	H	prediction of someone's future according to his/her sign of the zodiac

C Complete each sentence with a word formed from one of these verbs.

catch	censor	circulate	commentate	cover	criticise

1 The new gallery was given the seal of approval by *The Observer's* art _____, who wrote several enthusiastic articles about it.

2 Former champion John McEnroe has now made a name as a tennis _____.

3 Under the government's wartime _____ rules, all newspaper articles had to be checked by officials before being printed.

4 The tabloids have excellent _____ of scandal and sport: the quality papers deal with everything else.

5 The local newspaper's _____ fell dramatically when the editor was sacked.

6 That jingle from the teabag ad is so _____ that I can't get it out of my head.

D Choose the correct word or phrase from the pair in brackets to complete each sentence.

1 The actors have been _____ the play all this week. (rehearsing/repeating)

2 The audience applauded wildly when the director appeared on the _____ to take his bow. (scene/stage)

3 I've been watching a fascinating new _____ of art programmes. (serial/series)

4 Although the play has a large number of _____, it is comparatively easy to follow the plot. (characters/persons)

5 If you don't like that programme, you can always switch over to a different _____. (channel/canal)

6 The latest television dramatisation was filmed entirely _____ in a country village not far from here. (in the wild/on location)

7 Which _____ did Marlene Dietrich play in her last film? (role/performance)

8 There's a wonderful _____ of 'A Midsummer Night's Dream' in *The Evening Herald.* (critic/review)

E Complete the sentences with these words and phrases.

| standing ovation | soap opera | supporting roles | low-budget |
| prime-time | box-office success | subtitles | final curtain |

1 Despite being a critical disaster, the film was a huge _____.

2 The orchestra and their conductor were given a _____ at the end of the concert.

3 People who are addicted to a particular _____ seldom miss an episode.

4 It wasn't until the _____ fell that the audience voiced their disapproval by hissing and booing.

5 At the local arts cinema, foreign films are usually shown with _____, and only occasionally dubbed.

6 Compared with most American blockbusters, it was a _____ film, as very little funding was available.

7 Programmes on _____ television attract the greatest number of viewers.

8 Although the lead actor and actress were excellent, the _____ were very well acted too.

F Answer these questions as fully as you can, in conversation or in writing.

1 Which medium do you find

a) most informative? b) most sensational? c) most biased?

2 How can we avoid being brainwashed by prejudiced views or propaganda?

3 Is there a gap in the media market? What kind of new magazine, newspaper, TV or radio programme would you launch if you had adequate funds and a creative team behind you?

4 How important is the image or presentation of an organisation or public figure? Is employing a public relations firm a good way of improving this?

Success and fame

A Complete the text with these words. There are two more than you need.

public	reap	market	fame	wealth	ambition
respected	jet set	whizz-kid	success		
best-seller	rising	achieve	rocketed		
expanding	potential				

What is success? Achieving a long-held 1) _____? Earning a million by the time you're twenty-five? Joining the 2) _____? 3) _____ to the top of your chosen profession? Writing a 4) _____? 5) _____ means different things to different people, but one man has managed to 6) _____ all this in a very short space of time.

Jeff Packham was still at university when he realised the 7) _____ profits to be made from the sale of posters to an eager public. The poster stall he manned every Saturday was regularly surrounded by enthusiasts keen to snap up a bargain. So after graduating, he took out a loan, rented office space, and acquired a stock of posters. Soon his business was 8) _____ rapidly, and he was able to rent a warehouse, which he renovated and used as a centre for his operations. Other shops were opened in other parts of the country, and sales 9) _____. Hard-headed businessmen flocked to buy shares in this 10) _____'s company when it went public, and Jeff was able to 11) _____ the rewards of his hard work by taking time off to buy a house and get married.

He is still only in his mid-twenties, a father of two, and a 12) _____ businessman with a product which is a 13) _____ leader. To admirers of his achievements he points out that he has had to make sacrifices. 'It's difficult to maintain one's privacy,' he says. 'Once you are successful, you have to live in the 14) _____ eye, to a certain extent.'

B Make adjectives from these nouns, and check their meanings in a dictionary.

1 prodigy _____
2 dedication _____
3 ruthlessness _____
4 skill _____
5 notoriety _____
6 success _____
7 ephemera _____
8 stress _____
9 celebrity _____
10 legend _____
11 renown _____
12 talent _____

C Choose the correct word or phrase from the pair in brackets to complete each sentence.

1 The life of a child _____ can be fraught with difficulties. (prodigy/idol)
2 Garth left his small home town in the Midwest, lured by the bright _____ of New York. (lights/stars)

3 The rock group shot to _____ after appointing a new manager.   (publicity/stardom)

4 The _____ Dr Crippen, who was executed for poisoning his wife, was the first criminal to be apprehended by the use of radio-telegraphy.   (infamous/famous)

5 Ayrton Senna had already been world motor-racing _____ several times before his tragic death on the Imola circuit.   (champion/winner)

6 An ambitious person is committed to improving his or her _____ at work.   (status/rank)

7 The fans all waited excitedly at the stage door to get the singer's _____.   (signature/autograph)

8 The _____ of my neighbour's business was largely due to the world recession.   (failing/failure)

9 Princess Diana found the _____ of her privacy intolerable.   (intrusion/invasion)

10 Mr Sampson enjoys an excellent _____ as a heart specialist. (reputation/fame)

11 Many great geniuses receive only _____ recognition of their talents.   (posthumous/post-mortem)

12 Isabel's _____ came when her designs were spotted by a Paris fashion house.   (big break/window display)

13 People connected to the rich and famous often write diaries and memoirs for _____.   (longevity/posterity)

14 Sir Alfred Marks made his great fortune by identifying a(n) _____ in the market.   (gap/opportunity)

15 When Guy went back to the casino, he gambled his previous night's _____ on one turn of the roulette wheel, and lost them all. (earnings/winnings)

16 Many _____ these days are famous merely for being famous. (celebrities/gurus)

D Answer these questions as fully as you can, in conversation or in writing.

1 What are the advantages and disadvantages of maintaining a high profile in public life?

2 Do you think that people in the public eye are entitled to privacy, or should their privileged role expose them to public scrutiny at all times?

3 How would you define success? What area would you like to be successful in?

4 Do you think a person can become successful purely on his/her own merits, or is there always an element of influence or corruption?

5 Do you think the current cult of success, with massive salaries for company directors, and megastar status for singers, footballers and media personalities, reflects the achievements or the failures of our society? Are there other ways of rewarding high achievers, and what, in your opinion, should be rewarded?

Animals and their rights

A Complete the text with these words and phrases.

widespread	tested	experiments	livestock	climate
vivisection	consumers	factory farming		entertainment
activists	free-range		blood sports	opposition
	animal rights	cruelty		battery hens

People's attitudes to animals have changed considerably in the last two decades. Using animals in scientific 1) _____ and as a primary food source, once considered a human prerogative, is now being questioned by 2) _____ campaigners. There is also a 3) _____ revulsion against 4) _____ such as fox-hunting, and 5) _____ often endanger their own lives in an attempt to stop what Oscar Wilde called 'the unspeakable in pursuit of the uneatable'. Several cosmetics companies now claim that their products are not 6) _____ on animals, a policy which has been found to be popular with 7) _____.

Although the medical and scientific professions still maintain that 8) _____ is necessary for research purposes, there is more public 9) _____ to this than ever before. This change in the 10) _____ of public opinion means that using animals for 11) _____ is also frowned on. Zoos and circuses are sometimes accused of 12) _____, and are losing their popularity. Even in agriculture, changes are slowly being introduced in response to public concern about animal welfare. Many supermarkets now offer 13) _____ eggs to their customers, as well as eggs from 14) _____, and although 15) _____ is still widespread, farmers are aware that consumers are increasingly interested in the living conditions and even the feelings of 16) _____.

B Match the words in the lists to make compound nouns or well-known phrases, some of which may need a hyphen. Check their meanings in a dictionary.

1	book	A	fat
2	stag	B	crossing
3	dark	C	hole
4	puppy	D	party
5	zebra	E	tears
6	pigeon	F	eyes
7	crocodile	G	whistle
8	dog	H	worm
9	wolf	I	collar
10	cat's	J	horse

C Put these animal names into the correct sentences. You may have to change the form of the word, and/or add a hyphen.

whale sardine rat wolf horse parrot wild goose butterfly fly frog bird dog

1 Wouldn't you just love to be a _____ on the wall when Sarah tells him it's all over?

2 Could I have some water, please? I've got a _____ in my throat.

3 Even the great cellist, Dmitri Radovic, admitted to having _____ in his stomach before a concert.

4 From the helicopter the police had a _____ eye view of the accident.

5 Unfortunately Donald doesn't try to understand grammar rules. He just learns sentences _____ fashion.

6 Roger is extraordinarily selfish and possessive – a real _____ in the manger.

7 The old man led us all over town on a _____ chase, and so we never found the house we were looking for.

8 I'm afraid you're flogging a dead _____, Rupert. The boss will never agree to your proposal.

9 Caroline has cried _____ so many times before that people just don't believe her any more.

10 There's something strange about that plan of Mary's. I smell a _____!

11 Jane was having a _____ of a time at the party, and could hardly be dragged away.

12 When the train doors closed, we were packed like _____ and could not move an inch.

D Match each verb with the correct definition.

1	beaver away	A	move the head or body quickly downwards
2	duck	B	play or meddle (with something)
3	monkey about	C	confuse (someone)
4	worm your way	D	trouble, plague, bother (someone)
5	dog	E	work industriously
6	fox	F	insinuate yourself

E Answer these questions as fully as you can, in conversation or in writing.

1 If new medicines and cosmetics are not tested on animals, we will have to use humans as guinea pigs. What are your views on this?

2 How cruel do you think zoos and circuses really are? Animals kept in cages are certainly not free, but at least they are fed regularly and protected from danger and extinction. Do you think it is right for us to use animals for our entertainment?

3 What are the possible grounds for becoming a vegetarian, and which of them most appeals to you?

4 Why do you think people's attitudes towards animal rights have changed so radically, as described in Exercise A? Are the reasons historical, financial or sociological? Why do we not consider the rights of other species, like insects, plants or bacteria?

Language

A Complete the text with these words. There are two more than you need.

| literal   translation   nuances   dialect   metaphor |
| evoking   colloquial   original   authors |
| allusions   translators   interpreting |

At the World Congress of the International Federation of Translators in Brighton, selected 1) _____ shared a platform with their translators. 2) _____ is generally agreed to be the rendering of meaning from one language or 3) _____ to another. However, there is a central dilemma which all 4) _____ have to face, and which was discussed at length at the congress. How can readers of other nationalities understand all the 5) _____ and linguistic 6) _____ of particular writers? The translators' answer to this is to aim to capture the tone of the 7) _____, without translating it into 8) _____ language or slang. 9) _____ the flavour or atmosphere of the text is considered far more important than giving a(n) 10) _____ translation.

B Match the words on the left with the correct definitions.

1	pidgin	A	a word or phrase which reads the same backwards or forwards
2	jargon	B	non-standard, informal language
3	spoonerism	C	using the same letter to start each word in a sentence or a line of verse
4	onomatopoeia	D	unintentional confusion of two words
5	palindrome	E	a phrase or sentence difficult to say quickly
6	limerick	F	a simple language made up of elements of two or more languages
7	alliteration	G	five lines of comic verse
8	tongue-twister	H	using words whose sound imitates their meaning
9	malapropism	I	specialised language for e.g. a profession
10	slang	J	transposing the initial consonants of a pair of words

C Now match the terms in Exercise B with these examples.

1 You have deliberately tasted two worms and you can leave Oxford by the town drain.
2 Lend me five quid till tomorrow, will you?
3 Five miles meandering with a mazy motion
4 In the warm sunshine the bees buzzed round the hive.
5 Madam, I'm Adam.
6 The tractor feed is the part of the printer designed for handling continuous stationery.

7 Trespassers will be executed.

8 Peter Piper picked a peck of pickled pepper.

9 Me go house big-feller.

10 There was an old lady called Jane,

Who feared she was terribly plain,

But because she had wealth,

And, sadly, poor health,

She was proposed to again and again!

D Choose the correct word from the pair in brackets to complete each sentence.

1 The hall was packed for the visiting professor's _____ on eighteenth-century poetry.   (lecture/conference)

2 It was warm in the church, and some of the congregation found themselves dozing off as the vicar came to the end of his _____. (sermon/speech)

3 My aunt had a terrible _____ with her neighbour, which turned into a ten-year feud.   (argue/quarrel)

4 The mayor made a _____ in Italian, to welcome the delegates from Rome.   (speech/talk)

5 Wayne speaks English with a noticeable Canadian _____. (accent/dialect)

6 The two politicians had a heated _____ about capital punishment in front of the studio audience.   (debate/row)

7 The _____ of the word 'watch' is different from 'wash'. (accent/pronunciation)

8 The two old soldiers kept interrupting as each tried to finish his _____. 'No, no, it didn't happen like that!' they said, correcting each other.   (anecdote/history)

9 Every English _____ must have a working verb in it.   (phrase/ sentence)

10 Children often enjoy asking each other a _____, like 'When is a witch not a witch? When it's a sandwich!'   (puzzle/riddle)

E Answer these questions as fully as you can, in conversation or in writing.

1 How important do you think it is to learn standard English, or Received Pronunciation? Should regional accents and dialects be retained in any language, and taught to foreigners? Is there a social stigma attached to a non-standard accent in your country?

2 How different is written English from spoken English? Give examples. What differences are there in your language, spoken and written?

3 Does a language reflect the climate or location of the country where it is spoken? Does it reflect the character of people in that country? Give examples.

4 In what ways does learning a foreign language help to create international understanding?

5 What are the best ways of learning a foreign language?

Medicine and health

A Complete the text with these words and phrases.

transplants   heavy smokers   National Health Service
policy   emergency   patient   medical   bypass   collapses
cardiac   addicts   surgery   consultants   treatment   interim

Wythenshawe Hospital in Manchester maintains a 1) _____ of refusing to carry out heart 2) _____ operations on smokers. It is important to be clear about the views of the hospital 3) _____. They are happy to treat any smoker who 4) _____ and needs 5) _____ treatment, but they draw the line at carrying out expensive, non-urgent, preventive 6) _____ surgery on patients who refuse to stop smoking. There is a high risk of complications for 7) _____ during and after heart 8) _____, so many clinicians prefer to provide 9) _____ medical treatment, while encouraging the 10) _____ to give up smoking.

The death of a Manchester 25-cigarettes-a-day man, who died after being refused tests at Wythenshawe, has given rise to furious debate in 11) _____ circles. If this argument is taken further, drunken drivers could be denied emergency 12) _____, drug 13) _____ HIV treatment, and drinkers liver 14) _____. In other words, should any individual who can be shown to have contributed to his own medical problems be refused help on the 15) _____?

B Choose the correct word or phrase from the pair in brackets to complete each sentence.

1 John's been off work for a week with flu, and he still feels rather _____.   (under the weather/full of beans)

2 Chickenpox is a children's infectious _____, but adults can catch it too.   (disease/sickness)

3 The _____ who performed the operation visited the patient soon after she came round.   (physician/surgeon)

4 Don't worry, I can assure you that this medicine produces no _____ at all.   (side effects/results)

5 I'd like to visit Patricia, now that she's out of intensive care, but I'm not sure which _____ she's in.   (ward/cell)

6 Your state of health must be good before you can become a blood _____.   (giver/donor)

7 Although Bob recovered fairly quickly from the accident, he had to have plastic _____ to remove facial scars.   (operation/surgery)

8 Mrs Wright took her son to the weekly baby _____, to have him weighed and to check that he was making good progress. (hospital/clinic)

9 If someone collapses in the street, it may be necessary to give them _____ aid until the ambulance arrives.   (emergency/first)

10 Most food experts now criticise the use of drastic slimming _____. Instead, they recommend a programme of exercise and balanced eating.   (regimes/diets)

11 Medical students are usually encouraged to watch operations in the operating _____, as part of their training.   (room/theatre)

12 You'll need to take your _____ to the chemist's, Mrs Hall. (prescription/recipe)

13 When Jayne cut her hand, we had to drive ten miles to Bristol, as our local hospital has no _____ department.   (acute/casualty)

14 Have you ever had to have a blood _____? (transference/transfusion)

15 Trying to dress yourself with your arm in a _____ is almost impossible.   (bandage/sling)

C Decide whether the definitions are true (T) or false (F). Give the correct definition if necessary.

1 *Bacteria* are a group of micro-organisms, many of which cause disease.

2 *Organically* grown food is food grown without artificial pesticides or fertilisers.

3 Someone who is *vulnerable* to infection can resist infection well.

4 A *paediatrician* specialises in elderly people's health problems.

5 An *epidemic* is a widespread occurrence of a disease.

6 *Obesity* means having extremely low blood pressure.

7 An *injection* is a means of giving food to patients who cannot swallow.

8 *Antibiotics* are drugs used to fight infections.

9 *Homeopathy* involves treating people's joints and muscles with exercise and massage.

10 An *X-ray* is a photograph taken with special equipment which can show if bones are broken or internal organs damaged.

D Answer these questions as fully as you can, in conversation or in writing.

1 What are your views on the ethical problems raised in the text in Exercise A?

2 Do we all have a right to free medical treatment, provided by the state, or should we make our own provision for health care, using private health insurance?

3 How can we reconcile the fact that the demand for health care these days is unlimited, whereas health budgets are limited? What priorities would you set if you were Health Minister? How important is health education?

4 What do you expect, and what do you get, from your family doctor? Which do you think is more important, the consultation or the prescription?

5 What factors have the greatest effect on our health?

6 What do you think of alternative medicine? Is it just a fashionable fad that will not last long, or might it replace orthodox medicine in the end?

UNIT 47

Danger and risk

A Match the words or phrases to make common expressions connected with danger and risk. Use each word or phrase only once.

1	a narrow	A	the risk
2	raise	B	folly
3	the odds are	C	of mind
4	a false sense	D	overboard
5	risk life	E	escape
6	run	F	and sound
7	take	G	a charmed life
8	peace	H	the alarm
9	bear	I	and limb
10	safe	J	heavily stacked against
11	be swept	K	sensible precautions
12	sheer	L	of security

B Now use the phrases from Exercise A in their correct form in these sentences.

1 I had a very _____ on my way to work this morning. I was just crossing the road when I was nearly mown down by a car jumping the lights.

2 If you choose to drink and drive, you _____ of being arrested and sent to prison.

3 Mrs Geeson was very relieved to see her sons come home _____ from their canoeing trip on the River Ardèche.

4 Two men are still missing from their yacht in the Indian Ocean. It is feared they may have _____ by a freak wave and drowned.

5 Douglas should never have attempted to climb Mont Blanc. With his heart condition, it was _____.

6 You will only have complete _____ if you insure yourself carefully against every possible disaster.

7 Tony seems to _____. He's already been involved in a shipwreck, two car accidents, a helicopter crash and a supermarket fire, and has come out of all of them without a scratch.

8 If you are going mountain climbing in winter, you are advised to _____, such as wearing the right clothing, and taking the correct equipment with you.

9 I can't believe that Sabina is going to _____ on that parachute jump. Of course, she's doing it for charity.

10 As there had never been an accident at that pit before, the miners were lulled into _____, and became careless.

11 When one of the walkers was injured, two of the group stayed with him, while another boy set off down the mountain to _____.

12 The _____ the missing fishermen, but the search for them will be resumed at first light, if weather conditions allow.

C Match the words on the left with the correct definitions.

1	intrepid	A	dangerous
2	hazardous	B	difficult living conditions
3	survivor	C	food and other necessities
4	hardships	D	extremely brave
5	endurance	E	someone still alive after an accident or a disaster
6	foolhardy	F	to put someone or something in danger
7	sponsor	G	(providing) the money needed
8	provisions	H	having a fixed aim, being single-minded
9	jeopardise	I	being able to put up with difficult conditions
10	funding	J	someone who is hurt or killed, e.g. in an accident
11	determination	K	someone who provides money for a venture
12	casualty	L	carelessly, rashly adventurous

D Now complete the text with the words from Exercise C, in their correct form.

The small team of scientists who have recently been exploring the Brazilian rainforest endured many 1) _____ before they reached home. Some commentators felt that it was 2) _____ of them to set out without proper 3) _____ from government or commercial 4) _____. They had very little equipment, and ran short of 5) _____ after six weeks, so that extra food and supplies had to be airlifted to them. At one point, the team admitted later, they all began to think that there would be no 6) _____ from this extremely 7) _____ and poorly planned expedition. Their leader, Professor Ralph Blackwood, has since been criticised for 8) _____ his colleagues' lives in the name of science. Fortunately, however, they were clearly 9) _____ and resourceful men, with the necessary grit and 10) _____ to succeed in their undertaking. 'We needed all our stamina and 11) _____,' one of them told our reporter, 'to get out of that jungle alive.' They returned home with no 12) _____.

E Answer these questions as fully as you can, in conversation or in writing.

1 Statistics show that people are more likely to have a road accident near their home than when they are further away. Why do you think this might be so?

2 What is the greatest danger you are aware of in your daily life? Do you do anything to protect yourself from it? How likely is it to happen?

3 Make a list of what you consider to be dangerous sports. Should these be banned? Should people have to pay for their own medical care if they are injured in sports?

4 Do you enjoy taking risks? What kind of risks do you deliberately run?

5 What types of danger should we warn small children about? What is the best way of preparing school-age children for potentially dangerous situations?

The environment

A Complete the text with these words. There are two more than you need.

damage	obliterated	irrigation	developing	resources
drought	environmental	tribal	environmentalists	
source	construction	conservation	rugged	scale

Problems arose in the 1990s over the Indian government's giant dam project in the 1) _____ Narmada Valley, where many of Rudyard Kipling's stories are set. The Narmada River rises in the heart of central India and flows westwards to the Arabian sea. According to officials, the planned 2) _____ of two huge dams and 3) _____ canals would provide water for drinking and agriculture in an area worryingly prone to 4) _____. The Narmada dam project would also offer a major 5) _____ of electricity to power-starved regions. As part of its commitment to 6) _____ countries, the World Bank originally offered India a $450 million loan. However, critics argued that the dam project represented 7) _____ and cultural destruction on a 8) _____ so massive that the benefits would pale in comparison to the 9) _____ it would cause. They pointed out that more than 200,000 people would be uprooted and rehoused, and ancient 10) _____ cultures would be 11) _____. Despite intense pressure from 12) _____, the project is currently going ahead.

B Choose the correct word or phrase from the pair in brackets to complete each sentence.

1 There are very few unexplored areas left in the _____. (world/cosmos)

2 Barnaby spent all his life working on the _____, like his father and grandfather before him.   (earth/land)

3 After a long day in the town, you really appreciate the fresh air of the _____.   (nature/countryside)

4 Some market gardens find labour costs for casual workers so high that they allow the public to _____ the produce themselves. (pick/pick up)

5 The children watched open-mouthed as the meteor blazed across the evening _____.   (heavens/sky)

6 From the helicopter the navigator could see the red cliffs of the Devon _____.   (coast/shore)

7 It is hoped that recent advances in medical research will enable us to _____ many of the diseases which currently kill a large number of people worldwide.   (devastate/eradicate)

8 The air in the centre of town was thick with _____ from the hundreds of vehicles in the traffic jam.   (smoke/fumes)

9 South Africa is a country of great beauty and immense natural _____.   (sources/resources)

10 The travellers gazed in awe at the _____, a beautiful stretch of clear, fresh water surrounded by snow-capped peaks.   (lake/sea)

C Find adjectives connected with these nouns and verbs, and check their meanings in a dictionary.

1 tropics	9 region	17 disposal
2 globe	10 protect	18 biodegrade
3 town	11 congestion	19 solve
4 countryside	12 conifer	20 produce
5 nature	13 pollute	21 problem
6 scenery	14 climate	22 pole
7 mountain	15 disaster	
8 coast	16 replace	

D Match the words to make common expressions connected with the environment. Use each word only once.

1 health	A warming
2 fossil	B bank
3 unleaded	C effect
4 ozone	D fuels
5 acid	E footprint
6 carbon	F hazard
7 greenhouse	G rain
8 pressure	H layer
9 sea	I petrol
10 global	J group
11 sewage	K levels
12 bottle	L disposal

E Answer these questions as fully as you can, in conversation or in writing.

1 What is your greatest environmental concern, and why?

2 What can the individual do to reduce pollution of the environment?

3 What should governments do to tackle pollution?

4 Are you optimistic or pessimistic about the future of our planet? Explain why.

5 What sources of energy are most environmentally friendly? Discuss their pros and cons.

6 Is there a need for a world population policy and, if so, what would you like to see included in it?

Right and wrong

A Match the words or phrases to make common expressions connected with right and wrong. Use each word or phrase only once.

1	pangs	A	crime
2	a point	B	stricken
3	gross professional	C	values
4	conscience-	D	of civilised society
5	standards	E	problem
6	cook	F	of honour
7	family	G	abiding
8	law-	H	of conscience
9	a heinous	I	misconduct
10	an ethical	J	the books

B Complete the text with these words.

devious	corrupt	rival	loyalty	integrity	accused
blame	bribed	reproached	disgrace	hoodwinked	
	espionage	conscience	traitor		

Rupert worked as a food scientist with Mixo, a large company producing packet cake-mixes and instant desserts. His wife, Josie, had a similar job with a 1) _____ company, Whizzo. So when both companies almost simultaneously produced a new instant strawberry mousse, Rupert's boss hit the roof and 2) _____ him of selling industrial secrets.

'You've 3) _____ us all!' he shouted furiously. 'How much did Whizzo pay you to give the details of Strawberry Dream to your wife? It's industrial 4) _____!'

'Sir,' stammered Rupert in reply, 'I don't know how it happened. It's true that Josie and I were talking about mousse some time ago – perhaps that gave her the idea. I promise you, my commitment and 5) _____ to Mixo have always been one hundred per cent!'

'Get out of my sight, you 6) _____ little worm!' growled his boss.

Although Rupert was sure in his own mind that he was not to 7) _____ , he was upset that his professional 8) _____ had been called into question, and he felt that his colleagues considered him a 9) _____. At home, when he 10) _____ his wife for getting him into such hot water, she flew into a temper. 'I'm in 11) _____ at work too!' she cried. 'Whizzo think *I* was 12) _____ to reveal the secret mousse recipe. Just because we had the same idea at the same time, they assume we're both 13) _____ . Well, Rupert, we're both going to carry on working with a clear 14) _____!'

C Now complete the sentences with words from the box in Exercise B.

1 Judge Clark is renowned for his _____ and high principles.
2 Guy Trilby passed state secrets to a foreign power, and is therefore regarded as a _____ by most people.
3 Hugh is entirely trustworthy. His _____ to the organisation cannot be questioned.
4 Fortunately, James's _____ little plan to discredit the manager and gain promotion for himself did not succeed.
5 Sarah _____ herself for not confessing the truth earlier.
6 That man must have _____ you completely. Didn't you see through his story?

D Make adjectives from these nouns and verbs, and check their meanings in a dictionary.

1 honour   7 fraud
2 ethics   8 deceive
3 suspect   9 vice
4 pettiness   10 sin
5 bankruptcy   11 sacrifice
6 scandal   12 betray

E Choose the correct word or phrase from the pair in brackets to complete each sentence.

1 If you make a false statement to the Inland Revenue, you may be accused of _____.   (tax evasion/tax avoiding)
2 During the earthquake, gangs of youths _____ the electrical goods stores in the centre of town.   (stole/looted)
3 Dropping litter in the street is not a crime, but a(n) _____. (misdeed/offence)
4 Big Ed tried to avoid arrest by _____ the policemen who came to take him away.   (bribing/corrupting)
5 Whoever stole the money must come forward. If the _____ does not own up by the end of the day, the whole school will be punished. (wrongdoer/culprit)
6 As a family man, Terry has many _____. He never takes the kids out to the park, or helps with the housework.   (vices/shortcomings)
7 Julie seems to have no moral standards at all. She is completely _____.   (amoral/immoral)
8 I'm afraid your assistant has _____ the trust you placed in him, and leaked the whole story to the press.   (betrayed/deceived)

F Discuss the following ethical questions, in conversation or in writing.

1 Is shoplifting a serious crime?
2 Should euthanasia, or mercy killing, be allowed under any circumstances?
3 What is your definition of dishonesty? Should we always tell the complete truth?
4 To whom should your first loyalty be? To your family, friends, country, religion? Or to something or someone else?
5 What should be the criteria for selecting families to adopt or foster children?
6 Who should teach children the difference between right and wrong?

UNIT 50

Money and finance

A Complete the text with these words.

factors	expenditure	increase	wealth	poverty	income
material	economists	level	satisfaction		

Surveys show that, contrary to public expectation, 1) _____ does not always bring happiness. At 2) _____ level – that is, for the poorest fifth of the population in advanced economies – there is of course an 3) _____ in well-being for every £1000 increase in 4) _____. Beyond that, however, there is almost no improvement in people's 5) _____ with their lives relative to any rise in their 6) _____ of income. Strangely, market 7) _____ maintain that the purpose of the market is to maximise the satisfaction of 8) _____ wants, largely by encouraging personal 9) _____. However, according to most recent studies, there is little connection between the 10) _____ contributing most to people's happiness, such as a good family life or friendships, and their incomes.

B Match the words to make common expressions connected with money or finance. Use each word only once.

1	spending	A	card
2	profit	B	economy
3	credit	C	tax
4	market	D	test
5	per capita	E	margin
6	income	F	instalment
7	monthly	G	GNP (gross national product)
8	pocket	H	account
9	means	I	power
10	current	J	money

C Decide whether the definitions are true (T) or false (F). Give the correct definition if necessary.

1 Banks charge you *interest* when you borrow money from them.
2 A *wholesaler* buys from a retailer and sells to the public.
3 *Gross* profits are calculated after tax.
4 A *recession* is a period of economic growth.
5 If you have a bank account, you normally receive a *statement* at regular intervals.
6 People who are very well-off could be called *impecunious*.
7 A *stockbroker* handles clients' financial investments.
8 Running up an *overdraft* means spending more than you have in your bank account.
9 A *bargain* is a purchase obtained at a surprisingly low price.
10 When *inflation* is high, prices do not rise very much.

11 If you take out a *loan*, you are lending money to someone.

12 If an item is *under guarantee*, the manufacturer is obliged to replace or repair it free of charge.

13 A *bonus* is an extra charge added to your hotel or restaurant bill.

14 If a company goes *bankrupt*, it cannot pay its debts.

D Choose the correct word or phrase from the pair in brackets to complete each sentence.

1 It's easier to pay electricity and gas bills by _____. (direct debit/mail order)

2 The Robinsons are having difficulty in meeting the _____ repayments on their house. (credit/mortgage)

3 Sandra's uncle left her £10,000 in his _____. (will/testament)

4 I'm afraid you are already three months _____ with your rent, Miss Hughes. (in arrears/in debt)

5 Mr Micawber owed money to so many people that his _____ used to crowd round his house, demanding satisfaction. (creditors/debtors)

6 The spirit of _____ helps private enterprise to thrive. (concurrence/competition)

7 The property developer was obliged to declare his annual _____ to the Inland Revenue for tax purposes. (profit/gain)

8 When the customer's cheque _____, the store manager refused to deliver the goods. (rebounded/bounced)

9 No _____ has been spared on the grandiose public buildings which continue to rise in the new capital city. (cost/expense)

10 We don't accept cheques, I'm afraid. Please pay in _____. (card/cash)

11 Remember to keep the _____ in case you need to ask for a refund or replacement. (recipe/receipt)

12 If you show your student card, you may qualify for a _____. (decrease/discount)

13 Please make sure you have the correct change for the _____ before boarding the bus. (fee/fare)

14 Mrs Maitland has some _____ Picasso sketches in her private collection. The insurance premiums she has to pay are astronomical. (worthy/priceless)

15 People on a limited budget have to try to live _____, even if it means going without luxuries. (by all means/within their means)

16 The _____ from the village fair are earmarked for a local charity. (funds/proceeds)

E Answer these questions as fully as you can, in conversation or in writing.

1 What difference would it make to your life if you won a large sum of money – in a national lottery, for example?

2 Do you have a budget? Do you wait until you have enough cash to buy something, or do you use credit? What are the advantages and disadvantages of using credit?

3 Do you think everyone should save for a rainy day, or enjoy spending money while they have it?

Recycling

Choose the correct word or phrase to complete each sentence.

1 I presume you declare any private _____ to the appropriate authorities.
a) income b) revenue c) interest d) allowance

2 Derek had no experience of white-water canoeing, so it was extremely _____ of him to try and shoot the rapids.
a) hazardous b) intrepid c) perilous d) foolhardy

3 Meg had a _____ escape when she was hang-gliding yesterday.
a) narrow b) close c) near d) slender

4 The five-hour _____ which was performed on Mrs Brown's hip was expensive but effective.
a) treatment b) operation c) medicine d) therapy

5 Peregrine Thorpe _____ the rewards of his hard work when he was given the chair of classics.
a) got b) obtained c) reaped d) collected

6 I can't understand Juan's Spanish, because he speaks a regional _____.
a) dialect b) jargon c) accent d) slang

7 When the lift finally started moving, we were all packed inside like _____.
a) fish b) anchovies c) sardines d) dates

8 Mrs Taylor decided to buy a new coat by _____ order, as she didn't have time to look round the shops.
a) postal b) mail c) banker's d) standing

9 I usually switch off the television when the _____ come on.
a) commercials b) posters c) slogans d) advertising

10 'When do you have to hand in that report?' 'The _____ is Thursday 12th April.'
a) lifeline b) byline c) headline d) deadline

11 The police accused the bank employee of _____, after financial irregularities were uncovered in his department's accounts.
a) fraud b) hoodwink c) swindle d) cheating

12 When the accused was found guilty of reckless driving, he asked for five other _____ to be taken into consideration.
a) crimes b) offences c) shortcomings d) misdeeds

13 *The Gloucester Gazette* wanted to boost its _____ by targeting a younger market.
a) circulation b) readers c) coverage d) market

14 The soldier who saved the lives of three of his comrades was given a _____ award.
a) prenatal b) posthumous c) postprandial d) predicted

15 You never quite know what Ken is up to – he's rather a dark _____.
a) dog b) fox c) wolf d) horse

16 Tina took her four-year-old daughter to the children's hospital for an appointment with a _____.
a) paediatrician b) pedestrian c) philologist d) philatelist

17 For my _____ of mind, promise you'll wear a life jacket in the boat.
   a) satisfaction   b) contentment   c) peace   d) calmness

18 The burglar suffered _____ of conscience when he realised he had unwittingly stolen the little girl's teddy bear.
   a) pains   b) aches   c) stabs   d) pangs

19 In attacking the old lady, the youth committed a _____ crime.
   a) heinous   b) naughty   c) bad   d) evil

20 The World Health Organisation has stated that smallpox has been almost completely _____.
   a) uprooted   b) eradicated   c) obliterated   d) extinguished

21 John's amateur dramatic group are _____ 'My Fair Lady' this weekend. The first performance is on Wednesday.
   a) rehearsing   b) repeating   c) playing   d) practising

22 Once the new Marketing Manager's ideas were implemented, sales _____ and the company made huge profits.
   a) plunged   b) lifted   c) rocketed   d) achieved

23 I can't possibly make the announcement now – I've got a _____ in my throat!
   a) fish   b) toad   c) bird   d) frog

24 Cosmetics companies who claim not to _____ their products on animals are gaining a large share of the market.
   a) test   b) try   c) experiment   d) practise

25 Looking at old photos in family albums often _____ happy memories of the past.
   a) creates   b) evokes   c) makes   d) reminds

26 The week of exams left Miranda exhausted, and she's still rather _____.
   a) low down   b) full of beans   c) under the weather
   d) in worse condition

27 It was a complicated, subtle text, and the translator was not sure he had captured all its _____ of meaning.
   a) allusions   b) tones   c) shadows   d) nuances

28 What a mad thing to do! You could all have been killed! It was _____ folly!
   a) merely   b) only   c) sheer   d) wild

29 The President, flanked by his bodyguards, made a powerful _____ on the steps of the White House.
   a) speech   b) talk   c) lecture   d) sermon

30 Because Trevor had started a fight in the playground, he was in _____ for the rest of that day.
   a) punishment   b) exile   c) dishonour   d) disgrace

31 Blood _____ are needed urgently, as the national blood bank reserves are getting low.
   a) volunteers   b) donors   c) givers   d) offers

32 Those who live on the _____ tend to have a less sentimental view of nature than city dwellers.
   a) country   b) soil   c) earth   d) land

UK government

A Read the text, then decide which word from A, B, C or D is most appropriate for each space.

The full name of the UK is the United Kingdom of Great Britain and Northern Ireland. Great Britain, strictly speaking, is the island comprising England, Wales and Scotland. Ireland, to the west of Great Britain, is the island made up of Northern Ireland, which is part of 1) _____, and the 2) _____ of Ireland (known in Irish as Eire).

Great Britain and Ireland belong to the whole group of islands known as the 3) _____ Isles, which includes all the Scottish islands such as the Hebrides, the Orkneys and the Shetlands, plus others such as Anglesey and the Scilly Isles. Most of these smaller islands are part of the UK and are 4) _____ from the mainland, although the Isle of Man (in the Irish Sea) and the Channel Islands (between England and France) are largely 5) _____. In fact, the Isle of Man's 6) _____, the Tynwald, was established more than 1000 years ago, and is thought to be the oldest legislature in continuous existence in the world.

Until 1999, all parts of the UK were governed from London. However, following 'yes' votes in the Scottish, Welsh and Northern Irish 7) _____, the British government set up a new Scottish Parliament and Welsh and Northern Irish Assemblies, 8) _____ many of its powers to these bodies.

For economic purposes, England is divided into nine large 9) _____; development agencies exist to improve their economic performance and to tailor national 10) _____ to regional needs. However, most individuals feel a much stronger attachment to their 11) _____, which in most cases represents a historical link with the past. There are over forty of these in England, of varying 12) _____, from tiny Berkshire to enormous North Yorkshire.

The citizens of the United Kingdom have British 13) _____. In addition, they are citizens of the European 14) _____, because the UK is a 15) _____ state.

	A	B	C	D
1	the UK	England	Great Britain	Scotland
2	Kingdom	State	Homeland	Republic
3	English	Scottish	British	United
4	legislated	administered	accounted	enforced
5	self-governing	democratic	self-elected	tolerant
6	monarch	chamber	regime	parliament
7	referendums	elections	polls	surveys
8	depositing	deliberating	devolving	deratifying

	A	B	C	D
9	provinces	regions	states	localities
10	ideas	ambitions	policies	suits
11	region	town	village	county
12	beauty	sizes	shapes	age
13	identity	rights	statehood	nationality
14	Union	Club	Charter	Parliament
15	member	participant	voting	partner

B Match the words and phrases on the left, connected with UK politics, with the correct definitions.

1	a constituency	A	all qualified voters
2	a candidate	B	when all MPs are replaced or re-elected
3	a Member of Parliament	C	someone who offers him/herself for election as an MP
4	the electorate	D	the container in which you put your vote
5	a by-election	E	someone elected to represent his/her constituents
6	a general election	F	the building where you go to cast your vote
7	a ballot box	G	a district that sends an MP to Parliament (or its residents)
8	a polling station	H	the largest party in Parliament which is not part of the Government
9	the Opposition	I	when one particular constituency votes for a new MP
10	a majority	J	the number of votes/seats by which a candidate/party wins an election

C Use words or phrases from Exercise B to complete these sentences.

1 The government's currently trying to woo the _____ by promising huge tax cuts. Supposedly, these would kick in after the _____, so they represent an attractive lure for the man or woman in the street.

2 Even my cousin is rather dismissive of the party's tactics, and she's standing as their _____ for her local _____!

3 She takes her politics very seriously, and says she wants to become a(n) _____ so that she can improve the way the country's governed.

4 The Leader of the _____ joined with the Prime Minister in condemning the latest terrorist outrages.

D Answer these questions as fully as you can, in conversation or in writing.

1 What is the difference between the United Kingdom, Great Britain and the British Isles?

2 What do you think of the largely symbolic role played by the sovereign in the British parliamentary system? What effect, if any, do you think the monarch has on British politics?

3 What are the pros and cons of a written versus an unwritten constitution?

4 Who should hold more power, local or central bodies? Which should take precedence, regional or national interests?

Conflict and revenge

A Match the words or phrases to make common expressions connected with revenge or forgiveness. Use each word or phrase only once.

1	settle	A	into your own hands
2	a fit	B	a grudge
3	take the law	C	your just deserts
4	turn	D	feud
5	an eye	E	old scores
6	get your own	F	of jealousy
7	get no more than	G	amends
8	make	H	and forget
9	forgive	I	for an eye
10	a family	J	back
11	bear	K	the hatchet
12	bury	L	the other cheek

B Choose the correct word from the pair in brackets to complete each sentence.

1 The two secretaries kept up their _____ for six months, and did not speak to each other unless they had to. (feud/argument)

2 Don't _____ him by pointing out his mistakes. (antagonise/exacerbate)

3 What was the Minister's _____ for giving his assistant the sack? (cause/motive)

4 When they heard of the atrocities committed by the occupying army, the exiled government vowed to _____ a terrible revenge if they ever regained power. (wield/wreak)

5 Throughout world history, countries have engaged in _____ for reasons of territorial aggression, or religious or racial hatred. (warfare/rioting)

6 The marriage guidance counsellor is hoping to bring about a _____ of both parties, to prevent a divorce. (redress/reconciliation)

7 Three villagers were shot in _____ for the killing of three soldiers. (reprieve/reprisal)

8 'Good! I'm glad you're hurt!' said Gloria _____. (enviously/vindictively)

9 Callers jammed the switchboard after a request was broadcast for information from _____ of burglary. (casualties/victims)

10 Max's feelings of _____ persisted, even though the company made every effort to placate him. (rancour/apprehension)

11 When Julian criticised her dress sense, Jacky _____ by commenting on his bald spot. (reprimanded/retaliated)

12 I wish you could have a discussion without getting _____! (aggressive/assertive)

C Complete the missing answers or clues in the crossword. All the answers can be found in Exercise B, but you may have to change the form of the word.

A _____ revenge
B _____ bitterness
C <u>14 across</u> a long-standing quarrel
D <u>15 across</u> people who suffer harm or injury
E <u>1 down</u> a feeling of wanting revenge
F _____ the state of competing with other people
G <u>7 across</u> a reason for doing something
H _____ punishment or compensation
I _____ a private family feud
J _____ to repay an injury, fight back
K _____ to put right a wrong
L <u>4 down</u> to re-establish friendly relations after a quarrel
M <u>11 down</u> to inflict (revenge)
N <u>3 across</u> to make someone hostile
O <u>6 down</u> the process of waging war
P <u>9 across</u> deep bitterness or hostility

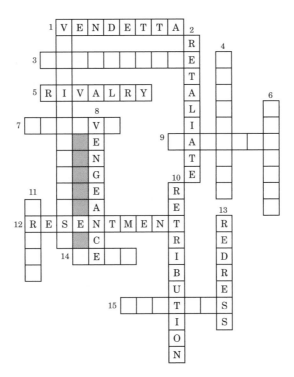

D Answer these questions as fully as you can, in conversation or in writing.

1 Can you think of occasions when you have tried to get your own back? Has it always worked?

2 Have you any personal experience of long-harboured resentment or family feuds? How can these problems be resolved?

3 How can the desire for revenge affect a) negotiation of disputed national boundaries? b) arrangements for a couple's divorce?

4 Should the desire for revenge play any part in the legal system or the punishment of criminals? How can an innocent victim be helped to come to terms with the effects of a crime committed against him/herself?

UNIT 54

Technology and progress

A Match the words to make common expressions connected with technology or progress. Use each word only once.

1	digital	A	crops
2	DNA	B	television
3	optimum	C	efficiency
4	remote	D	testing
5	cable	E	facility
6	market	F	control
7	solar	G	emissions
8	security	H	dish
9	satellite	I	tag
10	mobile	J	dispenser
11	playback	K	energy
12	carbon	L	leader
13	cash	M	highway
14	GM	N	phone

B Complete the text with these words. There is one more than you need.

integrated	monopoly	digital	initiative
encoded	revenue	investing	market
spreadsheet	system	PCs	compatible
lucrative	rivals	consumers	growth

Microsoft is the giant of the computer software market, and its quarterly 1) _____ exceeds ten billion dollars. It originally supplied the operating 2) _____ adopted by IBM for its 3) _____, and now sells its own phenomenally popular system, Windows. Building on the latter's success, the company developed carefully 4) _____ software products designed to be thoroughly 5) _____ with each other, but not necessarily with those of all other companies. Microsoft's business strategy has been widely criticised by its 6) _____, who have accused it of attempting to create a 7) _____, thus stifling healthy competition as well as harming the interests of 8) _____. Although it is currently the 9) _____ leader, the company cannot assume that the unprecedented 10) _____ in software sales will last for ever. Therefore, in order to maintain its market position, it has joined the telecommunications industry in 11) _____ heavily in cable technology, in order to create a so-called 12) _____ highway capable of delivering digitally 13) _____ video, the internet and other services to the home. This concept is likely to be a very 14) _____ one for Microsoft and any other companies associated with the 15) _____.

C Complete the sentences with these words and phrases. Use each expression only once.

robot	electromagnetic field	closed-circuit
security tags	microchip	remote control	streamline
solar	white goods	optimum efficiency	anti-nuclear
central locking	programme

1 When a man with a shotgun took his girlfriend hostage, the Maryland police decided to send a _____, operated by_____, into the building to disarm him.

2 Parents of a 13-year-old leukaemia victim are suing their local electricity company on the grounds that the _____ in their son's bedroom contributed to his death.

3 Police attempted to hold back the _____ protesters as they surged towards the parliament building.

4 Contrary to popular belief, _____ energy can still be collected and stored even on a cloudy or misty day.

5 Most supermarkets and department stores have a system of _____ television in operation twenty-four hours a day.

6 Customers are requested to ensure that all _____ are removed from garments at the time of purchase.

7 The board of directors is currently seeking to _____ the decision-making process at management level.

8 Hoover, Zanussi and Bosch are all well-known manufacturers of _____.

9 The electronics and computer industries have been revolutionised by the development of the _____.

10 The _____ of a centrifugal pump is related to its speed of rotation.

11 Most cars these days have a _____ system, enabling all doors to be locked by turning just one key.

12 You can _____ the central heating to come on at set times, using a time switch connected to the boiler.

D Decide whether the definitions are true (T) or false (F). Give the correct definition if necessary.

1 A *catalyst* is a person or thing that causes a change.

2 A *gadget* is a large electrical appliance.

3 *Data* is another word for information.

4 A *trolley* is a two-wheeled cart for carrying shopping.

5 *Radiation* is the emission of energy in the form of rays.

6 A *sophisticated* machine is a complex one.

7 A *socket* is a device attached to a flex, used to make an electrical connection.

8 A *vehicle* is a means of transport with wheels.

E Answer these questions as fully as you can, in conversation or in writing.

1 What, in your opinion, was the greatest technological achievement of the twentieth century?

2 Which area of technology do you think deserves further research and development, and why?

3 Name three gadgets or other pieces of equipment which you feel are indispensable to your comfort, and explain why.

Work and study

A Match the words to make common expressions connected with employment. Use each word only once.

1	trade	A	salary
2	curriculum	B	pay
3	aptitude	C	retirement
4	sick	D	action
5	industrial	E	prospects
6	promotion	F	union
7	probationary	G	test
8	short	H	period
9	monthly	I	vitae
10	early	J	list

B Choose the correct word or phrase from the pair in brackets to complete each sentence.

1 If you work longer than your contract stipulates, you will be paid _____. (flexitime/overtime)

2 Every year there are at least 50,000 _____ for that particular examination. (applicants/candidates)

3 People who are unable to find work may be eligible for unemployment _____. (payment/benefit)

4 Dr Brewer decided to spend his _____ year on research into comparative religions. (secondment/sabbatical)

5 As the shipyard had run out of orders, all the workers were made _____. (redundant/sacked)

6 Chris really is very talented, but he can't possibly expect to make a _____ from his painting. (profession/living)

7 University students who take out a _____ to pay for their studies may be seriously in debt when they graduate. (loan/mortgage)

8 I hope *Jane Eyre* will be on the _____ again next year. (studies/syllabus)

C Choose the correct word to complete each sentence.

1 When Lucinda graduated, she had no idea which _____ to choose.
a) living   b) business   c) career   d) work

2 The sales manager failed to negotiate a suitable _____ with his Japanese counterpart.
a) deal   b) transaction   c) business   d) accord

3 The job you've applied for isn't _____. It's only temporary, I'm afraid.
a) long-lasting   b) permanent   c) eternal   d) durable

4 Pete has a well-paid position with a local _____.
a) firm   b) association   c) house   d) society

5 When you send in your application, remember to supply the names of two _____.
a) umpires   b) judges   c) supporters   d) referees

6 The day-to-day running of the school is handled by the headteacher, who is responsible to the _____ of governors.
a) board   b) table   c) committee   d) meeting

7 Silvio was the first member of staff ever to be _____ for gross professional misconduct.
a) dispatched   b) sacked   c) released   d) shot

8 Employers are often less interested in an applicant's academic _____ than in his or her experience.
a) papers   b) certificates   c) qualifications   d) degrees

9 Gary accepted the job in Lisbon, although he would only be _____ half his previous salary.
a) winning   b) gaining   c) deserving   d) earning

10 Depending on their circumstances, university students live on a _____ from the bank, an allowance from their parents or income from part-time jobs.
a) loan   b) pension   c) fund   d) purse

D Complete the sentences with these expressions. There is one more than you need.

on-the-job training	achieve his potential
enter the labour market	off sick on the dole
on leave	wage dispute picket line

1 Peter lost his job in 1998 and has been _____ ever since.

2 Kirsty feels this is an inopportune moment to _____, so she is planning to continue her studies instead.

3 We attach very little importance to the fact that you have no experience of computers, because you will be given the necessary _____.

4 When we took on Craig Henderson a couple of years ago, we hoped he would become a high-flyer. But I'm afraid he has completely failed to _____.

5 Staff morale is at an all-time low, largely owing to the recent _____.

6 During the strike, the union organised a 24-hour _____ outside the gates, to discourage people from entering the factory.

E Answer these questions as fully as you can, in conversation or in writing.

1 How much freedom and choice should children be given at school? How important do you think rules and discipline are?

2 Suggest ways of improving a country's education system.

3 How would you balance work and leisure, if you had a free choice?

4 How important is it to have high educational qualifications when looking for a job?

5 What qualities would you look for in
a) a boss?   b) a colleague?   c) a subordinate?

6 What are the advantages and disadvantages of
a) single-sex education?   b) boarding schools?

c) freelance work?   d) early retirement?

Different lifestyles

A Match the words to make common expressions connected with different lifestyles. Use each word only once.

1	fast	A	tension
2	standard	B	image
3	poverty	C	of living
4	child	D	durables
5	welfare	E	level
6	nuclear	F	state
7	working	G	flyer
8	disposable	H	parent
9	consumer	I	benefit
10	single	J	family
11	subsistence	K	class
12	racial	L	income
13	self	M	pace
14	high	N	trap

B Complete the text with these words. There is one more than you need.

> renovation   habitation   bare necessities   polarised   threats
> brave   victimising   plight   support   demolish
> sympathise   cottage   belongs   survival   evict

A Welsh district council has refused to pay for the 1) _____ of a tiny two-room stone 2) _____ , and has declared it unfit for human 3) _____. The cottage 4) _____ to Miss Heather Morton, who has lived there since her childhood. She manages with only the 5) _____ of life, as there is no electricity or piped water. She wants to stay in the 150-year-old cottage, but the council is determined to 6) _____ her and 7) _____ the building. Her 8) _____ has 9) _____ the community. A few of her neighbours 10) _____ the council's decision, but most 11) _____ with Miss Morton and accuse the council of 12) _____ an elderly lady. Despite the council's 13) _____, Miss Morton intends to 14) _____ out the next few winters in her home, with her five dogs for company.

C Decide whether the definitions are true (T) or false (F). Give the correct definition if necessary.

1 *Materialism* is an excessive interest in money and material possessions.
2 A *status symbol* is a possession which is regarded as proof of the owner's social position.
3 An *acquisitive* person is someone who asks too many questions.
4 *Affluence* is the power exerted by one person over another.
5 *Slums* are squalid, overcrowded areas of a city.

6 *Squatters* are people who illegally occupy houses or land.

7 The *metropolis* is the capital or main city of a country.

8 *Tramps* are people who travel around on foot, with no permanent home.

9 *Priorities* are young couples who are buying their first home.

10 An *au pair* is a person who insists on equal opportunities.

11 A *busker* is someone who plays an instrument in a public place and asks passers-by for money.

12 A *New Age traveller* is a person who travels around the country, camping wherever he/she feels like it.

D Choose the correct word or phrase from the pair in brackets to complete each sentence.

1 Many housing estates and blocks of flats were put up in the building _____ of the 1980s. (surge/boom)

2 People are encouraged to live _____ these days, by making excessive use of credit facilities. (in the red/beyond their means)

3 Residents of the _____ enjoy good social amenities without the noise and bustle of living in the town centre. (downtown/suburbs)

4 It is becoming fashionable to dress in _____ clothes snapped up from junk shops and jumble sales. (second-hand/antique)

5 Some people opt out of the _____ and take early retirement. (rat race/grindstone)

6 A house can be seen as a comfortable dwelling to bring the family up in, or as a lucrative _____. (investment/profit)

7 While some householders have open-plan gardens, others feel the need for high fences, guard dogs and _____ lights. (privacy/security)

8 Tastes in interior decoration vary from the plain, simple, farmhouse style to the _____ , expensive decor you find in many town houses. (tasty/sophisticated)

9 If a marriage does not work out, the couple often split up, share out their assets, and live _____. (separated/apart)

10 So many celebrities have a private life which is quite different from their public _____. (picture/image)

11 In certain countries, _____ visitors is always done in hotels or restaurants, while in others it is considered more hospitable to invite guests to the home. (entertaining/greeting)

12 It is difficult for people in serious _____ to get out of the spiral of borrowing and paying interest on ever-increasing loans. (credit/debt)

E Answer these questions as fully as you can, in conversation or in writing.

1 What factors make a lifestyle challenging or rewarding?

2 How do you account for the current interest in the material aspects of life, rather than the spiritual? Do you think this is a temporary aberration, or purely a more realistic approach which will last?

3 Can you give reasons for the widening gap between rich and poor in developed countries as well as the Third World? Is there a long-term solution to this problem?

4 What would your ideal lifestyle be, if you had no financial considerations or family responsibilities to take into account?

Belief and superstition

A Match the words or phrases to make common expressions connected with belief or superstition.

1	dabble	A	account
2	mind	B	pokery
3	extra-sensory	C	telling
4	sleight	D	in the occult
5	jiggery-	E	magic
6	far-	F	perception
7	burden	G	of proof
8	unidentified	H	illusion
9	fortune	I	of hand
10	black	J	over matter
11	optical	K	fetched
12	eyewitness	L	flying object

B Decide whether the definitions are true (T) or false (F). Give the correct definition if necessary.

1 A *premonition* is an intuition of a future happy event.

2 A *charlatan* is someone who pretends to have knowledge he or she does not possess, especially in medicine.

3 To *levitate* means rising or causing to rise and float in the air.

4 A *seance* is a meeting where spiritualists try to receive messages from the spirits of the dead.

5 *Astrology* is the study of the planets and stars.

6 A *poltergeist* is a spirit which makes noises and moves objects.

7 *Telepathy* means being able to understand, and communicate with, people's thoughts.

8 A *clairvoyant* is someone who knows exactly what happened in the past.

9 To *haunt* means to visit a person or a place regularly. (used of ghosts)

10 A *sceptic* is someone who does not believe a person or an idea.

11 To *dowse for water* is to hunt for water by holding a forked stick over the ground.

12 *Fringe medicine* refers to alternative treatments, many of which are not generally recognised by the traditional medical establishment.

13 A *cult* is a sect devoted to the practices of a particular religion or set of theories.

14 An *atheist* is someone who believes in God.

15 *The evil eye* is a look or glance superstitiously supposed to have the power of inflicting harm.

16 *Old wives' tales* are superstitious beliefs passed on by word of mouth.

17 *Witchcraft* is the art of using magic to make certain, usually evil, things happen.

18 A *totem pole* is a carved post set up by certain Native Americans as a tribal symbol.

C Fill in the missing words, all beginning with **m.**

1 People sometimes see a ☐☐☐☐☐☐ , of an oasis or water, in the desert. It recedes as they approach it.

2 A ☐☐☐☐☐☐ is a person who claims to carry messages between the dead and the living.

3 The unicorn is a ☐☐☐☐☐☐☐☐ beast.

4 Do you believe the Loch Ness ☐☐☐☐☐☐ exists?

5 ☐☐☐☐☐ is the art which supposedly influences events by the use of spells.

6 A ☐☐☐☐☐☐☐ is a surprising event attributed to a supernatural cause.

7 The cult members were ☐☐☐☐☐☐☐☐☐☐ by their fascinating but manipulative leader, and agreed to do whatever he wanted.

D Choose the correct word to complete each sentence.

1 His story appeared completely _____ at the time, and we were all taken in.
a) gullible   b) believable   c) credulous   d) honest

2 When the police found her, she was living under a(n) _____ name.
a) assumed   b) fraudulent   c) bogus   d) fake

3 Adam was only able to pass the entry test by _____.
a) duping   b) fooling   c) cheating   d) deceiving

4 I am afraid I cannot give _____ to Humphrey's account of what happened.
a) truth   b) belief   c) faith   d) credence

5 The journalists asked the Prime Minister to _____ the date of the next election.
a) predict   b) foretell   c) presage   d) prevaricate

E Answer these questions as fully as you can, in conversation or in writing.

1 What superstitious habits are common in your country?

2 Do you need proof before you can believe anything, or do you take some things on trust? Give examples.

3 Discuss whether you think the following situations are supposed to bring good or bad luck:

a) a black cat crossing your path

b) walking under a ladder

c) arranging something for Friday the 13th

d) driving a green car

e) breaking a mirror

f) taking the last sandwich on a plate

g) catching the bride's bouquet as she leaves for her honeymoon

h) treading in a cowpat or dog mess, or being hit by bird droppings.

4 Astrology, palmistry and reading tea leaves or tarot cards are all ways of trying to predict the future. Do you believe in any of them?

Time and memory

A Match the words on the left with the correct definitions.

1	decade	A	a hundred years
2	diary	B	a chart showing the days and months of a year
3	epoch	C	a clock in a tall wooden case
4	century	D	ten years
5	calendar	E	a personal record of daily events
6	stopwatch	F	a watch used for timing sporting events
7	timer	G	a person descended from someone
8	grandfather clock	H	a device which can be set to ring after a period of time or to switch on a system
9	ancestor	I	a period of time in history
10	descendant	J	a person from whom someone is descended

B Choose the correct word or phrase from the pair in brackets to complete each sentence.

1 The old man often used to _____ happily about the past. (reminisce/recollect)

2 When Allen was asked the all-important question, his mind was _____. (a total blank/total recall)

3 At least the photos are a _____ reminder of that wonderful holiday. (durable/lasting)

4 Eleanor brought back several interesting _____ of her trip to South America. (memorials/souvenirs)

5 When the boy was asked for an explanation, he _____, making up a story about a long-lost uncle. (procrastinated/prevaricated)

6 Too many people indulge in unnecessary _____ for the past. (recall/nostalgia)

7 My aunt has taken the wrong keys again. She's so _____. (absent-minded/open-minded)

8 The memory of the beggar's face _____ Sam for a long time. (hampered/haunted)

9 Any event recorded by history is a(n) _____ event. (historic/historical)

10 The village church dates back to _____ times. (ancient/antique)

11 Aya spent a whole week _____ facts and figures for her statistics exam. (memorising/remembering)

12 Olga Berkov has furnished her London flat in striking _____ style. (contemporary/day-to-day)

13 I expect you'll receive a reply from the Education Department _____. (at last/sooner or later)

14 Please make sure you arrive at eight _____. (on the dot/on the spot)

15 Have you seen the long-range weather _____? They say there'll be gales this weekend. (prediction/forecast)

16 Please note that Little Theatre performances always start _____.
Latecomers will not be admitted until the interval. (in time/on time)

17 Of course the hero marries the heroine _____ of the story, and
they live happily ever after. (in the end/at the end)

18 I used to be able to reel off my French irregular verbs just like
that, but I'll have to _____ my memory before next week's test.
(arouse/refresh)

19 I only met her briefly, but I'm sure I would _____ her again.
(recognise/memorise)

20 The young boy politely gave up his seat to the _____ lady who
had just hobbled on to the bus. (elder/elderly)

C Fill in the missing words.
The first letter of each is
given.

1 I can't remember his name. It's on the `T` | | of my tongue.

2 You must remember! Think! `R` | | your brains!

3 Warren never remembers anything. He's got a memory like a
`S` | | | | .

4 The cathedral was built in the Middle `A` | | | .

5 The new President took over immediately from his
`P` | | | | | | | | | .

6 The standing stones at Woodhenge date back to
`P` | | | | | | | | | | times.

7 It's `H` | | | time you told him the truth.

8 Rosemary thought she would never get over Colin's death, but with
the `P` | | | | | of time she began to come to terms with it.

9 Time `F` | | | when you're enjoying yourself.

10 Much of our information on the mediaeval way of life has come from
`D` | | | | | | originally written by monks.

11 Only `P` | | | | | | | | will be able to judge whether the
Prime Minister made the right decision or not.

12 With `H` | | | | | | | | the Government realised they had
blundered, but it was too late to rectify the situation.

D Answer these questions
as fully as you can, in
conversation or in writing.

1 Describe any historic events which occurred in the year of your birth.
Which events that have happened since then are the most important,
in your opinion?

2 Choose the three dates that you consider the most important
historically, and give reasons for your choice.

3 What different systems are there for improving memory? Do these
work, and if so, why?

4 Find out as much as you can about the life and achievements of a
historical figure, and write an essay or give a talk about him or her.
Could this person have achieved as much in a different historical
period or not?

5 Describe your first memory, your most embarrassing memory, and
your happiest memory.

Travelling and transport

A Match the words to make common expressions connected with travelling. Use each word only once.

1	steering	A	reservation
2	off-	B	shoulder
3	central	C	hour
4	Highway	D	calming
5	hard	E	carriageway
6	rush	F	peak
7	high	G	crossing
8	dual	H	wheel
9	pedestrian	I	season
10	filling	J	Code
11	traffic	K	holiday
12	package	L	station

B Decide whether the definitions are true (T) or false (F). Give the correct definition if necessary.

1 The *flight recorder* is a plane's co-pilot.

2 A *traffic jam* occurs when heavy traffic moves slowly, if at all.

3 *Commuters* travel considerable distances from home to work.

4 *Off the beaten track* is used to describe an isolated, relatively unknown place.

5 A *berth* is a type of camp bed.

6 You put coins into a *parking meter*, to pay for time to park there.

7 A *tachograph* measures a vehicle's fuel consumption.

8 An *itinerary* is a plane or train timetable.

C Complete the text with these words. Use each word only once. There is one more than you need.

resort	luxury	picturesque	lounging	cuisine	facilities
range	cruise	brochure	self-catering	spectacular	
overseas	excursions	accommodation	inclusive		

Welcome to the wonderful world of Portland Holidays! In our latest
1) _____ we are sure you'll find the widest 2) _____ of holidays
on the market. You can pamper yourself at the five-star Portland
Sheraton in the well-known 3) _____ of Los Reyes, where 4) _____
for sports and nightlife are second to none. Or you can 5) _____
around the island on a 6) _____ yacht, 7) _____ on deck in the
warm Mediterranean sunshine, and admiring the 8) _____ scenery.
Alternatively you might prefer to take a 9) _____ apartment in one
of the 10) _____ fishing villages. Here you can sample the authentic
local 11) _____, with its famous seafood specialities, and go on a
variety of 12) _____ to places of cultural and archaeological interest.
Our prices are 13) _____ of all flights and 14) _____ , and
represent excellent value. Book now!

D Complete the missing answers or clues in the crossword.

A _____ a long, difficult journey, often on foot
B 11 down a road around a town, not through it
C 15 across a house in the country or at the seaside
D _____ a fee to be paid when using a bridge or motorway
E 9 across a central island with traffic moving round it
F 8 down a small room on a ship
G _____ a small house in the mountains, usually of wood
H 2 down a holiday where everything is included in the price
I 3 across an overland or hunting expedition, especially in Africa
J 14 down passing through
K _____ the place where a train or bus ends its journey
L 4 across a piece of paper showing you have paid to travel
M 5 across a booklet advertising holidays
N 6 down (travelling) across a country
O _____ sections of a train (e.g. 1st class)
P 13 across 'You must be tired after your long _____.'
Q 12 down the London Underground
R _____ a cheap flight booked by a package tour company
S 1 down state of complete tiredness

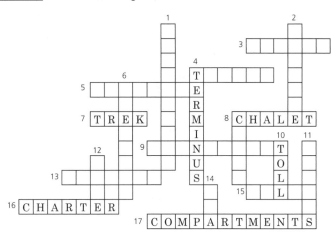

E Answer these questions as fully as you can, in conversation or in writing.

1 What are the advantages and disadvantages of travelling in remote areas? What preparations would you make for a holiday trekking in the foothills of the Himalayas, or exploring the Brazilian rainforests, or crossing the Sahara Desert by jeep?

2 What traffic control or traffic calming measures can you suggest to improve life for pedestrians in towns?

3 What do you think the best means of transport is

a) for a short journey across town to work every day?

b) for an evening at the cinema or theatre?

c) for a touring holiday in Europe?

Books and reading

A Choose the correct word from the pair in brackets to complete each sentence.

1 All Shakespeare's plays are out of _____, as he has been dead for over seventy years. (copyright/playwright)

2 Before publication, an author usually checks the _____ sent by the publishers. (manuscript/proofs)

3 If you go on holiday to a country where you don't speak the language, you probably need a _____. (phrasebook/guidebook)

4 I'm afraid I lost interest in the book. The _____ was too complicated. (plot/theme)

5 I probably won't buy anything from the bookshop. I'll just _____ . (peruse/browse)

6 You'll get an idea of what the book is about by glancing at the _____. (dedication/dust-jacket)

7 Is this the latest _____ of *The Evening Herald*? (volume/edition)

8 To appreciate historical novels you need a good _____. (imagination/fantasy)

9 Have you done the exercises? Look the answers up in the _____. (key/bibliography)

10 The information should be clearly presented in well-planned _____. (sectors/paragraphs)

11 Most modern poetry doesn't _____. (verse/rhyme)

12 Some of the best writers can be interpreted both _____ and metaphorically. (laterally/literally)

13 'Is that the end of the story, Mummy?' 'Let's turn over the _____ and see.' (page/sheet)

14 I really enjoyed the suspense. It's one of the best _____ I've ever read. (romances/thrillers)

15 The new biography of Gandhi is rather expensive, so I think I'll order it from the _____, rather than buying it. (bookshop/library)

B Fill in the missing words. The first letter of each is given.

1 I never buy H[ ][ ][ ][ ][ ][ ][ ] books, as they're so expensive. I just wait till they come out in paperback.

2 Karl Marx's works have been T[ ][ ][ ][ ][ ][ ][ ][ ] into most of the world languages.

3 It was impossible to attract Mike's attention. He was so E[ ][ ][ ][ ][ ][ ][ ][ ] in his book.

4 *Never Look Back* has already sold 100,000 copies and is going to be another B[ ][ ][ ]-[ ][ ][ ][ ][ ][ ] for Alexander Fleming.

5 In the opening C[ ][ ][ ][ ][ ][ ] of the novel, the young boy has a terrifying experience which will haunt him throughout his life.

6 Many people have a favourite A[ ][ ][ ][ ][ ] and read all his or her books avidly.

7 Thomas Hardy is better known for his [P ☐ ☐ ☐] than for his poetry.

8 Yet another [B ☐ ☐ ☐ ☐ ☐ ☐ ☐] of D.H. Lawrence has just been published, with some new insights into his unhappy adolescence.

9 Could I borrow your [C ☐ ☐ ☐] of *Macbeth* for this afternoon's lesson? I seem to have left mine at home.

10 Children's books are often lavishly [I ☐ ☐ ☐ ☐ ☐ ☐ ☐ ☐ ☐ ☐] by accomplished artists.

C Match the words on the left, connected with books or reading, with the correct definitions.

1	a whodunnit	A	a book from which information may be obtained
2	an atlas	B	an alphabetical list of names or topics referred to in a book
3	a reference book	C	a section at the end of a literary work, in the form of a commentary
4	an index	D	imaginative writing based on recent or future scientific discoveries
5	a satire	E	a passage taken from a book, play etc.
6	plagiarism	F	a crime novel
7	an epilogue	G	a collection of poems or literary passages
8	an extract	H	the act of taking ideas, passages etc. from another writer
9	science fiction	I	a complete list of items (e.g. for sale)
10	a catalogue	J	a work in which topical issues, politics etc. are ridiculed
11	non-fiction	K	a book of maps
12	an anthology	L	factual writing

D Answer these questions as fully as you can, in conversation or in writing.

1 What, for you, are the ingredients of a good book? How would you set about writing a best-seller?

2 Will reading become a thing of the past, as more people watch videos and use computers in their spare time?

3 How do a country's history, customs, economic situation, climate and language development affect the literature it produces? Give examples.

4 Write a review of a book you have read recently. Either recommend it, or say why, in your opinion, it is not worth reading.

5 People read for various reasons: for relaxation, to acquire information, for escapism, to help further their studies or career, for fun, to keep up with current events.

Decide which of the above are true for you. If you do not read much, explain why reading does not appeal to you.

Law and order

A Match the words or phrases to make common expressions connected with law and order.

1	tackle	A	police
2	riot	B	sentence
3	open	C	oath
4	prison	D	custody
5	under	E	the problem
6	take into	F	hooligans
7	commit	G	concern
8	soccer	H	bail
9	public	I	a crime
10	release on	J	prison

B Complete the text with these words and phrases. Use each word or phrase only once.

reach a verdict   deterrent   charged   court
criminologists   evidence   plead   sum up   lawyers
offenders   jury   acquitted   pass sentence
committed   offence   witnesses   stand   defendant

A person who is 1) _____ with a serious 2) _____ in Britain has to 3) _____ trial, and 4) _____ guilty or not guilty in 5) _____. During the case the judge and 6) _____ will examine all the 7) _____ presented by both sides, and listen to the cross-examination of any 8) _____ called by the defence and prosecution 9) _____. Finally the judge will 10) _____ the case in legal terms, and the jury will retire to 11) _____. If the 12) _____ is found guilty, the judge will 13) _____ on him, but if he is found not guilty, he will be 14) _____. His sentence will be heavier if he has 15) _____ the same offence previously, though some 16) _____ argue that the number of persistent 17) _____ suggests that prison is not necessarily the most effective 18) _____.

C Complete the missing answers or clues in the crossword. You will find some of the answers in Exercise B.

A	2 down	the place where trials are conducted
B	14 down	Handcuffs go on these!
C	_____	a policeman's rubber weapon
D	18 across	a reason or apology for doing or not doing something
E	8 down	a judge in a lower-level court
F	12 across	a violent public protest
G	_____	a theory or system of fairness for everybody
H	_____	a young person whose behaviour is uncontrolled and destructive or violent
I	15 across	something which puts people off committing a crime

J 3 down   The accused was found innocent and was _____.

K 10 across   'I have no option but to report this incident to the _____.'

L _____   repeated relapse into crime

M 11 across   another word for prison

N 13 across   the person who listens to evidence in court and decides on a punishment

O 5 down   A juvenile _____ is a young person who commits minor crime.

P 4 across   a lawyer who represents his/her clients in court

Q _____   someone in prison

R _____   a formal accusation of an offence or crime

S 16 across   money paid as a punishment for an offence

T 19 across   to attack and rob violently in the street

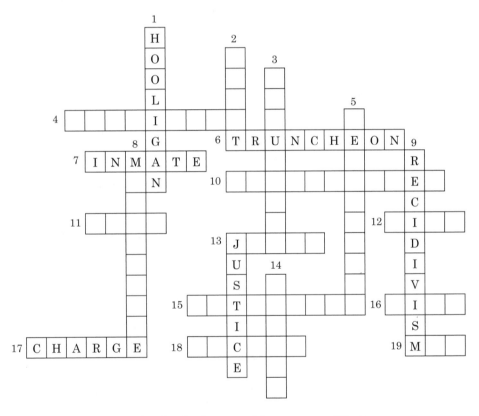

D Answer these questions as fully as you can, in conversation or in writing.

1 How could law and order be improved in your town? Is it a question of investment in police training and manpower, or should ordinary citizens become more involved (as in neighbourhood watch, patrolling or vigilante schemes)?

2 What is the worst miscarriage of justice you can remember in recent times? Does this make you sceptical about the fairness of the legal system and the courts?

3 Do you see prison as a means of punishment, or rehabilitation, or a cross between the two?

Recycling

A Choose the correct word or phrase to complete each sentence.

1 Jane was full of _____ towards her stepmother.
   a) retribution   b) resentment   c) reprisal   d) vengeance

2 Factories are having to _____ all production processes and, in some cases, the workforce too.
   a) slim   b) simplify   c) streamline   d) train

3 Digitally _____ messages can be delivered via cable direct into our homes.
   a) numbered   b) dialled   c) encoded   d) deciphered

4 Josie makes a good _____ from her freelance work.
   a) profession   b) job   c) living   d) earnings

5 When Wilson's company was hit by the recession, he decided to take early _____.
   a) redundancy   b) retirement   c) resignation   d) redeployment

6 Who needs more than the _____ necessities of life?
   a) naked   b) pure   c) bare   d) sole

7 The _____ of the abandoned orphans in Romania has aroused the world's pity.
   a) sadness   b) trouble   c) case   d) plight

8 I'm afraid Jennifer's very _____. She believes everything she's told.
   a) gullible   b) trustworthy   c) credible   d) honest

9 People can make themselves walk on nails or through fire. It's a question of mind over _____.
   a) body   b) material   c) matter   d) facts

10 If you aren't sure what day the 24th is, look it up on the _____.
   a) calendar   b) diary   c) agenda   d) dairy

11 With _____, it's easy to see that a mistake has been made.
   a) rear view   b) overlook   c) retrospect   d) hindsight

12 In August we always go to this wonderful little Greek village, miles from anywhere and really off the beaten _____.
   a) road   b) track   c) path   d) lane

13 The woman accused of shoplifting was found not guilty and was _____.
   a) acquitted   b) liberated   c) excused   d) interned

14 You're not supposed to park on the hard _____ except in an emergency.
   a) lane   b) shoulder   c) leg   d) area

15 While the yacht sailed on, I went to my _____ and changed my clothes.
   a) deck   b) cabin   c) bunk   d) cockpit

16 Some people prefer to watch a film first, and then read the _____ in the paper.
   a) critic   b) revue   c) review   d) criticism

17 We can always find out what books the author consulted by referring to the _____.
   a) index   b) bibliography   c) key   d) dust jacket

18 The old man did not notice it had begun to rain. He was so _____ in feeding the pigeons.
   a) concentrated   b) obsessed   c) engrossed   d) fascinated

19 Several influential pressure _____ are campaigning for a reduction in the current prison population.
   a) groups   b) charities   c) points   d) members

20 Burglar alarms on cars and houses may act as a _____ to the casual thief.
   a) prevention   b) deterrent   c) stopper   d) precaution

21 A lot of old _____ were settled in the New York gangland killings of the 1960s.
   a) quarrels   b) criminals   c) scores   d) feuds

22 I had a strong _____ that a disaster would occur, and it did.
   a) premonition   b) prediction   c) forethought   d) anticipation

23 Don't worry if you run out of money at the weekend. You can always get some from the cash _____.
   a) desk   b) dispenser   c) counter   d) card

24 We should never have quarrelled like that. Let's bury the _____ and forget all about it.
   a) axe   b) argument   c) hatchet   d) subject

25 It is often difficult for a householder to _____ squatters and regain possession of his or her property.
   a) eliminate   b) withdraw   c) evict   d) vacate

26 When the teacher asked Amanda what the chemical formula was, her mind was a total _____.
   a) void   b) empty   c) nothing   d) blank

27 If you have a(n) _____ control handset, you don't even need to get out of your chair to change TV channels!
   a) distant   b) electronic   c) far   d) remote

28 As a result of the recent rise in the divorce rate, there are far more _____ parents than there used to be.
   a) single   b) only   c) unique   d) separate

29 I was really hoping to get the job, as they'd put me on the _____ list, but in the end they appointed someone else.
   a) interview   b) short   c) top   d) good

30 Geraldine always brings back beautiful little _____ from her African trips.
   a) memorials   b) reminders   c) souvenirs   d) memories

31 The Shorter Cambridge Dictionary consists of two _____, A – L and M – Z.
   a) volumes   b) editions   c) tomes   d) issues

32 When Delia's brother Mike pulled her hair, she got her own _____ by kicking him under the table.
   a) back   b) fun   c) revenge   d) retaliation

33 Some of the villagers thought the old woman had the _____ eye.
   a) black   b) evil   c) magic   d) wicked

B Read the text, then decide which word from A, B, C or D is most appropriate for each space.

E-STYLE!

Remember all that advice people used to give you about how to lay out a 1) _____? Well, the good thing about 2) _____ is that you don't need to worry about most of that. No need to put your 3) _____ in the top right-hand corner or wherever. No need to say 'Dear Dan' if you don't want to. Some people do, however, add a 4) _____ at the bottom of their 5) _____ – it usually contains all their 6) _____ details.

In 7) _____ of general style, though, it's a good idea to keep it short and sweet. 8) _____ that people are paying to 9) _____ your mail, so try not to add to their 10) _____. You'll find your email style tends to be much more 11) _____ than in conventional correspondence, as most people see it as an extended form of conversation. Of course, your mail won't look at all 12) _____ if it's so ungrammatical or badly spelt that no one can understand it!

Most 13) _____ mail features headings and text that scream at you in capitals. This is 14) _____ as the equivalent of shouting, and looks rather rude, so it's better not to annoy people by doing it.

	A	B	C	D
1	telegram	fax	heading	letter
2	communication	electronics	email	websites
3	address	surname	phone number	file number
4	dedication	signature	autograph	postscript
5	message	memo	folder	report
6	contract	private	contact	factual
7	matter	terms	course	regard
8	Remind	Bear	Remember	Recall
9	store	send	forward	download
10	receipts	bills	invoices	accounts
11	stylish	looser	lazy	informal
12	impressive	impressed	impressing	impressively
13	rubbish	junk	recycled	direct
14	thought	considered	looked	regarded

C Think of **one** word only which can be used appropriately in all three sentences in each group.

1 I should have _____ that document I was working on today.
She _____ all her old love letters in case she wanted to re-read them.
Toby fell overboard, but his friends _____ him from drowning.

2 My brother has no idea of the problems his arrival will _____.
It makes no difference to me whether I _____ for the photos or not.
The detective decided to _____ as a social worker in order to gain the suspect's confidence.

3 A man is being _____ by the police in connection with the assault.

The elections were _____ in the first week of May, according to custom.

Fortunately for me, my good luck _____, and I managed to get the job.

4 Deborah must _____ an excellent chance of passing the exam if she revises properly.

Our MP has made the decision not to _____ for re-election.

If there's trouble, you'll have to _____ your ground and defend yourselves.

5 I cautiously _____ the car into the last space in the car park.

When it came to signing the contract, the buyers _____ out of the deal.

As he did every evening, Dick _____ up all his files on disk.

D Complete the text by making a new word from each word given in capitals.

SIGN OF THE TIMES

The pen-and-paper signature is dying. In fact, it may soon be dead. There is now legislation in force

1) _____ which gives the same legal status to WORLD

2) _____ signatures as handwritten ones. What DIGIT

does this mean? Well, where 3) _____ affairs are FINANCE

concerned, it usually means a series of numbers

allocated to each individual. Once the right 4) _____ GROUND

checks have been carried out, we can all 'sign'

electronic 5) _____ with what, to all intents and CORRESPOND

purposes, is our very own 6) _____ signature. PERSON

Naturally, the numbers and our top-secret

7) _____, which we can choose for ourselves, must WORD

all remain totally 8) _____. This is clearly in the CONFIDE

interests of our own 9) _____. In many ways, this SECURE

new type of signature has done much to 10) _____ STREAM

the process of business communication.

Humour, puns and jokes

Humour is notoriously difficult to understand in a foreign language. Many **jokes** in English are based on lexical ambiguity and therefore require an in-depth knowledge of advanced vocabulary. A **pun** is the use of a word or phrase which exploits such ambiguity, usually for humorous effect, and is a play on words. In order to understand puns in English, watch out for the different meanings a word can have.

The **punchline** is the culminating point of a joke or funny story, which gives it its humour. It often gives a different answer from what might normally be expected.

A Think of **two** different meanings for each of these words. Then choose the correct word to complete each joke.

pride	spring	skate	dressing	trunk	spotted
spirits	branch	scales	hailing	refuse	crane

1 What would you do if someone offered you a bag of rubbish? _____.

2 If you met an arrogant lion with a troublesome family, what would you say to him? *Watch that _____ of yours!*

3 What bird is good at lifting weights? *A _____.*

4 What's worse than raining cats and dogs? _____ *taxis.*

5 Waiter, there's a twig on my plate. *All right, sir, I'll get the _____ manager.*

6 Why doesn't anybody with a watch go thirsty in the desert? *Because a watch has a _____ in it.*

7 Why did the lobster blush? *Because it saw the salad _____.*

8 What kind of fish is most useful on ice? *A _____.*

9 What did the guard say to the elderly elephant getting off the train? *I'll help you with your _____.*

10 Why do leopards never manage to escape from the zoo? *Because they're always _____.*

11 What did the barman say when the ghost asked for a drink? *Sorry, sir, we don't serve _____.*

12 Which part of a fish weighs the most? *The _____.*

B Look at the first lines of these jokes and think what answer you would expect. Then match them with the correct punch lines.

1 I feel like a banana.

2 Waiter, will the pancakes be long?

3 What's the best thing to buy as a parting gift?

4 How did you find your steak, sir?

5 When is a door not a door?

A When it's ajar.

B Really? Which platform?

C To keep up the conversation.

D Extremely tired.

E A comb.

6 Why do they put telephone wires so high?

7 What are you growing in your garden?

8 One of my ancestors died at Waterloo.

9 Why do birds fly south in winter?

10 Waiter, do you serve shellfish?

F Quite by accident. I moved a few peas, and there it was.

G You don't look like one.

H Because it's too far to walk.

I No problem, sir. We serve anybody.

J No sir. Round.

> Most jokes are designed to be told, not written down, so the **sound** is more important than the spelling. Don't worry if you don't immediately see the joke when you read it. If you say it out loud, the meaning is more likely to become clear.

C What is the key word in each of these jokes, and how can it be spelt or spoken differently to acquire a different meaning?

1 What's black and white and red all over? *A newspaper.*

2 What runs around forests making animals yawn? *A wild boar.*

3 Why do you always lose if you play cards in the jungle? *Because there are so many cheetahs.*

4 Where does Dracula get all his jokes? *From his crypt-writer.*

5 Why is the theatre such a sad place? *Because the seats are always in tiers.*

6 How do you make a gold pie? *Put fourteen carrots in it.*

7 What animal do you eat for dessert? *A moose.*

8 Why is getting up at 4 am like a pig's tail? *Because it's twirly.*

9 What did the ram say to his girlfriend? *I love ewe.*

D Read the first line of each joke. Then think up a punchline, using one of the phrases in the box and making changes to it if necessary. Sometimes there is a clue in brackets to help you.

> no time like the present
> here today, gone tomorrow   make a clean getaway
> drop me a line   take a dim view of things   to make ends meet
> unidentified flying object   Morse code

1 What did the barber say to the client as he finished shaving his head? (hair)

2 What did the astronomer see in his frying pan?

3 How did the Vikings send secret messages? (Norse)

4 What did the boss say when deciding when to hand over a clock as a farewell gift to a member of staff?

5 What's the best way to communicate with a fish?

6 Why does a poverty-stricken dog chase its tail?

7 Why did the thief take a bath?

8 Have you heard the one about the man who always wore sunglasses?

E Use the words in capitals to make longer words that fit the spaces in this text about a particular type of recurring joke.

Responding to 1) _____ insults that have been thrown at you is a 2) _____ way of honing your sense of humour. The great 3) _____ George Bernard Shaw was a contemporary of Winston Churchill's. GBS 4) _____ invited Churchill to the first night of one of his plays, 5) _____ two tickets with a note which said, 'One for yourself and one for a friend – if you have one.' Churchill lost no time in writing back, saying that 6) _____, due to pressure of work, he would be 7) _____ to come, but could he have tickets for the second night – 'if there is one.'

This joke was 8) _____ more recently by a prominent 9) _____ in the Labour Party, when speaking to a colleague and 10) _____ rival of his. The two men found themselves in the same meeting, despite being 11) _____ enemies. The colleague 12) _____ rose to excuse himself, saying that he had arranged to phone some friends, 13) _____ the statesman immediately handed him a small coin (enough for a brief local call) and said 14) _____, 'There you are. Go 15) _____ and phone them all!'

PROVOKE
WONDER
PLAY

THOUGHT
CLOSE

FORTUNATE
ABLE

DATE
POLITICS
TERM

SWEAR
APPEAR
UPON

WIT
HEAD

F Match these jokes with their punchlines, and explain why people might find them funny.

1 Who invented the 5-day week?

2 What happened to the piglet who wanted to act in a Shakespeare play?

3 What kind of boats do vampires like?

4 How do ghosts pass through a locked door?

5 What did the sea say to the sand?

6 What's the difference between a nightwatchman and a butcher?

7 Where do astronauts leave their spaceships, when in town?

A Blood vessels.

B One stays awake and the other weighs a steak.

C At parking meteors.

D Nothing. It just waved.

E He ended up as Hamlet.

F Robinson Crusoe. He had all his work done by Friday.

G They use a skeleton key.

Idioms

An **idiom** is an expression whose sense is not easily deduced from the meanings of the individual words that form it. Verb tenses and pronouns can be changed but otherwise an idiom must be treated as a unit of language. For example, *kick the bucket* is an idiom which means *die*. Another word for *bucket* is *pail*, but this cannot be used instead of *bucket* in the idiom.

An idiom must be used accurately and in an appropriate situation.

A Complete the sentences with these idioms, in the correct form. There are two more than you need.

> watch your step   give someone the cold shoulder
> take the biscuit   have a bone to pick with someone
> give someone the slip   take someone/something for granted
> on the tip of your tongue   tongue in cheek
> make a mountain out of a molehill   pull someone's leg
> out of the question   get your own back
> down in the mouth   play second fiddle

1 Look, the party's going to be quite easy to arrange.
 Don't _____.

2 You live next door to Julia Roberts? No! You must be
 _____.

3 We can't possibly stop for a snack on the way home. Sorry, it's
 _____.

4 Send Max into my office when he arrives, will you? I've got
 _____ with him.

5 Sally, you're looking rather _____. Has anything
 happened?

6 You know Stuart borrowed my stapler yesterday and didn't return
 it? Well, I've just seen my calculator on his desk! That really
 _____!

7 Although police were watching all the ports, the escaped convict
 managed to _____ and stow away on a cross-channel
 ferry to France.

8 I don't think Nigel meant what he said. His remark was rather
 _____.

9 When smoke from Mr Reeve's bonfire dirtied Mrs Ward's washing,
 she _____ by throwing the contents of her dustbin over
 the fence into his garden.

10 I'll remember his name in a moment. It's _____.

11 If you're going to see the Head today, _____. She's in a
 really foul mood, for some reason.

12 I'm afraid Derek doesn't really appreciate all his sister does for him.
 He just _____.

B Match the idioms on the left with their meanings.

1	get (hold of) the wrong end of the stick	A	specify exactly
2	put your finger on	B	make an embarrassing mistake
3	go like a bomb	C	go out of control, work erratically
4	come to terms with	D	look serious, avoid smiling
5	put your foot in it	E	terrify you
6	keep a straight face	F	eventually accept
7	go haywire	G	boast about yourself
8	keep your head	H	misunderstand
9	make your hair stand on end	I	have a very good relationship
10	blow your own trumpet	J	be nervous
11	have butterflies in your stomach	K	not panic
12	get on like a house on fire	L	be very successful, sell well

C Idioms often include animal images. Choose the correct animal idioms to complete the sentences. Use each idiom only once.

> red herring   bee in his bonnet   dark horse   lame duck
> barking up the wrong tree   whale of a time
> get the lion's share   sort out the sheep from the goats
> flogging a dead horse   let the cat out of the bag
> dog-eared   putting the cart before the horse

1 That's the third time Vijay's put forward that suggestion. He's got a _____ about it.

2 There are lots of good candidates, but the three-day selection process is bound to _____.

3 You'll never persuade Simon to change his views on smoking. You're _____, I'm afraid.

4 Areas with high unemployment often _____ of EU subsidies.

5 Don't, for heaven's sake, _____! Elise mustn't even guess at the truth!

6 Strangely enough, the boss had organised the new training programme before he even interviewed the first applicant, rather _____, if you ask me.

7 Nobody knows anything about Gerry's past. He's a bit of a _____.

8 I'm afraid we've got a _____ for a leader. She's lost three elections so far, and looks like losing the next.

9 The class spent twenty minutes discussing school lunches before the teacher realised it was a _____, and insisted they return to the main topic.

10 It certainly wasn't my sister you saw in the cafe. You're _____ there!

11 'Did you enjoy the party?' 'Oh, I had a _____! I couldn't drag myself away!'

12 Here's my copy of *Pride and Prejudice*. I've read it so often I'm afraid it's rather _____.

D Match the idioms on the left, all connected with colour, with their meanings.

1 a red-letter day
2 black and blue all over
3 out of the blue
4 white-collar (worker)
5 in the red
6 green-eyed monster
7 white elephant
8 the green light
9 see red
10 yellow streak

A owing money
B jealousy
C non-manual, clerical
D an important day
E signal to go ahead
F badly bruised
G cowardly characteristic
H become very angry
I unwanted, useless possession
J unexpectedly

E Choose the correct word from the pair in brackets to complete each sentence.

1 Nicole smokes continuously. She's a real _____ smoker. (chain/ring)

2 We'll go _____, shall we, and each pay for our own drinks? (French/Dutch)

3 You can't see a thing in the attic. It's _____ dark up there. (pitch/coal)

4 The window cleaner lost his balance and nearly fell off his ladder. It was a _____ shave. (narrow/close)

5 You'll never persuade Sam to help you decorate the house – he's _____ idle. (bone/wood)

6 You like that china cabinet? I was so lucky, I bought it for a _____ at a jumble sale. (tune/song)

7 I'm sorry, I can't understand this leaflet at all. I can't make head or _____ of it. (tail/foot)

8 Are you two still talking _____? I know your work's fascinating, but can't you find something more relaxing to talk about?! (job/shop)

9 I just want to say a big thank you to all my wonderful customers. Drinks on the _____ for everyone! (table/house)

10 Vincent Ryan? Do you know, that name rings a _____. I'm sure I've heard of him before. (bell/buzzer)

11 It's 6.30. Shall we call it a _____, and go and get a bite to eat? We can finish off the report tomorrow. (stop/day)

12 Kathy and Dee have been at _____ ever since they started sharing an office. They don't even speak to each other now! (deadlock/loggerheads)

13 I'd love to be a fly on the _____ when Mary hands in her resignation. (ceiling/wall)

14 We thought we might have trouble finding the house in the dark but it was a piece of _____, thanks to Paul's directions. (cake/cheese)

15 Since our argument, I've been having second _____ about going on holiday with Isabel. (thoughts/worries)

Proverbs and similes

> **A proverb** is a common saying. It may be a famous quotation, a practical tip or the result of bitter experience! Often people only say the first half of a proverb, and the second half is understood. Proverbs are surprisingly frequent in everyday conversation, so it is useful to be able to recognise and use them.

A Match these beginnings and endings of proverbs, and then say what each proverb means.

1 Too many cooks	A is another man's poison.
2 One man's meat	B keeps the doctor away.
3 The early bird	C calls the tune.
4 Don't count your chickens	D while the sun shines.
5 An apple a day	E is worth two in the bush.
6 Marry in haste,	F before they're hatched.
7 He who pays the piper	G catches the worm.
8 A bird in the hand	H saves nine.
9 Make hay	I repent at leisure.
10 A stitch in time	J spoil the broth.

B Decide which of these proverbs is suitable for each situation. There is one more than you need.

> A You can't judge a book by its cover.   B The more the merrier.
> C It never rains but it pours.   D Every cloud has a silver lining.
> E Waste not, want not.   F There are plenty more fish in the sea.

1 You are trying to persuade your parents to invite a large number of friends to your 21st birthday party.

2 You broke your leg skiing, but in your three months' sick leave from work you had time to teach yourself conversational Italian.

3 You are encouraging a friend to save water and not leave taps running.

4 You are discussing a neighbour's problems. Not only has the poor woman lost her job, but now her eldest son has been sent to prison.

5 You are surprised to hear that Samantha at work, who looks so quiet and shy, drives a red Porsche and is often seen at nightclubs.

C Choose the correct word to complete each proverb.

1 Don't look a gift horse in the _____. (mouth/eyes/stable)
2 A rolling _____ gathers no moss. (snowball/pin/stone)
3 Let sleeping _____ lie. (cats/dogs/babies)
4 A little learning is a _____ thing. (dangerous/wonderful/useful)
5 _____ news is good news. (Some/Recent/No)
6 _____ was not built in a day. (Paris/Rome/London)
7 One swallow does not make a _____. (summer/drink/nest)
8 A leopard cannot change his _____. (skin/spots/hide)
9 You can't teach an old _____ new tricks. (dog/peasant/monkey)
10 It's no use crying over spilt _____. (blood/wine/milk)

D Match these beginnings and endings of proverbs, and then say what each proverb means.

1 While the cat's away,   A shouldn't throw stones.
2 People who live in glasshouses   B 'twixt cup and lip.
3 There's many a slip   C that blows nobody any good.
4 It's an ill wind   D less speed.
5 Nothing venture,   E flock together.
6 More haste,   F without fire.
7 There's no smoke   G make light work.
8 It's the last straw   H nothing gain.
9 Birds of a feather   I the mice will play.
10 Many hands   J that breaks the camel's back.

> **A simile** is a comparison of two things, usually introduced by **like** or **as**, and is used to emphasise or illustrate an idea.

E Match each of these adjectives or adjective phrases with one of the twelve similes.

> healthy   unflappable   very pale   tough   well-behaved
> hard of hearing   extremely short-sighted   crazy
> without shame   obvious   ancient   defunct

1 as cool as a cucumber _____
2 as good as gold _____
3 as bold as brass _____
4 as white as a sheet _____
5 as hard as nails _____
6 as dead as a doornail _____
7 as blind as a bat _____
8 as fit as a fiddle _____
9 as deaf as a post _____
10 as mad as a hatter _____
11 as plain as the nose on your face _____
12 as old as the hills _____

F Form correct similes to complete the sentences, using *as* or *like*, the word in brackets, and a word or phrase from the box. There is one more than you need.

two short planks	out of water	bull	thin	rock
bell	red	judge	mule	

1 You won't need another check-up for a while, Mr Ferguson. Your chest is _____. (sound)

2 She was so embarrassed! She went _____. (beetroot)

3 Do you know, Andy barged right in without a by-your-leave! He's just _____. (china shop)

4 Mandy hasn't got used to being a student again. She misses her job, and hasn't made any new friends yet. At the moment she feels _____. (fish)

5 That lad doesn't understand a thing you say to him. He must be _____. (thick)

6 At least you don't need to think about losing weight! You're _____! (rake)

7 I didn't mind the police breathalysing me at all, because luckily I was _____. (sober)

8 You simply cannot make her change her mind. Once she's decided something, that's it. She's _____. (stubborn)

G Match the two halves of the sentences correctly. They all contain similes with *like*, some involving idiomatic usage.

1 The photographers clustered round the actress   A just like one of the family.

2 They treated me very kindly,   B like wildfire.

3 He avoids family holidays   C like a ton of bricks.

4 In a very short time the rumour spread   D like hot cakes.

5 Jeff's new board game is selling   E like a drowned rat!

6 I've got absolutely soaked. I look   F like the plague.

7 He can't put a foot wrong, or Janet comes down on him   G like bees round a honeypot.

H Match each of these similes with the appropriate situation.

A as brown as a berry   B as pleased as Punch   C as safe as houses
D as large as life   E as thick as thieves   F as strong as an ox
G as quick as a flash   H as like as two peas in a pod
I as light as a feather   J as right as rain

1 being completely out of danger _____

2 being big and strong _____

3 feeling delighted _____

4 doing something extremely fast _____

5 being completely recovered after an illness _____

6 seeing two very similar-looking people _____

7 having a good suntan _____

8 seeing someone you thought was dead or missing _____

9 picking up something weighing very little _____

10 seeing two people co-operating closely _____

Newspaper language

Newspaper headlines often use the present simple to describe an action that has already taken place: • *France wins World Cup*
the passive with the verb **to be** omitted: • *President re-elected*
and the infinitive with **to** to refer to a future action: • *Star to wed dustman*
To keep the headline as short and snappy as possible, no unnecessary words (e.g. auxiliary verbs, articles) are used.

Nouns are frequently piled up in headlines to make compound nouns: • *Government bribe scandal*. There is often a play on words to catch and hold the reader's interest.

A Match these verbs used in headlines with their definitions, using a dictionary if necessary.

clash	top	woo	wed	flee	rock	axe	dog
name	go	up	net	clear	cut		

1 be higher than
2 marry
3 shock severely
4 disagree
5 sack, dismiss
6 reveal the identity of
7 raise, increase
8 try to persuade
9 reduce
10 gain, win
11 acquit
12 be a source of worry to
13 resign, leave, disappear
14 run away from

B Explain these headlines in your own words.

1 TRIO SAVED IN CLIFFTOP DRAMA
2 MOTORWAY CRASH TOLL RISES
3 PM'S PLEDGE ON JOBS
4 POLICE BAN ON LONG HAIR
5 FISH SHOP BLAST RIDDLE
6 RAILMEN'S BID SET TO FAIL
7 DRUGS HAUL AT HEATHROW
8 BRIBES CASE SHAKES CABINET
9 AID FOR QUAKE VICTIMS
10 PIT PERIL LIKELY

C Look at the headlines and choose the correct synonym from the box for each word in italics.

disappointment	election	weapons	angry outburst
hurried visit	ambassador	employment	negotiations

1 *Arms* haul in attic
2 Anglo-French *talks* off
3 November *jobs* rise
4 Madrid *envoy* to resign
5 *Blow* for English cricket
6 High *poll* turnout expected
7 Education chiefs in *storm*
8 Pope's *dash* to Poland

Borrowed words

A **borrowed word** has originally come from another language. When it is assimilated into English, it may keep its original meaning, or acquire an alternative or additional meaning. It may also be pronounced differently from the original.

A Complete the sentences with these borrowed words or phrases.

faux pas	vice versa	bona fide	ad lib
post-mortem		persona non grata	
blasé	non sequitur	spiel	contretemps
alibi	curriculum vitae	coup d'état	née

1 We could go first to Rome, and then to Florence, or _____, if you have urgent business in Florence.

2 A _____ appears to have taken place in the province of Murumba, where an army general is now reported to be in control.

3 He can easily prove he's a _____ resident, just by showing his passport.

4 When you apply for that job, don't forget to enclose a _____ with your letter of application.

5 I'm afraid I made an awful _____ the other day. I asked Marianne how her husband was, quite forgetting he died last year!

6 Nobody likes the new accountant in Jack's office. He's _____ as far as we're concerned.

7 A _____ was carried out on the victim, to establish the exact cause of death.

8 You looked so confident and _____ about it all that I thought you must have parachuted before!

9 What he said had very little connection with what we were discussing – it was a complete _____, in fact.

10 Dick had a bit of a _____ with a traffic warden this morning – that's why he's late.

11 Fellow graduates will be pleased to hear that Caroline Parrott, _____ Neill, has become a director of Pelco Insecticides Ltd.

12 Yet another double-glazing salesman rang up last night, but at least his _____ was short and to the point!

13 If you forget your lines, you'll just have to _____. The audience won't notice a thing!

14 The police were unable to charge Jefferson, as he had an unshakeable _____ for the time when the robbery had been committed.

B Match the borrowed words on the left with their definitions.

1	cuisine	A	hiding place or hidden store
2	siesta	B	ahead of fashion, daring
3	wanderlust	C	summary
4	paparazzi	D	type (literary or artistic)
5	cache	E	relationship or understanding
6	forte	F	prestige
7	avant garde	G	urge to travel
8	rapport	H	afternoon sleep
9	genre	I	photographers desperate for photos of celebrities
10	vigilante	J	style of cooking
11	kudos	K	strong point
12	résumé	L	self-appointed guard

C Complete the sentences with these borrowed words or phrases.

> alfresco   tête-à-tête   incognito   quid pro quo   macho
> verbatim   carte blanche   kamikaze   ad infinitum
> aplomb   entrepreneur   in camera

1 I was delighted when Mrs Starr asked me to furnish her house for her. She gave me _____ to order whatever I needed.

2 We could go on _____ considering the various options, but I think it's time we made a decision.

3 It was such a warm evening we decided to have a little _____ supper in the garden.

4 The two of them were enjoying a quiet _____, over coffee.

5 The judge decided to hold the hearing _____ , as it was important to protect the children from unnecessary publicity.

6 John recovered quickly from the shock of seeing his sister, and said with great _____, 'Wonderful to see you back so soon, Denise!'

7 The photographer made an almost _____ attempt to retrieve his camera from under the wheels of the double-decker.

8 'I think I owe you a _____ ,' smiled the manager. 'If you take on the extra responsibility now, I'll make sure you get promotion next year.'

9 My neighbour is an up-and-coming _____. He owns several shops, and is always on the lookout for a new business opportunity.

10 Jane's husband seems a big, tough, _____ type. Yet you should see him changing the baby's nappies!

11 I think that man looks just like Mel Gibson. It *could* be him, travelling _____. He wouldn't want to be bothered by autograph-hunters.

12 At the public meeting, the discussion was recorded _____ by the council secretary, although some of the protesters did not express their points very clearly.

Words with two or more meanings

A Complete the sentences with these words.

degree	initial	pound	coach	trip
common	surgery	very	suit	plot

1 Sadly, beggars have become a _____ sight in many of our cities.

2 There were some _____ teething troubles when the no-smoking rule was first introduced, but most people have accepted it now.

3 Please come to the _____ to consult the doctor if at all possible. He only makes house calls in cases of serious illness.

4 My heart began to _____ as I cowered behind the door, watching the handle turn slowly.

5 Maria had arranged to see the specialist on Monday. That _____ morning the letter arrived from the clinic, with her blood test results.

6 In his spare time Sam used to _____ the under-14 football team.

7 I suppose I'll have to wear a _____ and tie for the interview.

8 Be careful not to _____ over the children's toys in the hall.

9 I wish I'd bought a programme. Then I might have been able to follow the _____! Who was it who died in Act 1?

10 On graduation day, Mohamed's parents turned up to see their son receive his _____.

B The words you used in Exercise A have more than one meaning. Match each one with one of these definitions.

1 a long-distance bus _____

2 unfenced land which anyone may use _____

3 operations on hospital patients _____

4 a British monetary unit (=100p) _____

5 extremely _____

6 a short journey _____

7 to conspire (against someone) _____

8 the first letter of a name _____

9 to be appropriate for _____

10 a measurement of heat or angle _____

C Think of a word that has both meanings, and write it in the box.

1 a company [_____] unyielding, strict

2 limbs [_____] weapons

3 a written message [_____] a part of the alphabet

4 a stick used in golf [_____] a group of members who share an interest

5 magic words [_____] to write a word correctly

6 part of a tree [_____] a large suitcase

7 used for smoothing metal or manicuring nails [_____] a collection of papers under a name or heading

8 a bird's mouth [＿＿＿] this tells you what you have to pay

9 a living green thing [＿＿＿] a factory

10 new [＿＿＿] a book (fiction)

11 similar to [＿＿＿] to enjoy

12 to reserve [＿＿＿] pages bound together for reading

13 completely [＿＿＿] rather, fairly, not very

14 a white fish [＿＿＿] only

D Think of **one** word only which can be used appropriately in all three sentences in each group.

1 The government's overthrow should _____ as a reminder of the transience of power.

Delia continued to _____ on the board for a further five years.

Toss the salad in the dressing before you _____ it to your guests.

2 If you buy a new car from an established dealer, it should _____ a twelve-month guarantee.

Unfortunately the ice wasn't thick enough to _____ the boy's weight, so he fell into the lake.

If you _____ that argument to its logical conclusion, you'll need to buy bigger premises.

3 There was a deafening _____ of thunder just over our heads.

You can ring up the town hall to check that you're on the electoral _____.

I bought a cheese and tomato _____ and ate it in the park.

4 The summer is our busy period. It's difficult for me to _____ time off then.

It is expected that government forces will _____ the city by the end of the week.

I decided to _____ Peter's advice if I was made redundant again.

5 Sally doesn't _____ any interest at all in her work.

Don't bother to get up, I can _____ myself out.

Even relatively unknown artists will be able to _____ their work in the new gallery.

6 I had almost finished the exam, when the drilling began again outside the window and _____ my train of thought.

Tourists started leaving the resort when the warm weather _____ at the end of August.

I'm not sure which newspaper first _____ the story, but now it's common knowledge.

7 There is great public _____ over the addition of unnecessary chemicals to our food supply.

As it's just a small family-run _____, I don't suppose we'll ever float it on the stock exchange.

What happens when the new policy is implemented is of no _____ to me.

Confusing words

A Choose the correct word from the pair in brackets to complete each sentence.

1 I think we could improve this dish with a _____ use of seasonings. (judicious/judicial)

2 Sharon, who's seven, _____ bickers with her little sister Anne. They're always fighting! (continually/continuously)

3 Mrs Hodge was sent to _____ for shoplifting, as it was her third offence. (goal/gaol)

4 It was very _____ of Trevor to refuse to co-operate with us. (childish/childlike)

5 By improving the interview process, we are hoping to achieve more _____ treatment of immigrants into this country. (human/humane)

6 Did you notice the _____ your remarks had on Gregory? He was quite shocked! (effect/affect)

7 Many businesses have suffered as a result of the world-wide _____ recession. (economic/economical)

8 The examiner decided that he could not mark the paper, as the candidate's handwriting was _____. (eligible/illegible)

9 What would you _____ me to do in my situation? (advice/advise)

10 That new hairstyle seems to _____ you – it looks just right on you. (suit/suite)

11 When the police frogmen came to the surface, they reported that they had discovered the _____ on the river bed. (corps/corpse)

12 Katie has always written up her _____ every night, ever since she was a schoolgirl. (diary/dairy)

13 The _____ of the story is 'Look before you leap'! (moral/morale)

14 My _____ reason for moving to the Lake District was to be nearer my family. (principle/principal)

B If the word in italics in each sentence is correct, put a tick. If not, write the correct word.

1 Stephen has always preferred *classic* music to pop.

2 My neighbour is a very *practicable* man – always repairing or making something.

3 Can you believe it? The bus was *stationery* for twenty minutes, while we all sat there fuming!

4 Tim and Mick went to India and Australia *respectfully.*

5 The President's New Year banquet is one of the capital's most important *social* gatherings.

6 *Loathe* though I am to criticise, I must say I thought the bread was rather stale.

7 It was extremely *official* of the policeman to demand to see our passports, and quite unnecessary.

8 I believed everything he told me. But then my friends always say I'm far too *credible.*

9 The marines disembarked from the *troupe* carrier onto the beach.

10 Add one *desert* spoon of sugar to the mixture.

11 From what you say I *imply* that you are not satisfied with your current job.

12 Vivienne is attending an *intensive* secretarial course.

C There are many pairs of confusing words which sound the same (called homophones), but which have different spellings and meanings. Match each word in the box with the correct definition. (Other definitions may also be possible.)

pier/peer	medal/meddle	wave/waive	core/corps
pare/pair	gambol/gamble	course/coarse	horse/hoarse
ore/oar	fare/fair	tears/tiers	beer/bier	guilt/gilt
sweet/suite	canvass/canvas	aisle/isle	

1 to peel (fruit, vegetables etc.) _____

2 untreated metal _____

3 gold paint _____

4 to bet money _____

5 an award for service given _____

6 to greet by lifting a hand _____

7 a series of lessons or medical treatments _____

8 a group of soldiers _____

9 water from your eyes _____

10 an artist paints on this _____

11 to interfere _____

12 an equal _____

13 two of something _____

14 awareness of having done wrong _____

15 an alcoholic drink made with hops _____

16 a passage between rows of seats _____

17 the centre of an apple _____

18 rough, common _____

19 an island _____

20 just, right _____

21 a set (chairs, rooms) _____

22 a jetty _____

23 an animal you ride _____

24 to ask for votes _____

25 to jump around playfully _____

26 used for rowing _____

27 money you pay for transport _____

28 rows placed above each other _____

29 to not insist on/enforce _____

30 used for carrying a dead body _____

31 having a sore throat _____

32 with a sugary taste _____

Spelling and punctuation

Notice how these words ending in **-y** change:
- *hurry~hurries, penny~pennies, worry~worried, obey~obeyed, play~plays*
Exceptions are: • *say~said, pay~paid*

Remember that most adjectives add **-ly** to become adverbs, but if the adjective ends in **-y**, this is replaced by **-ily**, and if it ends in **-le**, the final **-e** is replaced by **-y**.
But note: • *whole~wholly* (See **Unit 14, Adverbs**.)

When adding the suffixes **-ed** and **-ing** to words, remember that

a one-syllable words ending with one vowel and one consonant (except **x** and **w**) double the final consonant: *drip~dripping*

b most words ending in silent **-e** lose the **-e**: • *rate~rating*

c longer words ending with one vowel and one consonant usually double the consonant if the stress is on the final syllable: • *begin~beginning*
There are a few exceptions, e.g. *travelling, kidnapping*.

A useful spelling rule is '**i before e except after c**'. This is used for /i:/ sounds where there is **ei/ie** confusion, e.g. *believe*. There are some exceptions, e.g. *seize, counterfeit*.

A Tick the words which are spelt correctly, and correct any which are not.

1 hurrys	6 chief	11 happening	16 bowwing
2 happily	7 flaping	12 ruinning	17 comfortabley
3 wholy	8 married	13 taxing	18 friendily
4 instaling	9 separateing	14 plaied	19 becoming
5 ageing	10 deceit	15 rolling	20 siege

B Choose the correctly spelt word or phrase from the pair in brackets to complete each sentence.

1 Although Tina and Matt are married, they keep their money in _____ accounts. (seperate/separate)

2 During the incubation period, the female bird is totally _____ on the male for food. (dependant/dependent)

3 Daphne has always been _____ in collecting antiques. (interessted/interested)

4 It's a pity I didn't _____ this information earlier. (receive/recieve)

5 Don't _____ your nerve! I know it's dangerous, but you can do it. (loose/lose)

6 Pete is having his films _____ at the photographic shop on the corner. (developed/developped)

7 It's the hospital's _____ to ensure that proper precautions are taken to protect patients from infection. (responsability/responsibility)

8 Unemployed actors often make good money by doing voice-overs for television _____.   (advertisements/advertisements)

9 Now that my uncle has retired, he won't have to commute to Brussels _____.   (anymore/any more)

10 Our plans for the summer are not _____ yet, but we'll let you know as soon as we've decided.   (definite/definate)

11 No sooner had the helicopter landed _____ it was ordered to take off again.   (then/than)

12 Young children have the habit of saying the most _____ things in public.   (embarassing/embarrassing)

C In **most** lines of the text there is a spelling mistake. Write the correct spelling next to the number on the right. Tick any lines that are correct.

British universities are currently gearing up for there new	1 _____
intake of students. 'It's bean complete chaos this year,' one	2 _____
registrar told me. 'Because of problems with the computerised	3 _____
application system, we still don't no how many new students	4 _____
we'll be getting.' It now appears that, far from having to many	5 _____
first-year students, universities will not have enough, and it is	6 _____
doubtful weather full government funding will be available to	7 _____
university departments witch have not met predicted targets.	8 _____
As a result, both students and officials are calling for a revue	9 _____
of the hole university entrance procedure, from application to	10 _____
acceptance. It is generally felt that confusion has rained for	11 _____
far too long.	12 _____

Capital letters are used for the first letters of people's titles and names, geographical names, historical periods and events, languages and nationality nouns or adjectives, days of the week, months, festivals, planets and stars (but not *the sun* or *the moon*), named buildings, titles of creative works, organisations and political parties, and at the beginning of every sentence.

D Correct this text by rewriting it with capital letters where necessary.

plans for a spectacular pop concert in falmer park, just outside portsmouth, have been submitted to hampshire county council. the open-air event, featuring the singer neil silver and his backing group the raiders, is planned for wednesday 6th july and friday 8th july, to coincide with portsmouth arts festival as well as the tour de france. the organisers, gigs unlimited, say the show will have a french theme to fit in with the cycle race. the proposal will be considered at a special meeting on thursday 12th may.

local people are divided on the issue. while some welcome the influx of visitors and the increase in trade that the concert will bring to portsmouth, others are predicting an invasion of new age travellers. hampshire's chief constable edward lang-jones is, however, confident that he has adequate manpower to deal with any disturbance that might occur.

The apostrophe is used

a to show that a letter or letters have been omitted:
  • *Who's there?* • *I'd like some help.* • *It's Monday today.*

b to show possession: • *my wife's birthday*

c to indicate plural forms with dates and letters of the alphabet: • *the 1980's*
  • *How many t's are there in 'getting'?*
It is not correct to use the apostrophe for any other plurals, or for the possessive
pronouns *its, hers, ours, theirs.*

Note also that **s'** is used for the possessive of plural nouns. But irregular plurals like
men add **'s**: • *my parents' house* • *the men's uniforms*

E Rewrite the sentences to include apostrophes where necessary, and say which of the above uses (**a**, **b** or **c**) is involved in each case.

1 Her aunts been in hospital for years.
2 It isnt easy to create new jobs in a recession.
3 Would you take Mr Browns file to the teachers room, please?
4 His is a family company, which was founded in the 1920s.
5 Hes so meticulous. He always dots his is and crosses his ts.
6 Has anyone seen Jamess pen?
7 The childrens toys are all over the floor.
8 Celias friends cant come next week.
9 The Bennets house is far larger than the Joneses.
10 Toms plan wont work as well as his fathers.

Commas are used

a to separate items in a list (but not usually before *and*): • *cows, sheep and pigs*

b to divide clauses or phrases: • *If he had seen you, he would have said hello.*

c to show a difference in meaning in relative clauses (see **Unit 13**).

F Say which of the above uses of the comma (**a**, **b** or **c**) is involved in each of these sentences.

1 The manager explained that, if he had known we were coming, he would have made other arrangements.
2 Unless I hear from you by tomorrow, I shall assume the meeting is off.
3 You can sail any kind of dinghy, cruiser, yacht or surfboard in the harbour.
4 The rescuers, who had no extra provisions with them, had to be rescued themselves.
5 I decided to go to Paris with my cousin, who lives in Cornwall.
6 Who's been invited? Let's see – John, Angie, Brett and Simon.
7 The Sales Manager has been all over Europe, except to Austria.
8 Louise's mother, who is almost 92, has never left her home town.

Recycling

A Tick any of the sentences which are correct. Rewrite any in which the idiom or proverb is not in its usual form.

1 I did most of the work, so I should get the bear's share of the money!

2 Many hands need washing.

3 Nothing venture, nothing gamble.

4 The entry test is bound to sort out the wolves from the lambs.

5 Sorry, I thought *you* were getting married next week, not Janice. I often get the wrong end of the stick.

6 Waste not, if you want to save the world.

7 A stitch in time is a very good idea.

8 Rafael couldn't make head or tail of the instructions, so he had to ask Paco to put up the tent.

9 The early bird calls the tune.

10 Make hay in the sunshine.

11 The lorry whizzed past me but luckily didn't touch me. It was a narrow shave.

12 Don't count your chickens before they lay eggs.

13 If you don't blow your own trombone, nobody else will.

14 Birds of a feather make nests in spring.

15 You're looking rather down in the face these days. Is life really that bad?

16 An apple a day is worth two on the bush.

17 Guess who turned up yesterday out of the sky?

18 Every cloak has a silken lining.

19 Poor old Mrs Hyde kicked the basket last week, and was buried yesterday.

20 The children took it for granted that they would be allowed to watch the late film.

B Fill in the boxes with a suitable word or phrase to complete each sentence. In each case, a letter is given to help you.

1 As the weather was so wonderful, we decided to eat [ ][ ][ ][ ][ ][ ][O] on the patio.

2 The whole cast noticed the immediate [ ][P][ ][ ][ ] between the director and his leading lady.

3 If you think I'm going to go on working for you [ ][ ] [I][ ][ ][ ][ ][ ][ ][ ] , think again! I'm leaving tomorrow!

4 At the Red Lion Hotel you will be able to sample the delights of our local [ ][U][ ][ ][ ][ ] , with dishes such as fresh salmon, wild rabbit and roast pheasant.

5 You will have to supply full details of your financial background if you wish to be considered [E][ ][ ][ ][ ][ ][ ] for a scholarship.

6 Considering that he had just been made to look a complete fool, I thought he carried it off with amazing [ ][ ][ ][ ][B] .

7 Bodyguards surrounded the royal limousine, trying in vain to protect the princess from the attentions of the [ ][ ][ ][ ][ ][z], who were crowding round with their cameras.

8 As we wish to encourage more mature students to take the course, we are prepared to [w][ ][ ][ ] the fees in your case, so you'll only have your accommodation to pay for.

9 Medical experts recommend us to have a short [s][ ][ ][ ][ ] in the afternoon. Apparently a nap after lunch helps our digestion and our concentration.

10 Robbers stashed gold bullion away in a garden shed five years ago. Today their [ ][ ][h][ ] was discovered by a small boy.

C Think of a word that has both meanings, and write it in the box.

1 smart matching business clothes [ ][ ][ ] to look good on

2 to fall (over something) [ ][ ][ ] a journey

3 to conspire [ ][ ][ ] the story of a play or film

4 the first letter of a name [ ][ ][ ][ ][ ] early, at the beginning (adj)

5 a doctor's office [ ][ ][ ][ ][ ] hospital operations

6 unfenced land for general use [ ][ ][ ][ ] usual

7 a unit of British currency [ ][ ][ ][ ] to beat or thump

8 to train (students or sportsmen) [ ][ ][ ][ ] a type of bus

9 extremely [ ][ ][ ] particular, exactly that one

10 a unit of temperature [ ][ ][ ][ ] university studies diploma

11 weapons [ ][ ][ ] limbs

12 only [ ][ ][ ] a white fish

13 a large suitcase [ ][ ][ ][ ] main part of a tree

14 a nation or people [ ][ ][ ] a speed contest

D Tick any of the sentences which are correct. Rewrite any similes which are incorrect.

1 Louisa was so frightened she looked as white as a daisy.

2 The grandchildren behaved extremely well. They were as good as gold.

3 Do you know, Gerry came to work in his slippers the other day! He's as mad as a monkey!

4 She doesn't really feel happy here, does she? She's like a fish on the beach.

5 The judge could not tell the difference between the pair of twins. They were as like as two eggs in a basket.

6 I thought the manageress would panic when she saw the mess the hooligans had left but, no, she was as calm as a cucumber.

7 Without his glasses, Uncle Jock is as blind as a bat. He can't see a thing.

8   He had no trouble moving the piano, all on his own. He must be as strong as a bull!

9   Christine marched into her boss's office, as bold as a brick, and demanded a pay rise.

10 I've heard that joke dozens of times before. It's as old as the mountains.

11 You'll never be able to bring Vincent round to your point of view. He's as stubborn as a mule!

12 The new model Ford have brought out is selling like a bomb.

13 When the student nurse realised her mistake, her face went as red as a postbox.

14 Don't worry about your money. It'll be as safe as houses in my keeping.

E Complete the text by making a new word from each word given in capitals.

ANNABELLE'S DIARY

Decided to go 1) _____ to check my bank balance   LINE

this morning and was shocked to discover I have an

2) _____! Can't think how it happened – maybe my   DRAFT

salary got paid in late. Decided to ring up the bank.

Was a bit 3) _____ about it – I suppose I felt as if I   APPREHEND

was in 4) _____ somehow. Had visions of losing my   GRACE

credit rating and of staring 5) _____ in the face a   POOR

few months down the line! But calmed down when I

spoke to a nice 6) _____ man, who said it was no   FLAP

big deal. Apparently now there's an economic

7) _____ on, it's happening to lots of their   RECEDE

customers. I even managed a few 8) _____   HUMOUR

comments while we sorted it all out. He's sending me

a handy 9) _____ on 'Ways of Managing Your   LEAF

Money' – not sure how useful it'll be, but you won't

catch me 10) _____ it!   CRITIC

UNIT 72

Collocations

Collocations are combinations of words which are frequently used together in a way that sounds natural and correct. These words 'collocate' with each other, and approximate synonyms are very often unacceptable:
- *a hard frost* (NOT *strong* or *rigid*)   • *a sorry state of affairs* (NOT *apologetic*)
- *catch a cold* (NOT *take* or *capture*)   • *come to a standstill* (NOT *approach* or *go*)

Strong collocations are ones which are extremely common or instantly recognisable. They may be **fixed collocations**, where no other words collocate to produce the same meaning:
- *for the time being, a breach of the peace, power of attorney*

Many **idioms** are, in fact, fixed collocations, but the broad difference between idioms and collocations is that the component parts of idioms, which may refer to animals, colours, objects etc, make their meaning much less predictable. (See **Unit 64** on Idioms.)

There are also **open collocations**, where a number of different words may be used to complete the word group. Sometimes there seems little difference between the alternatives:
- *keep to/stick to a diet, do your best/utmost to persuade him, have/hold/bear a grudge*

but in other collocations a different word can change the meaning:
- *gather/lose momentum, lingering/serious scruples, call for/offer up a sacrifice*

A Choose the correct word from the pair in brackets to complete each sentence. All the collocations include the verb *call*.

1 I paid for this week's petrol and you paid for last week's, so we don't need to settle up. We can call it _____. (quits/evens)

2 Poor Ruth had to accept her father's decision to cancel her trip. She's not earning yet, so he calls the _____. Perhaps she can go when she's paid off her overdraft! (melody/tune)

3 I can't quite call to _____ the incident you mention. Late 1980s, did you say? I expect it'll come back to me. (memory/mind)

4 You two are getting married? Wonderful news! This calls for a _____! (ceremony/celebration)

5 The fact that he was prepared to falsify documents calls into _____ his fitness to carry out his professional duties. (discussion/question)

6 I'm simply exhausted! Let's call it a _____! We can always finish tomorrow. (day/night)

7 When several of the demonstrators were arrested, the organisers called _____ to the protest. (an ending/a halt)

8 I thought Josh would lose his temper with his little brother Harry and call him _____, but he managed to stay surprisingly calm. (names/insults)

9 If Ross tells me one more time about his Porsche, I'll call his _____ and ask him to take me for a drive in it! That'll teach him a lesson! (game/bluff)

B Choose the correct word from the box to complete the collocations, all connected with the word *light*. There are two more words than you need.

set	years	by	face	travelling
first	make	shed	let	come	reading	in

1 I set my alarm so that I could wake up at _____ light, before anyone else was stirring.

2 It is hoped that the current research will _____ light on the hitherto unknown causes of this terrible disease.

3 Clara always makes a point of _____ light, with just a change of clothes rolled up in a small backpack.

4 The principal announced that the culprit would be _____ off lightly, as long as he or she owned up immediately.

5 The full story didn't _____ to light until a fifty-year-old diary was unearthed in an attic.

6 The cut was bleeding quite badly, but Nicki was determined to _____ light of it, and said it was just a scratch.

7 Will's _____ lit up as he entered the room and saw the long table groaning with food. He suddenly realised how ravenous he was.

8 Well, I got my first job soon after leaving school. It seems light _____ away now, but I can still remember how excited I was.

9 _____ the light of recent events, the government will shortly be making an announcement on the action it plans to take.

10 With mounting rage, Daisy tore up the letter, threw the pieces into the grate, and _____ light to them with a match.

C Choose the correct expression from the box to complete the collocations, all connected with *heat*.

hot off the press	hot under the collar
get into hot water	hotting up	piping hot
in the heat of the moment	blowing hot and cold
a heated discussion	take the heat off you
just so much hot air	a hot potato

1 Hazel regretted what she had said _____.

2 When I entered the house, I could hear _____ going on in the kitchen.

3 I'm not sure the project will be going ahead – the boss is _____.

4 Make sure that meat pie's _____ before you eat it.

5 If Neil resigns, at least it'll _____ for a while.

6 Things are _____ at work now we're approaching the peak tourist season.

7 I got all _____ when they asked to see my driving licence.

8 You'll _____ if your mother finds out.

9 Immigration is such _____ that few politicians can agree on it.

10 I didn't pay any attention to what he said – it's _____.

11 Here's the council's list of sports centres, _____.

D Read the text, then decide which word from A, B, C or D is most appropriate for each space.

A BLAST FROM THE PAST

In recent years, museums around the world have 1) _____ a campaign to tell us as much about extinct species like dinosaurs as possible. They have been 2) _____ and abetted in their endeavours by film directors like Steven Spielberg and by the public's passion for prehistoric creatures. Now the Natural History Museum in London has 3) _____ delivery of a Tyrannosaurus rex, which is the most sophisticated model of a dinosaur ever built. It draws on a 4) _____ of information gleaned from important finds over the last thirty years, and is a 5) _____ cry from the dry-as-dust fossils and skeletons that used to be the best a museum could offer – this creature looks, sounds and even smells like a dinosaur. It incorporates state-of-the- 6) _____ movement sensors, so that it can respond to the approach of a 7) _____ being by lunging terrifyingly with its hideous mouth 8) _____ open. Its first victims were a class of primary school pupils, 9) _____ into the prehistory section by their teacher. When Tyrannosaurus rex became 10) _____ of their movements, it lashed its three-metre tail, threw up its great head and bellowed. This stopped the school children in their 11) _____, and they gazed up at the huge animal, transfixed.

The model took a team of Japanese engineers three months to construct, and cost in the 12) _____ of £220,000. This dinosaur was known to be a messy eater; it probably flattened its prey under a massive foot, then ripped it to 13) _____ with its teeth and claws. Because of the decaying food that would have lodged between its teeth, it must have had truly revolting breath, but the museum curators 14) _____ the line at allowing their model to stink of rotting flesh. Instead, they arranged for it to give off a swampy smell, like badly cooked spinach.

	A	B	C	D
1	authorised	pioneered	validated	spearheaded
2	aided	helped	assisted	supported
3	ordered	announced	taken	completed
4	treasure	heap	harvest	wealth
5	distant	far	remote	prolonged
6	art	science	method	technology
7	whole	human	hated	hesitant
8	broad	all	wide	right
9	shepherded	manhandled	hoodwinked	mollycoddled
10	sensible	aware	alert	acquainted
11	path	steps	shoes	tracks
12	region	lines	area	roundabout
13	fragments	shreds	morsels	chunks
14	toed	ruled	drew	measured

New language

Many **new words or phrases** are connected with people's work or lifestyle. They reflect current social trends, political movements, technological and scientific developments, and popular interests. The most frequently used expressions are called *buzz words*.

A Complete the text with these words and phrases. There are two more than you need.

proactive	dotcom	cutting edge
keyhole surgery		text messages
user-friendly	biodiversity	latte
counsellor	grassroots	name of the game
healthcare	asylum seeker	body piercing
sell-by dates	number cruncher	raves

MOVING SWIFTLY ON

Modern society is made up of all kinds of people, doing all kinds of things. You might be a computer whizz-kid, at the 1) _____ of technology, doing your best to make soft- and hardware 2) _____ for the consumer. Or you might be a senior hospital consultant, pioneering techniques such as 3) _____ while bemoaning the inadequacies of 4) _____ funding. You might be a 5) _____, a financial expert, assessing the risks of investing in hi-tech 6) _____ companies. Perhaps you're a teenager, campaigning to protect the 7) _____ of the natural world; or you might be into having fun at weekend 8) _____, with 9) _____ from your friends constantly appearing on your mobile. You could be an 10) _____, hoping against hope that you will be accepted into a new community, or a 11) _____, working hard to mend relationships and heal psychological wounds. You may be a parent, providing the best you can for your family by buying organic food and religiously checking 12) _____ on supermarket products, or a 13) _____ politician, nostalgic for the values of the past, or a student, struggling to get by on a student loan and seeing your debts spiralling out of control.

Whoever you are, you probably accept the need to be 14) _____ rather than reactive, in today's socio-economic climate. Our work and lifestyles are constantly evolving. Innovation is the 15) _____, and although the speed of change can be quite alarming, most of us realise it is necessary for progress.

There are many new words which are **abbreviations**, formed from the initial letters of a group of words:
- *GM* (genetically modified), *TLC* (tender loving care)

If the new word is pronounced as a word, and not as separate initials, it is an **acronym**:
- *AIDS* (Acquired Immune Deficiency Syndrome)

B Complete the sentences with these items. What do they mean in full? Which one is the true acronym?

BSE	aka	PIN	RSI	asap	PC	TLC	OTT

1 You'd better not write your _____ number down anywhere, in case someone sees it.

2 Rolf's been looking really down in the dumps lately. What he needs is some _____.

3 Chris has been off work for ages. Apparently she's suffering from _____ and is planning to sue the company.

4 'Have you heard? Doug in Sales has been sacked for sending in his reports late!' 'That's a bit _____, isn't it?'

5 'Who's your sister's getting married to?' 'Oh, he's a local radio DJ. Terry Murphy, _____ the Prince of Cool!'

6 Pete, can you e-mail me the invoice reference _____? Then I can arrange immediate payment.

7 I don't think Rhona likes being called an actress. She says 'actor' is more _____.

8 The incurable brain condition found in cattle, _____, is commonly known as mad cow disease.

When a new gadget is invented or a new phenomenon develops, a name is sometimes created for it by telescoping two existing words together to form a new one:
- *brunch* (a meal between breakfast and lunch), *smog* (a combination of smoke and fog)

These new words are known as **portmanteau words** and they are often first seen on shop signs, in advertisements for products, or in media reviews.

C Which portmanteau words match these definitions?

1 a video camera which also records sound

2 a film about the life of a particular person

3 a documentary filmed like a soap opera

4 the jargon or 'babble' used by psychotherapists

5 a TV programme in a series focusing on situational comedy

6 an airport for helicopters

7 an estimate which is based largely on guesswork

8 a diary or log posted on the internet

D Complete the text with these informal expressions. There are two more than you need.

big time	the full monty	vegging out
a bad hair day	been there, done that
a couch potato	gobsmacked	crying foul
cherry-picked	to die for
drop-dead gorgeous	get a life

Fed up with work? Having 1) _____? Don't worry, you've always got the next episode of *I'll Be There For You* to look forward to when you get home from the office. *IBTFY*, the Aussie version of the American smash-hit sitcom, *Friends*, is all set to clean up 2) _____, so that's good news for the ATV production company, who 3) _____ the best locations from an admittedly stunning range on offer. Oh, 4) _____, I hear you say, with *Neighbours*, *Home and Away* and so on. Ah, but this is different. For a start, you'll be 5) _____ by the stunning leading actor, George Rooney, who's guaranteed to get the girls swooning. He's supported by a great cast, including the 6) _____ Fran Jacobs, whose clothes are 7) _____. The plotlines are inventive, the jokes come thick and fast, and as the credits roll, you're left wanting more. *IBTFY* is 8) _____, all right. So don't feel bad about being 9) _____ and 10) _____ in front of the TV – just switch on and enjoy!

E Choose from the list A–J the best phrase to fill each gap. Use each phrase only once. There are more answers than you need.

SHORT OF FUNDS

You see, I started the job with the highest of hopes. I mean, I'd never really thought of fund-raising as a career, but 1) _____ it's a job, isn't it? It pays the bills. Well, it would have done 2) _____. That was the trouble. First they wanted me to phone their *previous* sponsors, then they said I should forget them and concentrate on attracting *new* donors. And of course, I was having to input everything 3) _____ – you wouldn't believe the things it could do! I wasn't getting on well with my boss either – you could tell 4) _____. Who knows why? I must have done something to upset her. But when she discovered I hadn't raised any money at all in the whole three months I'd been there, 5) _____ and I found myself out on my ear.

Well, I never liked it much there anyway. Being unemployed 6) _____. I've got enough money to tide me over till about September. I'm still looking around for something else, but if there's absolutely nothing and 7) _____, I might try and set up my own business on the internet. It can't be that difficult, can it?

A push comes to shove
B it all went pear-shaped
C on this all-singing, all-dancing computer
D in your face
E I just wasn't her flavour of the month

F it took off
G isn't the end of the world
H if they hadn't kept moving the goalposts
I on a level playing field
J at the end of the day

Plural and feminine forms

> **Plurals** of the majority of nouns are formed by adding **-s** or **-es**. In nouns ending in **-o**, both forms are occasionally possible. Nouns ending in **-f** or **-fe** normally change to **-ves** in the plural, although there are some exceptions.
>
> There are a number of **irregular plural forms**: • *child~children, man~men, woman~women, foot~feet, mouse~mice*, etc.
> Certain nouns do not change at all in the plural: • *deer, sheep, fish, salmon*

A Give the correct plural form of these nouns, using your dictionary if necessary.

1 mosquito	6 casino	11 echo	16 video
2 piano	7 shampoo	12 potato	17 kangaroo
3 avocado	8 ghetto	13 hero	18 radio
4 volcano	9 rodeo	14 studio	19 biro
5 motto	10 tomato	15 concerto	20 solo

B Follow the instructions for Exercise A.

1 leaf	6 child	11 hoof	16 sheep
2 goose	7 house	12 postman	17 life
3 deer	8 mouse	13 belief	18 louse
4 foot	9 roof	14 half	19 knife
5 wife	10 tooth	15 wolf	20 self

> Some plural nouns look singular, e.g. *police, people*, and some singular nouns look plural, e.g. *a means, a crossroads*. Some singular nouns referring to groups of people can be used with either a singular or a plural verb, e.g. *army, government, orchestra, team*. Uncountable nouns, e.g. *information, furniture*, have no plural form.

C Decide whether you should use a singular (S) or plural (P) verb after these nouns. In some cases both are possible.

1 family	6 jury	11 accommodation	16 means
2 news	7 scenery	12 people	17 army
3 staff	8 cattle	13 police	18 knowledge
4 series	9 crossroads	14 information	19 advice
5 air	10 water	15 sand	20 training

D Match each of the twelve nouns with one of these collective nouns. Some of them can be used twice.

flight	bunch	flock	gang	swarm	shoal	pack	herd

1 keys	4 criminals	7 bees	10 geese
2 steps	5 sheep	8 cows	11 carrots
3 cards	6 fish	9 wild dogs	12 ants

There are three categories of plurals for **words of classical origin** in English.

1 Anglicised plurals, adding **-s** or **-es**: • *bonuses, circuses, operas, viruses*

2 Classical plurals, retaining Greek or Latin forms: • *criterion~criteria, automaton~automata, diagnosis~diagnoses, larva~larvae, nucleus~nuclei, stimulus~stimuli, appendix~appendices, curriculum~curricula*

3 Classical plurals in formal contexts, but Anglicised plurals for general use:
• *cactus~cacti/cactuses, formula~formulae/formulas, referendum~referenda/referendums*

Compound nouns either form plurals in the usual way by adding **-s**:
• *girlfriends, sit-ins*
or by pluralising the first element: • *sisters-in-law, passers-by*

E Give the correct plural(s) of these nouns. Use your dictionary if necessary.

1 nucleus	6 aquarium	11 circus	16 virus
2 formula	7 brother-in-law	12 cactus	17 appendix
3 boyfriend	8 bonus	13 breadwinner	18 larva
4 press-up	9 stimulus	14 opera	19 bacterium
5 take-off	10 criterion	15 diagnosis	20 automaton

Although most nouns in English do not have separate **masculine or feminine forms**, there are a number of exceptions. A common feminine ending is **-ess**, although with some words, e.g. *poet, priest, murderer*, the **-ess** ending is becoming less common.

F Give the feminine form of these nouns, if there is one. Use your dictionary if necessary.

1 heir	6 actor	11 doctor	16 uncle
2 fiancé	7 sculptor	12 manager	17 landlord
3 masseur	8 emperor	13 host	18 cousin
4 monk	9 hero	14 barman	19 headmaster
5 nephew	10 widower	15 bridegroom	20 steward

G Match the group nouns on the left with the appropriate nouns on the right.

1 congregation	A sportsmen
2 cattle	B computer programmes
3 orchestra	C cows
4 cutlery	D worshippers
5 crockery	E paper and pens
6 team	F tools, machines
7 stationery	G cups, plates and bowls
8 fuel	H petrol
9 equipment	I musicians
10 software	J knives, forks and spoons

Prefixes and suffixes

> **A prefix** is added to the beginning of a word. The most common use for a prefix is to make an adjective, adverb or verb negative, or to give it the opposite meaning.

A Form the opposite of these adjectives by adding the correct prefix. Choose from **un-, im-, il-, in-, ir-, dis-, non-**.

1 attainable	7 aware	13 satisfied	19 legible
2 existent	8 expensive	14 patient	20 rational
3 legitimate	9 conscious	15 complicated	21 perfect
4 resistible	10 tolerant	16 able	22 resident
5 accessible	11 likely	17 capable	
6 prepared	12 probable	18 enthusiastic	

B Form the opposite of these words by adding the correct prefix. Choose from **anti-, un-, dis-, mis-, de-**.

1 do	7 cast	13 classify	19 employment
2 approve	8 wrap	14 incentive	20 personalise
3 clockwise	9 embark	15 confirmed	21 fire (verb)
4 understand	10 centralise	16 mount	22 cyclone
5 used	11 climax	17 damaged	
6 briefing	12 prove	18 common	

C Match the prefixes **counter-**, **over-** and **co-** with these words.

1 worker	7 attack	13 espionage
2 balance	8 estimate	14 board
3 pilot	9 react	15 simplify
4 claim	10 director	16 educational
5 author	11 operate	17 due
6 priced	12 anxious	18 dose

D Match the prefixes **out-**, **ex-**, **re-** and **under-** with these words.

1 pouring	6 cooked	11 size	16 unite
2 wife	7 organise	12 distribute	17 assure
3 last	8 boyfriend	13 exposure	18 clothes
4 vote	9 elect	14 stay	19 achiever
5 direct	10 mine	15 claim	20 integrate

E Match the prefixes **a-**, **hyper-**, **mal-**, **mono-** and **neo-** with these words.

1 active	6 political	11 function
2 moral	7 sensitive	12 symmetrical
3 nutrition	8 syllable	13 adjusted
4 Nazi	9 classical	14 market
5 formation	10 critical	15 tone

A **suffix** is added to the end of a word, to make it into an adjective, noun or verb.

F Make adjectives from these verbs and nouns by using the suffixes **-able**, **-al**, **-ful**, **-ic**, **-ish**, **-ive**, **-less**, **-ous**, **-proof**, **-some**, **-ly** and **-y**. Make any necessary spelling changes.

1 fog	6 child	11 home	16 hope
2 help	7 tragedy	12 wash	17 imagination
3 destroy	8 fire	13 nostalgia	18 rely
4 befriend	9 humour	14 quarrel	19 drama
5 hate	10 magic	15 grace	20 reality

G Make nouns from these verbs and adjectives by using the suffixes **-al**, **-ance**, **-ence**, **-ety**, **-hood**, **-ion**, **-ity**, **-ment**, **-ness**, **-our**, **-ure** and **-y**. Make any necessary spelling changes.

1 depart	6 attract	11 satisfy	16 theoretical
2 entertain	7 arrive	12 rude	17 deliver
3 betray	8 emancipate	13 please	18 widow
4 pious	9 dark	14 maintain	19 available
5 behave	10 patient	15 advertise	20 tolerant

H Make verbs from these adjectives and nouns by using the suffixes **-en**, **-ify** and **-ise**.

1 horror	5 category	9 ideal	13 peace
2 wide	6 long	10 short	14 false
3 straight	7 high	11 critical	15 computer
4 real	8 intense	12 red	

I Use the words in capitals to form longer words to fit the spaces.

GUILTY OR NOT GUILTY?

Yet another 1) _____ athlete has been branded a cheat. NATION

A highly-qualified panel of experts has 2) _____ all the VIEW

evidence in the case of Anna Morris, who was sent home in

3) _____ from the Olympics after a random drugs test GRACE

proved positive. She continues to maintain her 4) _____, INNOCENT

however. Her defence is based on the alleged 5) _____ LIKELY

that her urine sample was tampered with, although the

authorities claim that no 6) _____ occurred in the REGULAR

handling of the sample.

Now Anna has been found guilty of taking an 7) _____ LEGAL

substance, and she is 8) _____ by the verdict. 'I find it HORROR

9) _____,' she told our reporter outside her home. 'It BELIEF

just isn't true! For me this verdict is simply 10) _____. ACCEPT

And although I 11) _____ there is very little chance of REAL

my 12) _____ in clearing my name, I'm still determined SUCCESS

to appeal against the ruling.'

False friends and word pairs

> **A false friend** (from the French 'faux ami') is a word which looks very similar to a word in another language. Learners may mistakenly assume that both words have the same meaning and use.

A Choose the best synonym (A or B) for each word on the left.

		A		B	
1	particular	A	private	B	special
2	nervous	A	irritable	B	apprehensive
3	spiritual	A	witty	B	concerned with religion
4	gymnasium	A	sports hall	B	grammar school
5	extra	A	supplementary	B	best quality
6	control	A	regulate	B	check
7	process	A	trial	B	procedure
8	exact	A	precise	B	correct
9	mark	A	brand	B	stain
10	souvenir	A	memento	B	memory
11	notorious	A	famous	B	infamous
12	sympathetic	A	compassionate	B	likeable
13	chef	A	boss	B	cook
14	public school	A	state school	B	private school
15	actual	A	current	B	real
16	critic	A	reporter	B	review
17	saucy	A	with sauce	B	impolite
18	sensible	A	practical	B	sensitive

B Complete each sentence with the correct word from one of these pairs.

waistcoats/vests	chips/crisps	insulated/isolated
aerial/antenna	meaning/opinion	bank/bench
birthday/anniversary	bargain/occasion	

1 It's Andrew's _____ today! He's 25, I think.

2 Their television doesn't have very good reception. I think their outside _____ needs adjusting.

3 In order to retain heat in winter, a house should be properly _____.

4 Could I have a packet of cheese and onion _____, please, to eat with my packed lunch?

5 Snooker players on television always take their jackets off, and play in their _____ and trousers.

6 I've told you what I think about it. Now what's your _____?

7 I'm exhausted! Let's sit down on this _____ for a moment.

8 You only paid £9.95! That's a wonderful _____!

C Explain the difference between these pairs by giving a short definition for each word or phrase.

1 warehouse   department store
2 recipe   receipt
3 block   notepad
4 smoking   dinner jacket
5 costume   suit
6 congealed   frozen
7 salute *(verb)*   wave to
8 pensioners   boarders
9 deranged   disturbed
10 prove   test

> The words in certain **word pairs**, linked with **and**, have a fixed order. They may refer to two things which go together, e.g. *salt and pepper*, two opposites, e.g. *black and white*, or just one idea, e.g. *high and dry*.

D Put the pairs of words into the correct order to make expressions linked by *and*. EXAMPLE: *ladies and gentlemen.*

1 chips/fish
2 women/children
3 ink/pen
4 bed/breakfast
5 butter/bread
6 dead/buried
7 rules/regulations
8 socks/shoes
9 in/out
10 pros/cons
11 wrongs/rights
12 law/order

E Choose the correct word from the pair in brackets to complete each sentence.

1 Make sure you get your facts and _____ together in good time for the presentation.   (figures/details)

2 Now that the property market is so unpredictable, it is not wise to invest all your savings in bricks and _____.   (cement/mortar)

3 Connolly looked really emaciated after his hunger strike. He was just skin and _____.   (skeleton/bone)

4 Simon rushed to and _____ in a panic, trying to collect what he needed.   (away/fro)

5 Fortunately the potholers were rescued and brought back to base, safe and _____.   (sound/unhurt)

6 Today the Prime Minister is out and _____ on the streets of the capital, meeting members of the public.   (about/busy)

7 When we lost the kitten, we searched for her far and _____, but there was no trace of her anywhere.   (near/wide)

8 As the tide went out, the remains of the wrecked ship were left high and _____ on the sand.   (dry/tidy)

9 Miss Hunt didn't laugh at Antony's slightly risqué joke, did she? I think she's rather prim and _____.   (proper/prudish)

10 We'll have to have a good clean-up before we go. We must leave the cottage spick and _____ for the next visitors.   (shining/span)

F Complete the sentences with these expressions. They are used in a less literal, more idiomatic way than those in Exercise E.

sick and tired   flesh and blood   hard and fast   odds and ends
song and dance   chalk and cheese   pins and needles
head and shoulders   wear and tear   tooth and nail
ins and outs   cut and dried   chop and change
cock-and-bull   neck and neck

1 For heaven's sake, losing your keys isn't the end of the world! Don't make such a _____ about it!

2 We can try claiming on our house contents insurance for _____ to the carpet, but I don't hold out much hope.

3 Penelope had been sleeping on her arm, and woke up with _____ in it.

4 The brothers aren't like each other at all. They're as different as _____.

5 You might find an elastic band in that box. I keep a few _____ in there.

6 Look, there's no point in trying to overturn the decision. It's all _____.

7 I'm surprised the old man didn't leave his fortune to his nephews. They were his own _____, after all!

8 I'm _____ of hearing the same old excuse, week after week. Use a bit of imagination and come up with a new one next time!

9 For thirty years the two next-door neighbours had fought each other _____ in the lawcourts.

10 There's no doubt that Glenda will win the competition. She's _____ above the other designers.

11 You weren't taken in by what he told you, I hope? It was a complete _____ story!

12 They're not so much rules as helpful guidelines. There's nothing _____ about them.

13 I thought you'd already decided on the Zanussi frost-free model. It's difficult to keep track when you _____ so much.

14 Let's meet for lunch tomorrow, and I'll explain the _____ of the proposal.

15 The horses were _____ in the final straight, but then the favourite pulled ahead and was first past the post.

UNIT 77

Ways of walking, talking, looking and laughing

A Complete the sentences with these words, in the correct form. There is one more than you need.

wade	plod	march	limp	hop	shuffle	tiptoe	
	ramble	stroll	toddle	stagger			

1 Today the whole family is going for a _____ over the hills, with a picnic.

2 We had to _____ into the water right up to our thighs in order to retrieve the beach ball.

3 Corinna proudly watched her one-year-old daughter _____ towards her across the sitting room.

4 The middle-aged woman _____ straight up to the duty officer's desk and demanded to see the head of CID.

5 Odette had polio when she was a child, and still walks with a slight _____.

6 The old man put his slippers on and _____ slowly out of the room.

7 The girls had all the time in the world. They decided to _____ along Regent Street to do a bit of window-shopping.

8 'Help!' cried the man, as he _____ into the shop clutching his chest. 'Get an ambulance! It's my heart!'

9 It was so late when Nina got home that she had to _____ upstairs, hoping Mr and Mrs Burdon wouldn't hear her.

10 Yawning, the security guard _____ round the premises for the tenth time that night. He was tired, his feet hurt, and he was looking forward to the end of his stint.

B Match these verbs of walking or moving with their definitions.

1	trudge	A	move by jumping from one foot to the other
2	stumble	B	stand idly or walk with frequent stops
3	skip	C	move on hands and knees
4	stride	D	walk unsteadily, stagger
5	saunter	E	walk heavily or wearily
6	loiter	F	walk lamely or awkwardly
7	totter	G	run quickly and/or playfully
8	hobble	H	walk with long steps
9	crawl	I	almost trip or fall while walking
10	scamper	J	walk in a leisurely way

C Choose the correct word for a way of talking from the pair in brackets to complete each sentence.

1 You'll have to _____ if you don't want the rest of the group to hear you. (mutter/whisper)

2 When the police managed to reach the potholer, he was barely conscious and _____ with pain. (sighing/moaning)

3 Ray feels frustrated when he goes to his Italian conversation class, as he can't _____ himself well enough. (talk/express)

4 Mr Mayhew has a lot on his plate at the moment. It's not surprising that he _____ at people sometimes. (snaps/retorts)

5 The official was so taken aback that he did not _____ a word, but just stared at us. (mention/utter)

6 My aunt always looks forward to a good _____ with her sisters whenever there's a family get-together. (gossip/argue)

7 The boys' parents _____ them for half an hour on the risks they had run. (lectured/warned)

8 There are several points of interest that the committee will be _____ at the meeting. (discussing/chatting)

9 Mrs Stephens _____ her son in from the garden. (called/shouted)

10 A colleague of mine had a childhood _____ which occasionally comes back if he gets nervous. (mumble/stammer)

D Complete the sentences with these words for ways of looking, in the correct form. Sometimes more than one word is possible.

spot	stare	gaze	recognise	glance	glimpse
	scrutinise	watch	peep	observe	notice
		peer	glare	examine	

1 The Prime Minister's car went through the village so fast that the onlookers didn't even catch a _____ of him inside.

2 The lecturer had left his glasses at home, so he was _____ at his notes, trying to read his writing.

3 As he joined the main road, the motorcyclist _____ quickly to the right, but unfortunately did not see the pedestrian on his left.

4 Kelly looked so different when I saw her recently that I hardly _____ her.

5 The antiques expert _____ the silver vase very carefully, while its owner watched in suspense.

6 When the climbers reached the top of the mountain they were delighted to see the mist disperse and the sun _____ through the clouds.

7 The whole coachload of tourists _____ in wonder at the Pyramids, stark and black against the desert sand in the moonlight.

8 Silke recorded the last episode of her favourite television serial on video, but somehow never got round to _____ it.

9 Old Mrs Gudgeon fell and broke her hip last week. She lives alone, but luckily her neighbour _____ that she hadn't drawn the curtains, went round to check up on her and called the ambulance.

10 There's a competition in the local paper this week. If you can _____ the deliberate mistake in the editorial, you might win a brand new Ford Mondeo!

E Match these verbs of smiling or laughing with their definitions.

1	guffaw	A	laugh with pleasure or delight
2	giggle	B	laugh disrespectfully or furtively
3	grin	C	laugh softly or to yourself
4	chortle	D	smile broadly
5	sneer	E	scoff or mock
6	snigger	F	laugh nervously or foolishly
7	jeer	G	smile scornfully or contemptuously
8	chuckle	H	laugh crudely or noisily

F Complete the sentences with these expressions with *laugh*, in the correct form.

> laugh all the way to the bank   Don't laugh   a laugh a minute
> no laughing matter   laugh someone out of it
> laugh in someone's face   laughable   Don't make me laugh
> laugh up your sleeve   laugh off   have the last laugh
> laugh on the other side of your face

1 Although the boxer looked quite badly cut and bruised, he staggered to his feet, _____ his injuries and insisted on continuing the fight.

2 You've decided to give up smoking? _____! You'll never be able to, not in a million years!

3 Have you seen the late-night comedy show on at the Festival Theatre? It's really funny, _____.

4 I thought I'd been so clever, getting myself an invitation to dinner at Linda and Pete's, but they _____ when they made me do all the washing-up!

5 Mark's married a wealthy heiress now, has he? He must be _____!

6 You can't possibly sell your house for so little. Really, what your buyer's offering you is _____.

7 The Minister went on with his speech. Meanwhile I was _____, waiting for him to make another embarrassing mistake.

8 You may think being in love is something to laugh at now, but you'll _____ when it happens to you one day!

9 When the probation officer tried to help Charlie, the youth just _____, saying he didn't want any help.

10 _____, but I've decided to sell up and move to a Greek island.

11 Take that smile off your face, Matthew! Bullying is _____ and will not be tolerated.

12 For some reason Pauline was in a foul mood, and it was impossible to _____.

Ways of holding and pulling
Words for light, water and fire

A Complete the sentences with these words, in the correct form. Use each word only once.

| draw | tow | lug | haul | jerk | drag | tug | wrench |

1 The breakdown lorry was called to the motorway to _____ away the Range Rover which had been involved in the pile-up.

2 The toddler _____ insistently at his mother's hand. 'Please can I have an ice cream?' he whined.

3 Paula felt too ill to go to work, but she managed to _____ herself out of bed to make some breakfast.

4 Jeremy gave the blind a sudden _____, and sunshine flooded into the room.

5 The plumber had some difficulty removing the bath tap, but finally, using all his strength, he managed to _____ it off.

6 Here's your homework file. I've been _____ it around with me all day. Quite heavy, isn't it?

7 The authorities had to use a crane to _____ the submerged wreck out of the water.

8 When he heard the shot, the bodyguard turned in a flash and _____ his own gun.

B Match these expressions with **drag**, **draw**, **pull** and **tug** with their definitions.

1 drag your feet or heels
2 pull your weight
3 drag someone's name through the mud
4 pull strings
5 draw a blank
6 a drag
7 pull the wool over someone's eyes
8 pull apart or to pieces
9 pull your socks up
10 tug at someone's heartstrings
11 pull yourself together
12 long-drawn-out
13 a tug of love
14 draw to a close
15 at daggers drawn with someone
16 pull out all the stops

A disgrace someone
B something boring
C very hostile towards someone
D get control of your feelings
E deceive or delude someone
F act with deliberate slowness
G be unsuccessful in finding something
H come to an end
I appeal to someone's emotions
J do everything you can to achieve something
K unnecessarily lengthy
L improve your behaviour
M criticise harshly
N do your fair share of work
O a dispute over the child of separated or divorced parents
P use influential friends or connections

C Make correct collocations by using these words and phrases after the verbs below. Some of the verbs have more than one collocation, and some of the phrases can be used more than once.

> your fists   forty winks   a concept   at straws   a flower
> the enemy soldiers   up courage   someone's brains   your eyebrows
> the nettle   your teeth   power   an audience
> his long-lost brother to his heart   your passport nervously
> a bag from an old lady   someone's imagination

1 grasp _____
2 pluck _____
3 clench _____
4 grip _____
5 snatch _____
6 seize _____
7 clutch _____
8 clasp _____
9 capture _____
10 pick _____

D Choose the correct word connected with light from the pair in brackets to complete each sentence.

1 As we came out of the cinema, we were _____ by the bright afternoon sunshine. (dazzled/glared)

2 In the garden the wet leaves _____ in the sunlight. (glimmered/glistened)

3 Anneka's eyes were _____ with rage as she tore up the contract. (glittering/flickering)

4 Some distance across the moors the traveller could just make out a faint _____ of light through the fog. (glimmer/sparkle)

5 The studio guests began to feel very hot under the _____ of the powerful television lights. (glare/flare)

6 The children saw another _____ of lightning light up the dark sky, and heard the clap of thunder a few seconds later. (flash/beam)

7 The surface of the lake _____ in the moonlight. (shimmered/dazzled)

8 When Frank opened the window, the candle on the table _____ briefly and then went out. (flashed/flickered)

9 The large diamond on Sophie's finger _____ as it caught the light. (shimmered/sparkled)

10 As the two men crept round the front of the house, they were suddenly caught in the _____ of a security light. (beam/glitter)

E Match these words connected with water with their definitions.

1 downpour (*noun*)
2 trickle (*verb*)
3 drip (*verb*)
4 shower (*noun*)
5 torrent (*noun*)
6 drizzle (*noun*)
7 canal (*noun*)
8 stream (*noun*)
9 puddle (*noun*)
10 gush (*verb*)

A   fine rain
B   a man-made waterway
C   to pour out suddenly and profusely
D   to fall in drops
E   a small river
F   a brief period of rain, snow or hail
G   a small pool of water on the road or pavement
H   to run or flow slowly and thinly
I   a heavy, sudden fall of rain
J   a fast, violent flow of water

F Complete the sentences with these words connected with fire. Sometimes more than one word is possible.

glow	smoke	embers	scald	swelter	flame
blaze	spark	burn	ashes	steam	scorch	sizzle	boil

1 In the darkness Michelle saw the red _____ of a cigarette and knew that Rod wasn't far away.

2 As the evening wore on and the fire died down, we put potatoes to bake in the _____, and ate them in our fingers.

3 Although police have not yet established the cause of the fire, it seems likely it was started accidentally by a _____ from a dropped match.

4 When the scouts put more dry wood on the bonfire, it began to _____ merrily, and the _____s leapt high into the sky.

5 Unfortunately my sister wasn't careful enough when ironing those trousers, so now there's a very noticeable _____ mark on the seat.

6 Benedict, be careful not to _____ yourself with all that boiling water.

7 Jason carefully _____ed open the letter while his mother was out shopping.

8 You'll _____ in that heavy jacket. Why don't you wear your linen one?

9 All that remained of their home after the fire was extinguished was a pile of sodden _____.

10 'There's no _____ without fire.' (proverb)

G Think of **one** word only which can be used appropriately in all three sentences in each group.

1 The taxi _____ up smartly in front of the Savoy Hotel.

The chairman _____ our attention to the third item on the agenda.

The child _____ a picture of the farmhouse where she used to live.

2 Whenever Maria wins a race, her parents simply _____ with pride.

He lay beside the fire's dying embers, watching them _____ in the dark.

People say that horses sweat, men perspire, and ladies gently _____!

3 I spent the first two golf lessons learning how to improve my _____.

Don't panic, Kylie! Get a _____ on yourself!

Several countries in the region are in the _____ of the worst recession for a hundred years.

4 Her long hair was _____ out behind her in the wind as she rowed towards the shore.

Refugees were _____ across the border, carrying their few possessions.

The little boy was calling for his mother, with tears _____ down his face.

5 Fighting _____ up again last night in areas of unrest.

The horse's nostrils _____ as he sensed imminent danger.

The flames from the burning building _____ into the night sky.

Recycling

A Fill in the boxes with a suitable word to complete each sentence. In some cases, a letter is given to help you.

1 I know you told me it was expensive, but could you tell me what the ☐☐☐☐☐☐ price was?

2 I had to haggle, but in the end I only paid £10 for the set. It was a real ☐☐☐☐☐☐☐☐.

3 There's a wooden ☐☐☐☐☐☐ by the pond, where I often sit and eat my sandwiches.

4 Have you read the wonderful ☐☐☐☐☐☐☐ in *The Guardian* of Barker's new play?

5 Surely you've heard of Spike Magee? He's the ☐☐T☐☐☐☐☐ bank robber who's on the run!

6 Try to use your ☐☐☐☐I☐☐☐☐☐ to make your composition as interesting as possible. Think up some new ideas!

7 Tell me more about your new ☐☐☐☐☐. Has he given you a pay rise yet?

8 As Chantal's parents are working abroad, she's a ☐☐☐☐☐☐☐ at a well-known girls' public school, and only sees her family during the holidays.

9 The doctor asked his patient to step on to the ☐☐☐☐☐☐ to be weighed.

10 Daphne collected all the traditional ☐☐☐☐☐☐☐ used by the village women in their cooking, and managed to get them published.

11 If you are tolerant, you accept that other people have different ☐☐☐☐☐☐☐☐☐ from you on all sorts of subjects.

12 This is a ☐☐☐☐☐☐☐ beach, which belongs to a hotel. Only the hotel guests are allowed to use it, not the general public.

B Complete the word pairs with words from the box, then give a definition for each pair.

wide	ends	dried	buried	neck	mortar	dry	nail
blood	bull	tear	needles	cheese	cons	dance	

1 dead and _____
2 a song and _____
3 bricks and _____
4 pros and _____
5 flesh and _____
6 cock-and-_____
7 far and _____
8 neck and _____

9 wear and _____
10 odds and _____
11 high and _____
12 chalk and _____
13 cut and _____
14 pins and _____
15 tooth and _____

C Read the text, then decide which word from A, B, C or D is most appropriate for each space.

HIDDEN DEPTHS

'I'll get soaked if I go out now,' said Hector. 'It's simply 1) _____!'
Jane threw him a 2) _____ of contempt. Is he a man or a mouse? she thought. Outside the teashop the wet cobblestones in the village square 3) _____ in the light from the streetlamps.

'Oh dear!' said Hector. 'I've spilt my tea!' Some children at a table near them 4) _____ quietly to themselves, as the ancient waitress 5) _____ slowly over to wipe the table. Jane looked down at her engagement ring, and the very small diamond 6) _____ back at her. She took a deep breath. I'll have to tell him, she thought.

'Er ... Hector,' she started. But was he even listening to her? He seemed to be 7) _____ to himself about something – just when she'd 8) _____ up the courage to tackle him. It really was *too* much!

Suddenly she realised that Hector had got up and 9) _____ casually over to the cash desk.

'OK, babe, hand over the takings!' he barked to the shocked waitress. '10) _____ the door, Jane,' he added. In a few moments they were out in the square with £57 in small change in a plastic bag. It had stopped raining, but Jane was so stunned she didn't even notice.

	A	B	C	D
1	drizzling	showering	pouring	dripping
2	stare	gaze	glimpse	glance
3	glistened	glimmered	glared	glittered
4	guffawed	sniggered	jeered	sneered
5	waded	sauntered	scampered	shuffled
6	sparkled	shimmered	beamed	dazzled
7	snapping	uttering	muttering	stammering
8	seized	plucked	gripped	snatched
9	marched	strolled	rambled	staggered
10	Stare	Examine	Peer	Watch

D Use the words in capitals to make longer words that fit the spaces in the text.

A POPULAR PAINTER

The American painter George Wesley Bellows (1882–1925) was the only son of an elderly couple who 1) _____ the Midwestern values of honest business practice and strict morality. From earliest 2) _____ he seemed determined to become an artist. Before graduating from Ohio State University, and in the face of stiff parental 3) _____, he moved to New York to study art. There he was strongly influenced by 'The Eight', or American Ashcan School. For the 4) _____ of his life, his work was characterised by

EXAMPLE

CHILD

OPPOSE

REMAIN

realist subject matter, 5) _____ which was a traditional   LIE

approach to composition. He was also fascinated by the

various systems of colour 6) _____ that painters were   RELATE

using at the time, and studied them in detail. The truly

7) _____ work that he produced in these early days   STAND

8) _____ and contributed to much of his later painting.   SHADOW

   Despite his 9) _____ with common, even low-life   IDENTITY

themes, he was elected an associate of the 10) _____   PRESTIGE

National Academy at the exceptionally early age of 27. One

of the reasons the Academy honoured Bellows, while

11) _____ approval from many of the other members of   HOLD

'The Eight', was the fact that there were 12) _____   MISTAKE

references to the old masters in Bellows' work. He was one of

the few artists who 13) _____ combined a modern verve   INSTINCT

and energy with an appreciation of artistic tradition, and his

almost 14) _____ appeal was therefore not surprising.   UNIVERSE

E Think of **one** word only which can be used appropriately in all three sentences in each group.

1 This is only a _____ estimate of the likely costs.
   The truck bumped along the _____ mountain track.
   I'm not taking the ferry if the weather's _____!

2 With a flourish the waiter _____ some pepper over the pasta.
   The sisters were _____ down by their years of exhausting work.
   The lorry _____ to a halt outside the factory gates.

3 All my worldly possessions are in three _____, due to arrive from Canada in a few days' time.
   Take your _____ with you, lads, in case you're offered a dip in the pool.
   Birds often like to nest in hollow tree _____.

4 Denise arrived home as the clock _____ midnight.
   Something _____ me the other day. I need a new job!
   Most people were still filing into the concert hall as the orchestra _____ up.

5 They're planning to dig over the vegetable plot in the _____.
   Nigel's had a _____ in his step ever since he started going out with Lynne.
   Luckily, the hikers were able to fill their water bottles from a _____, before continuing on their way.

6 The principal will have to _____ a decision soon.
   However busy Geraldine is, she's always careful to _____ time for her family.
   The bridegroom rose to his feet to _____ a short speech.

Formal letters

A **formal letter** may be written in many situations: to request information, to apologise for something, to make a complaint, to respond to a situation or to someone else's letter, to provide a personal reference, to draw someone's attention to something, to apply for a job, etc.

Letter writing conventions should be observed, with the **opening and closing phrases** as follows:

- *Dear Sir or Madam,*   or   *Dear Mr/Mrs/Ms/Miss/Professor/Dr Smith,*
- *Yours faithfully,*   or   *Yours sincerely,*
  (if you have used Sir/Madam)   (if you have used the person's name).

The correct **register** is crucial in a formal letter. You should:
- use complete sentences, with no slang, contractions or colloquial language
- make good use of linking words and paragraphing
- keep strictly to the point.

Sample question and answer

You belong to Fernbridge Cycling Club. Your local newspaper recently published a letter criticising cyclists' behaviour. At the same time, your club carried out a survey among its members. Read the extract from the letter, with your comments, and the survey results below it. Then write a **formal letter** to the newspaper in 180 – 220 words, giving the cyclists' point of view and making your own recommendation.

At last, wayward cyclists are being (targeted by police!) As a pedestrian

Sometimes the road is too dangerous for us   *not fair*

I'm fed up with (pavement cyclists) or those riding straight through

Of course this is irresponsible

(red lights on pedestrian crossings.) They're breaking the law. The

But we have to share it with motorists!

pavement is for pedestrians and the (road is for cyclists!)

Should Fernbridge have a complete cycle lane network?	YES 100%		
Should cycle lanes be protected by a barrier?	YES 98%	NO 2%	

Dear Sir or Madam,

As a member of Fernbridge Cycling Club, I was interested to read the recent letter from one of your readers about problems experienced with what he calls 'wayward cyclists'.

Naturally, it is extremely irresponsible of cyclists to ride on pavements or cross red lights, and fortunately there are very few cyclists who behave like this. However, they only do it because, when traffic is heavy, roads become too dangerous for them. It may be true in a legal sense that 'the pavement is for pedestrians and the road is for cyclists', but it does not work in practice, because we cyclists have to share the road with motorists. It is also unfair for cyclists to be 'targeted by police', as other road users, motorists in particular, are frequent offenders.

Cyclists need their own space, and this means giving them a network of wide cycle lanes, separated from the road, if possible, by a barrier or a safe distance. In my view, this is the only way in which conflict between pedestrians, motorists and cyclists can be avoided in future.

Yours faithfully,

Evelyn Lloyd

A Choose the correct sentence or phrase for a formal letter from these pairs.

1 a) I was wondering how things are going at the moment.

   b) I am writing to enquire whether satisfactory progress is being made.

2 a) At your earliest convenience

   b) As soon as you like.

3 a) We look forward to receiving your prompt reply.

   b) Hoping to hear from you soon.

4 a) Sorry I haven't written lately.

   b) I apologise for the delay in writing.

5 a) Please give my regards to your parents.

   b) All the best to your mum and dad.

6 a) Getting married! That's wonderful!

   b) May I offer my warmest congratulations on your forthcoming marriage.

7 a) I am extremely grateful to you.

   b) Thanks a lot.

8 a) Please don't breathe a word to a soul!

   b) I would appreciate your co-operation in keeping this matter confidential.

Here is some useful formal language for particular situations.

Apology I am writing to apologise for our failure to send your order.

I am extremely sorry to cause you this inconvenience.

I assure you nothing like this will ever happen again.

Request for information I would be grateful if you could send me full details/an up-to-date brochure.

I would like further information about the services you offer.

Application I am interested in applying for the post of bilingual secretary, which was advertised in *The Daily Herald* on 30th May.

I would like to apply for the post of Head of Science, which was advertised recently. My qualifications and experience, as you will see from my CV, make me a particularly suitable applicant.

Complaint I am writing to express my concern about the lack of facilities for disabled people.

With reference to your letter of 24 April, I would like to point out that my car was not parked in contravention of regulations when I was given a parking ticket. I must insist that you look into the matter further.

B Read this letter, and make any changes necessary to improve its style and layout as a formal letter.

Randalls Ltd
75 Central Drive
Northampton NN4 1SW

Hi Mr Randall,

I like the look of your ad in one of those computer mags I was reading recently. It might have been PC Direct. Or perhaps it was PC Plus. The thing is, I really need a computer. I'm writing a novel, you see, and I'm finding it hard typing it up every night on my old typewriter. So I think I should get a PC, probably something like your 386SX – 'now even better value than ever' according to your ad! What do you think? Could you write back as soon as possible, telling me a bit more about the PCs you offer? Do you deliver? Our car's being repaired at the moment – my son had a little accident in it the other day!

All the best,
Jerome Walsh

C Write one or more of these **formal letters**, in 280 – 320 words.

1 An English-language magazine is focusing on 'The World of Work' in a future issue, and the editor has invited readers to send in letters describing their personal experience of employment. You decide to send in a letter about your current job and your working routine, as well as the changes that you envisage making in the future.

2 You are going to attend university in Mexico City for a year on an international exchange programme. You want to know what the accommodation options are, and how much language training you will receive. Write a letter to the admissions tutor, explaining your concerns and asking for information.

3 You recently agreed to provide a personal reference for a friend of yours, who has applied for a high-powered job in a finance company. You have just received a request for the reference from the company's Personnel Director. Write a letter to the Director, stating how long you have known your friend, briefly describing your relationship with him/her, and expanding on his/her personal qualities.

4 You are applying for a post with a large multinational company. The advertisement requires you to send in your c.v. with a covering letter, explaining why you want the job and why the company should employ you. Write the letter, giving your reasons as persuasively as you can.

Informal letters

An **informal letter** is written to a friend, a relative, or someone you know, however slightly. It may therefore be quite correct to use slang, contractions, exclamations, direct questions and incomplete sentences, depending on the context. A formal register is not appropriate for an informal letter.

Some common **opening and closing phrases** are:
- *Dear* (name of the person you are writing to)
- *Yours,/Regards,/Kind regards,/Best wishes,/All the best,/Cheers,/Love,/Love from*
- (Your signature)

Sample question and answer

A friend of yours has written to you, asking for some advice. He wants to visit your country for three weeks this summer, and would like to know which places to visit, where to stay, and what clothes to bring. Write an **informal letter** to him, in 220 – 260 words, giving as many practical suggestions as you can.

Dear Stéphane,

I'm really pleased to hear you'll be coming to the UK this summer. Three weeks seems like a long time, but there's a lot to see – you'll be surprised!

You've got to spend some time in London to start with – the museums and galleries are brilliant. And then you should hop on the train to Cambridge, and wander round all the colleges that are open, and go for a punt on the river – you could do that as a day trip. I'd recommend Stonehenge – it's a very atmospheric stone circle, really old – and you could continue westwards to stay in Bath for a couple of days. Jane Austen called it 'the loveliest city in England'. It would be great if you could get up to Scotland – the Highlands are really worth seeing. It all depends on how much you can fit in.

Hotels are expensive here, but you could consider youth hostels. I might be able to arrange for you to stay with an aunt of mine while you're in London. She takes foreign students in the summer. I'll find out and let you know. And of course you're welcome to stay with us here in beautiful Yorkshire.

You'd better bring shorts in case it's hot (you never know!), jeans, a few T-shirts, a sweatshirt, some kind of waterproof jacket, and a decent shirt and trousers, in case you go somewhere smart.

Well, that's all I can think of at the moment. Let me know if there's anything else I can help with.

Cheers,

James

Here is some useful informal language for particular situations.

Apology I'm really sorry I haven't written lately.
I just haven't been able to get round/down to writing recently.
I've been so busy at work/with the move/with the children.

Reassurance I'm sure everything will be all right, just you wait and see.
Don't worry about them. They're old enough to take care of themselves now.
It wasn't dangerous at all. I followed the instructions very carefully.

Advice If I were you, I'd go in for engineering.
Have you ever thought of voluntary work?
What about moving into a bungalow rather than a flat?
I think you should consult an expert before deciding.

Polite refusal I'd love to, but I'm afraid I won't be able to make it this time.
I really don't think there's much chance of my boss changing his mind, so I'll have to miss the party.
It's nice of you to offer, but I don't think we'll need any more help. Thanks anyway.

A Match the formal expressions on the left with their informal equivalents.

1	furthermore	A	but
2	therefore	B	then/next
3	however	C	and another thing
4	in addition to	D	in spite of
5	notwithstanding	E	by the way
6	currently	F	I think
7	subsequently	G	as well as
8	incidentally	H	about
9	in my view	I	at the moment
10	approximately	J	so

B Find and correct the **ten** grammar and vocabulary mistakes in this informal letter.

Dear Susie,

Thanks very much for doing that babysitting last week. The kids have really enjoyed it, and also it gave me a chance to get on with my work with fewer interruptions as usual. I've just started an interesting new project on attitudes towards recycle, which the council are paying me. All very useful income, now than Paul's only working part-time.

I may have to ask you to look for them again. It could be next week, but the one after is more likely. I'll let you to know soon. What might I do without a friend like you?!

By the way, you know that little tax problem I mentioned to you? Well, in the end I rang up the tax office, and you wouldn't believe how helpful were they! They sorted it all out in no time. I'll try them again next time I'll get in a muddle.

Anyway, must dash. Hope you have a great time at Martha's. Will be in touch.

All the best,
Laura

C Rewrite this letter as if the Chairman of the Town Planning Committee were a friend of yours. Try to persuade him/her to take action on your behalf.

The Chairman
Rugley Council Planning Committee
St Anne's Hall
Rugley   CV21 2ZF

Dear Sir or Madam,

I am writing to protest in the strongest terms about Rugley Council's consent to the planning application submitted on 13 February 2002 by the developers, Haslers. Their proposal is a purely commercial one, with no thought given to the requirements or rights of residents in the Oxley Park area. We, the Friends of Oxley Park, are determined to resist any development of this beautiful and historic park, which has offered incomparable leisure activities to generations of Rugley residents. We are not only apprehensive about the disruption to our lives during the actual construction of the proposed blocks of flats, but we are also extremely angry that the town will be losing a public amenity which it will be impossible to replace.

We call upon you to reconsider your decision in the light of my remarks, bearing in mind the considerable public support for our stand. The petition handed in to the Council offices last Monday was signed by approximately five thousand people, as you are no doubt aware.

The Friends of Oxley Park are considering what legal action may be taken, in the event of your refusal to consult the wishes of residents. I can only reiterate that we are bent on opposing this ill-considered, blatantly profit-seeking proposal, and will fight tooth and nail for our voice to be heard.

I look forward to receiving your prompt reply.

Yours faithfully,
Gerald Portland
Secretary, Friends of Oxley Park

D You have moved away from home to a new job in an unfamiliar town. Your mother has written to ask how you are getting on. Read the extract from her letter and your diary. Then write a **letter** to her (in 180 – 220 words), giving her your news and apologising for not getting in touch earlier.

How are things going? What's the job like? And the flat? Are you making any new friends? Your father and I are worried about you – we haven't heard from you since you left.
Ring or write soon, won't you?
Love from Mum

May 3 Can't believe how busy it is at the office. Didn't even have time for lunch today! At least the flat's OK – when I finally get back to it!

May 7 Things quietening down a bit. Met a couple of nice people from accounts today, and agreed to play tennis with them after work.

May 10 The town is great – lots of things to do in the evenings. Think I'm going to enjoy it here! Must get round to telling the parents all about it.

UNIT 82

Articles

An **article** is a piece of writing for a newspaper, magazine or website. It may aim to interest and entertain as well as to inform. It should have an eye-catching heading, which will make the reader want to read on. Its style will depend on the topic and on the type of publication. It will often include some description and narrative.

Sample question and answer

Last summer you stayed with a family in a small town in England. A friend you made there has told you that the local newspaper is asking for articles about visitors' experiences of staying in the town. Read the extracts from your friend's letter and from your diary. Then write an **article** for the newspaper, in 180 – 220 words.

Remember what happened in the park? I think they'd like to hear what you thought about the family too. Go on – get yourself into print!

Gavin

JUNE 30 Such a nice family. Gave me a great welcome.

JULY 1 Went to open-air exhibition on Switzerland in the park. They realised I was Swiss and made me take part!

JULY 2 Went canoeing with Paul – great fun.

A HOME FROM HOME

'Don't mind us – we're all crazy!' That was how my English host family greeted me when I arrived at their home. It was a great welcome for a teenager like me, who was already feeling a bit homesick.

And so my stay in your beautiful town began. On my second day my host family, the Wilsons, took me to their local park, where there was an open-air exhibition about Switzerland. I was really interested, so I went up to one of the people in charge and told him I was Swiss. He got so excited he nearly had a heart attack. To cut a long story short, I was asked to stay there for the rest of the afternoon and answer people's questions. I suppose you could say I was a sort of living exhibit!

I forgot about being homesick after that. I began to settle in and felt I belonged. The next day Paul, the eldest son, took me canoeing on nearby Westbury Lake – that was fun too, and the scenery was amazing.

The fortnight passed by in a flash. There was so much to do and see. It was quite hard to say goodbye to the Wilsons (and believe me, they really are crazy!). But don't worry, I'll be back next year!

A Match each heading with the appropriate topic.

1	GREEN CARS	A	Places of architectural interest
2	BUILDING SIGHTS	B	Children's electrical design competition
3	UNDER THE SKIN	C	Armed forces head is resigning
4	BRIGHT SPARKS	D	Environmentally friendly vehicles
5	THE ANSWER'S A LEMON	E	Survey of the effects of cosmetics
6	ONE MAN AND HIS DOG	F	Benefits of cooking with citrus fruit
7	LOVE AT FIRST SIGHT	G	Local man's relative has left him a fortune
8	MILITARY CHIEF STEPS DOWN	H	Dead bodies discovered at bungalow
9	HOUSE OF HORROR	I	A shepherd and his highly-trained collie
10	BOB'S YOUR UNCLE	J	Romance between two film stars

B Put these sentences in suitable order to make a newspaper article, and think up a heading for it.

A The most famous picture of Nessie, the Loch Ness Monster, is one of the greatest hoaxes of the century, according to its perpetrator.

B 'I'll go on looking for as long as it takes,' said a determined Rory McGrath from his motor-home parked overlooking the loch.

C But now it appears that Colonel Wilson was one of a group of conspirators, who succeeded in hoodwinking Fleet Street and the gullible British public.

D However, true Nessie fans say that this disappointing discovery will not stop them from searching for the lovable monster.

E It was revealed today that Scotland's best-loved tourist attraction is definitely a sham.

F The photograph spawned the flourishing Nessie tourist industry, which grew up around the shores of the loch.

G The picture was taken in 1934 by a respectable medical expert, Colonel Robert Wilson, and appears to show the long neck of a sea serpent rising out of the loch.

H Another of the group confessed, just before his death last November, that the 'Nessie' in the picture was, in fact, a model made of wood and plastic.

C You have been asked to write an article for a health magazine on ways in which people can improve their general health and fitness. First, choose from statements a–m the ones you wish to include in your article. Then re-order them to make three paragraphs.

FITNESS FACTORS

a) Stress, at work and at home, can contribute to heart disease and stress-related disorders, such as migraine.

b) More fibre in the diet makes for better digestion and helps to prevent bowel cancer.

c) Excessive alcohol consumption can cause liver disease.

d) It is important to cut salt and fat intake, in order to reduce the likelihood of heart disease and circulatory problems.

e) Cigarette smoking can cause bronchial disease and lung cancer.

f) Eating fewer sugary foods will result in less tooth decay and better weight control.

g) Even passive smoking can cause lung cancer.

h) It is essential to maintain a well-balanced, varied diet, in order to provide the body with all its needs, and to control weight.

i) Alcohol is also addictive: if you must drink, it is better to limit yourself to a 'safe' number of units per week.

j) Exercise can be both enjoyable and healthy, as it controls the appetite, gives a feeling of well-being, reduces susceptibility to many diseases, and helps to eliminate stress.

k) Vitamins taken in fruit and vegetables help to give resistance to infection.

l) People may have to change their lifestyle, if it is producing excessive stress.

m) Habits which are harmful to health should be controlled.

Now write the complete **article** in 280–320 words, using any of sentences a–m and any of these linking words and phrases. Write your own introduction and conclusion. You should have five paragraphs altogether.

To start with, ...   For some, ...   For others, ...
Not only... but (also) ...   In today's health-conscious society ...
While/Whereas ...   In addition, ...
Another point to remember is that ...
A further factor to consider is ...   However, ...
So it seems that ...   On balance, ...   To sum up, ...

(There is a model answer on page 238 of the Appendix.)

D Now write an **article** in 220 – 260 words for a bookshop website.

BOOKWORMS UNITE!

Do you find reading books more enjoyable than watching TV or playing computer games? If so, then tell us why! We'll publish the best article on our website.

(There is a model answer on page 238 of the Appendix.)

Reports

A **report** may be written for an employer, a college principal, a team leader, or a group of colleagues, club members, consumers or people who share facilities. The main purpose is to provide factual information; it may also make suggestions or recommendations for future action. A report should be clearly organised, with a simple heading or title, and written in a formal or neutral style. Subheadings are helpful in making the different sections of the report clear to the reader.

Sample question and answer

Last summer you went on an international work camp. You have received a letter from the organisers asking you to write a report on it. Read the extract from the letter and your notes. Then write your **report**, in 180 – 220 words.

So if you could write a report for us, we'd be very grateful. We'd like to know your opinion of:

- the location   *too remote*
- the facilities   *old-fashioned tents, shower block too small and dirty*
- the food   *excellent, and lots of it!*
- the staff   *enthusiastic, the great atmosphere was down to them*
- the value or otherwise of the experience   *really valuable, made new friends*

We'd also like to know how we can improve things in future.

REPORT ON INTERNATIONAL WORK CAMP

The facilities

The work camp was on a remote farm, so leisure activities were limited to what participants could organise at the camp. The accommodation was in small tents, which were of a basic, old-fashioned design; they only allowed campers to crawl in and lie down, with no room for sitting or standing. The shower and toilet block often became seriously overcrowded, and could have been cleaned more regularly.

The food

This was excellent in every respect. Fresh, plentiful meals were served twice a day, morning and evening, and packed lunches were provided for participants to take to the fields.

The staff

All the staff were enthusiastic and welcoming. Nothing was too much trouble for them, and they went out of their way to create a happy atmosphere.

The value of the experience

It was immensely valuable for me. In addition to learning about fruit growing, I made a lot of new friends and learned about other people's customs and languages.

Recommendations

I would strongly suggest finding another site, closer to a village or small town, where evening activities would be available. A larger shower block should be provided, and regular cleaning arranged. However, my main recommendation would be to replace the old tents with new, more spacious ones.

Here is some useful language for writing reports.

This report is intended to ...	as a matter of urgency,
It appears that ...	It was extremely useful ...
In addition ...	I would strongly suggest ...
according to ...	It is interesting to note that ...
It is recommended that ...	On balance ...
to make recommendations	To summarise, ... / In conclusion, ...

A Your company recently sent you to an international conference. You have been asked to write a **report** about it for your colleagues, in 220 – 260 words. Before starting to write, you asked yourself some questions. Read your questions and answers.

1 When exactly was the conference? April 8 – 11
2 Where was it held? Aberdeen, Scotland
3 What was the name of the event? 15th Annual LinguaShow Conference
4 What was the company's purpose in sending me? to keep up-to-date
5 What were the highlights? lots of sessions, expert speakers, networking
6 What were the negative aspects? crowded snackbar, no quiet spaces
7 What lasting impressions was I left with? great experience
8 What suggestions or recommendations can I make, based on my attendance? interactive whiteboards in all schools?
9 Would I recommend sending a colleague next year? yes!

B Now complete the report by choosing the correct words from the box above. Also choose an appropriate subheading from the box opposite to complete the space before each section. (There is one extra heading which you do not need.)

Negative aspects	Conclusion	Where, when and why
Recommendations	Delegates' views	Positive aspects

Report on LinguaShow Conference

_____

This report is 1) _____ to summarise my feedback from the 15th Annual LinguaShow Conference, which took place in Aberdeen from April 8th – 11th. I attended as a delegate to help the company keep abreast of developments in teaching methodology, and in order to 2) _____ recommendations for implementation in our many language schools.

_____

It was extremely 3) _____ being able to sit in on workshops led by some of the best-known practitioners in the world. The huge variety of sessions available had to be seen to be believed. In 4) _____, the conference provided excellent opportunities for networking.

_____

At peak times, the refreshment facilities were overstretched and had difficulty in coping with the large numbers of delegates. It was often hard to find a quiet space for a conversation, or to mull over what had been said.

_____

It is clearly crucial for our language schools to keep up with teaching innovations. It is 5) _____ that, as a matter of 6) _____, we investigate the feasibility of installing interactive whiteboards in every classroom, and ensuring that staff are fully trained in how to use them.

_____

It is interesting to 7) _____ that there is now interactive web coverage of parts of the conference. However, on 8) _____, I think it is far more beneficial to the company to send a delegate in person. Attending the conference is an immensely valuable experience.

Proposals

A **proposal** is similar to a report, but whereas a report describes a past or present event or situation, a proposal focuses on the future. It is written for a superior or a peer group, and it must offer recommendations for action. It should be clearly structured, with separate sections and subheadings.

Sample question and answer

You are a student member of your college council. Your college principal has asked you to write a **proposal**, in 220 – 260 words, for improving facilities at the college in order to attract more overseas students. Make some specific recommendations in your proposal.

Proposal for improving college facilities

I have taken soundings among my fellow students, and I feel that I am speaking on their behalf when I make the following recommendations.

Library

The library is well stocked with a large selection of reference books, journals and worksheets. However, space is limited, so I suggest the room next door (currently in occasional use as a classroom) is knocked through to enlarge the library. Students can then use it for quiet study.

Multimedia rooms

The multimedia rooms have workstations and computers with high-speed broadband connections, but it is often impossible to find a free computer. These days, students expect to be able to stay in touch with friends and family by email, so I recommend doubling the number of computers. If necessary, a booking system could be instituted, in order to give all students a fair chance of using these facilities.

Classrooms

These are mostly spacious, but almost all of them have large south-facing windows and become very hot in summer. I suggest that air-conditioning units are installed in all classrooms. This feature could be mentioned in the college prospectus, as it would attract students from countries where air-conditioning is commonplace.

Dining hall

There are many complaints about the unimaginative food on offer, so I recommend replacing the current standard menu of two hot dishes at each meal with a wider-ranging buffet for students to help themselves from.

Conclusion

If my recommendations are acted on, I feel confident that Evergreen College will go from strength to strength and expand its recruitment of overseas students.

Here is some useful language for writing proposals.

I would therefore like to suggest ...	I am strongly in favour of ...
I trust that you will take ... into account	There is no question that ...
We look to the authorities to provide ...	I have taken soundings among ...
I hope you will give serious consideration to ...	on behalf of ...

A Your employer has asked you to find out from your office colleagues whether they would be happy for flexitime to be introduced at work. Read the comments they have made to you, before you think about writing a proposal.

No way! Over my dead body!   Molly, Reception

Mike and I would like 10 – 2 as the core time, when everyone has to be here. We'd probably both work from 8 till 4.   Jed, Design

Leaving at 4 would give me more time to go fishing.   Mike, Design

9.30 to 3 should be the core time. But who's going to answer the early phone calls if we all decide to start at 9.30?   Jasmin, Rachel & Steve, Accounts

Not sure. Shouldn't everybody be here from 9 to 5? But it's cheaper for me to play squash before 5, so why not?   Phil, Marketing

It'd be good to be free sometimes, to pick up Janie from school. Alan, Marketing

B Now rewrite the proposal in 180 – 220 words, in order to produce a more appropriate formal style, with subheadings and paragraphs.

Changes to the office timetable

I've asked everybody, and they all agree that flexitime would be a good idea. Well, Molly at Reception doesn't want it, but then she'll probably have to be here from 9 – 5 anyway, won't she? Jed and Mike in Design think the core time should be from 10 to 2. As you know, they always arrive and leave together, because they share a car to work. They say they'd most likely do 8 to 4. It'd give Mike more daylight hours to go fishing. But Jasmin, Rachel and Steve in Accounts want a longer core time. They think we should all be here between 9.30 and 3 pm. And they want to know who'll answer the phone in each department if *everybody* decides to start at 9.30! Phil and Alan in Marketing are the only ones who aren't sure about the plan. They say what about the poor customer? Shouldn't *all* the staff be here from 9 to 5? But they like the idea for themselves. You know Phil belongs to a squash club – well, it's cheaper before 5 pm. And Alan sometimes needs to be free in the afternoon to collect his daughter from school. So, all in all, people seem fairly well-disposed towards the scheme. I think our next step should be to fix a core time, and try it out for a month. Then we can review it.

(There is a model answer on page 239 of the Appendix.)

C Now do this task, in 220 – 260 words.

Write a **proposal** for your local council, on ways of improving the leisure and entertainment facilities in your town or village. Make some specific recommendations for future action.

Information sheets

An **information sheet** is written for people who need or would like help, advice or information. It may be produced by a local or national group publicising its activities, a commercial organisation trying to widen its market, or an administrative body aiming to inform or warn the general public.

It should be clearly organised, with an eye-catching heading and possibly sub-headings. Above all, the relevant points need to stand out.

Sample question and answer

You are helping to organise a four-day music festival attracting large numbers of young people. Write an **information sheet**, in 220 – 260 words, which:

- advises ticket-holders what (and what not) to bring with them
- suggests the best methods of travelling to the festival
- gives some tips on avoiding problems and gaining maximum enjoyment from the event.

FESTIVAL FUN AND FROLICS

Getting ready

Everyone's got their own idea of what to bring to a festival, but when packing, remember – less is best. Only bring essentials.

- Don't forget your ticket – you'll have to show it to get in
- If you're camping, only bring what you can afford to lose – no tent is secure
- No glass is allowed on the site, so forget those bottles
- Waterproof clothing is essential, and really comfortable footwear
- Bring a torch, for finding your way back to your tent in the dark.

Getting there

- Don't arrive before the gates open at 8 am on Wednesday 25th August
- You can get a combined coach and festival ticket from travel@buytickets.com
- There are extra trains to Castle Cary station, with a free shuttle-bus from there
- If you *have* to bring a car, check the car-sharing website www.liftshare.com

Getting the most out of it

We want you to stay safe and enjoy yourselves! So ...

- Use sunscreen to avoid getting sunburnt
- Don't store perishable food in your tent – it will soon go off and could make you ill
- Be prepared to wait – time becomes a vague concept at the festival
- Spread your cash around to avoid losing it all – some people keep their money and mobile phones in their boots while walking around!
- Think green – bag and bin your litter for recycling.

Have a great, unforgettable time!

A Alter the layout of this short information sheet in order to make it more striking. Think about subheadings and bullet points.

First Aid? Why do I need it?

It could be *your* loved one who needs your help. Don't you think you owe it to them to get some basic know-how? Don't worry if you know nothing about first aid. In only two hours the Heartbeat course will show you how to deal with someone who's choking, or with someone who's unconscious, how to control serious bleeding, how to check if someone is breathing, how to recognise a heart attack, and how to check if a person's heart has stopped and how to deal with them if it has. So what should you do next? Well, our highly-trained professional paramedics are leading the next public training session in April. Phone 676444 now to book your place on the course. You won't regret it. You might even save a life. Wouldn't that be worth a couple of hours of your time?

(There is a model answer on page 240 of the Appendix.)

B Look at these headings from information sheets, and say what kind of organisation produced them. Explain what you think the message of each sheet is.

1 Interested in our FREE ethical consumer magazine?

2 Great weekend breaks – don't miss out, book TODAY!

3 Annual Financial Report 2008 – 2009

4 Life's a Learning Curve – book a course today

5 Watch out for bogus callers – check their identity

6 Dream Holiday Giveaway

7 Be Streetwise – Stay out of Trouble

8 Save our local hospital!

9 Volunteers Needed – please help!

10 Important – Deadline 31st January

C Now write one of these **information sheets**, in 220 – 260 words.

1 You are the secretary of a college environmental group. You would like to increase your membership. Write an information sheet to be circulated to students, explaining your group's aims and activities.

2 You are organising a language conversation group in your town. Write an information sheet, which will be delivered to as many houses as possible, explaining what you envisage and asking people who are interested to contact you and/or attend the group's first meeting.

Essays

An **essay** is usually written for a teacher, or as part of an examination. You may be asked to write an essay on an extract from a longer text, a quotation or a set text. In Part 1 of the CPE Writing Paper you are required to write an essay summarising and evaluating the main ideas in two short texts. An essay should be carefully planned, use neutral or formal language, and show a logical sequence of ideas in a clear structure.

Sample question and answer

You have read this extract from a newspaper article on urban living. Your tutor has asked you to write an **essay**, in 280 – 320 words, responding to the points raised and expressing your own views.

Large cities hold a strong fascination. For many of us they act like a magnet, drawing us irresistibly to them. They offer amazing opportunities for work and play, but there is a price to pay, in terms of more expensive housing, greater exposure to crime, and reduced space for leisure activities. So, is urban living an outdated concept? Or is it the way forward? If so, how can we make our cities more attractive places to live in?

For many of us, a city is the place we grew up and the place we call home. We are accustomed to its bustle and noise and have come to expect its high standards of work and leisure opportunities. In the latter years of the 20th century, however, there was a rising feeling among some city-dwellers that the problems associated with urban living – inner-city crime, overpriced housing, air pollution, lack of green space – were beginning to outweigh the advantages. Consequently, there was a significant movement of urbanites out of the cities and into the countryside, to try a new, slower, more rooted way of life.

These days it is quite feasible to run a business from a remote farmhouse; a global market can be reached via the internet with ease. So the self-employed can earn a living as easily in a rural as in an urban environment.

Leisure and cultural facilities are still far better in towns, although what is on offer in rural areas has its own charm. However, transport is perhaps the greatest problem facing rural communities. Bus services may be infrequent – or even non-existent in the evenings – and taxis can be prohibitively expensive. It is for these reasons that many young people now stay in the cities, and others are moving back there from the countryside.

City councils are working hard and investing large amounts to improve living conditions for their residents. The provision of affordable homes for first-time buyers, an efficient public transport system, and parks and sports facilities make urban living more attractive than ever nowadays. People need to be encouraged to use the streets, to walk or cycle to work or the shops, and to feel safe at night as well as during the day. In a rural environment, there is often a strong sense of community. This is what is needed in our cities, so that we can truly enjoy living there.

A Match these informal remarks with their more formal equivalents.

1 Look, I'm absolutely sure that …
2 Loads of people say …
3 People have got it all wrong when they say …
4 I just can't stand …
5 I think … is a brilliant idea.
6 Don't you think that …?

A I am strongly opposed to …
B I am totally in favour of …
C I am convinced that …
D I would suggest that …
E Contrary to popular belief, there is no evidence that …
F Many people maintain that …

B Read this extract from a magazine article about whether famous people are entitled to keep their personal lives private. Then answer the questions.

Celebrities claim to be hounded by the paparazzi, who apparently allow them no privacy or space to 'be themselves'. But isn't it *their* fault, for seeking the limelight? Surely they must accept the consequences of fame along with its many rewards. Aren't we entitled to know the details of their personal lives? After all, we pay to watch them act or play football or present TV programmes – without us, they would not *be* celebrities!

1 What are the writer's main arguments?
2 What opposing views can you think of?
3 What is your personal opinion?
4 How would you organise the ideas you have written down, if you were asked to write an essay on this topic?

C Read the two texts, then write an **essay** summarising and evaluating the key points from both texts, in 240 – 280 words. Include your own views.

Eating meat is wrong

The painful confinement and violent death inflicted on animals that we raise for our food is barbaric. In our arrogance and selfishness, we pretend to be unaware of their suffering, but current research proves that there are high levels of stress in animals on factory farms and at abattoirs. Chickens, sheep, pigs and cattle are only seen in terms of their market value – our interest in the bottom line is one of mankind's least endearing traits – but we should respect them as living creatures and give up eating meat, to prevent their continued mistreatment and slaughter.

The right sort of meat

The main benefit of eating meat is that it provides an excellent source of high quality protein, which cannot be matched by any single vegetarian food. Humans are omnivores, and need meat as part of a balanced diet. However, there is a major problem with meat production in developed countries: the persistence of factory farming is harming the environment. The answer is to search out independent, small-scale meat producers who use sustainable farming methods, because having grass-fed, outdoor-reared animals is actually beneficial to the environment. That way you'll be able to enjoy your steak with a clear conscience!

(There is a model answer on page 240 of the Appendix.)

Reviews

A **review** is usually written for a newspaper, magazine or website. The aim is to give the reviewer's personal opinion about something he or she has experienced (a film, a book, a restaurant, a holiday, a website, etc). A review should describe the subject of the review, and will generally make a recommendation to the reader.

Sample question and answer

You have recently seen a staged version of a novel you have read. Write a **review** of the play, in 280 – 320 words, for a local arts magazine, saying what you think are the difficulties of creating stage plays based on books.

A PORTRAIT OF A LADY

Critics have called this 19th-century novel by the American author Henry James one of the wonders of world literature. It tells the story of Isabel Archer, an attractive young American heiress, who travels to Europe on a voyage of self-discovery. Having turned down an English lord and a wealthy American industrialist, Isabel marries Gilbert Osmond, a man who claims to care nothing for worldly possessions. The marriage is orchestrated by the charming Madame Merle. When Gilbert and Madame Merle reveal their true natures, however, Isabel has to confront her future alone.

The stage play based on the novel is written by Nicola Frei. The cast includes some household names you'll recognise from popular TV programmes. I'd particularly single out for praise Catherine McCormack, who plays Isabel, and who manages to portray her dual qualities of vulnerability and independence with consummate ease. The night I was there, the play, which is directed by veteran theatre director Peter Hall, received rapturous applause.

That's not to say, though, that a novelist's ideas are necessarily better expressed on stage than on the page. The detail and nuance of writing like James's is often lost when it is transferred to the physicality of the theatre. Swings and roundabouts, you may say – a play has the obvious advantage over a novel of showing us colour, action, sound. But novelists might reply that these are elements which may detract from the original purpose of the novel. Then there are the great abstract ideas, ideally suited to the medium of the novel – the pursuit of spiritual freedom, the power of love, the heavy hand of destiny. A really great scriptwriter is needed to make these concepts as powerful in the flesh-and-blood environment of a stage play as in the original novel.

Despite all this, I recommend you to catch *A Portrait of a Lady* before its run ends. I guarantee you will not be disappointed.

Here are some useful phrases for use in reviews.

> The book/film/programme/exhibition deals with/tells the story of/ focuses on/includes …
>
> The story/plot is based on …   The hotel/restaurant/café provides …
>
> I found the photography/acting/ending …
>
> The staff/whole cast are incredibly …
>
> It conveys a sense of …   It exudes an atmosphere of …
>
> Grant's acting/performance/portrayal of … was …
>
> Each chapter/scene is devoted to/involves …
>
> I was bowled over by …   I was most impressed by …

A Match these nouns, related to the cinema, theatre or radio/television, with their definitions.

1	cast	A	part of a television series
2	stage	B	where a film/programme is made
3	screen	C	actors in a play/film
4	studio	D	person financially responsible
5	broadcast	E	part of a play/film
6	plot	F	part of a theatre
7	stunt	G	radio/TV programme
8	scenery	H	clothes worn by an actor
9	producer	I	part of a cinema
10	costume	J	moveable background for a play
11	scene	K	dangerous action
12	episode	L	events or storyline

B These are adjectives you might use to describe a play, film etc. Divide them into two lists: positive and negative.

> boring   unusual   awful   informative   brilliant
> successful   fantastic   amateurish   stunning   original
> conventional   unimaginative   witty   fine   outstanding
> hopeless   predictable   thrilling   amazing   superb
> dreadful   horrible   great   pathetic   dull

C Choose the correct word or phrase from the pair in brackets to complete each sentence.

1 Barry Thomas wrote a stinging _____ of your friend's book in *The Times*.   (critic/review)

2 Fellini is one of Italy's best-known film _____. (directors/managers)

3 The actors had to learn their lines from the _____. (book/script)

4 It's a long play but fortunately there's a twenty-minute _____ after Act Two.   (pause/interval)

5 Spielberg's films are famous for their _____. (special effects/particular tricks)

D Now write this **review**, in 220 – 260 words.

Write a review of a recent film or TV programme you have seen, for an international student magazine website. Describe the film or programme, and say whether you would recommend it to other students, giving your reasons.

Set texts

You may be asked to write about a **set text** in the form of an article, an essay, a report, a review or (for CPE) a letter. Read the question carefully and plan your answer, using paragraphs with linking words and connected ideas.

Make sure you use the correct register and format. Refer to the story to support your opinions and to show you are familiar with the text.

Sample question and answer

As I Walked Out One Midsummer Morning by Laurie Lee.

'The main character in this book is Spain.' Write an **essay** for your tutor, in 280 – 320 words, giving a brief description of the book, discussing the statement above, and giving reasons for your views.

In the mid-1930s, a young man called Laurie Lee left England and spent a year tramping round Spain. He played the fiddle to pay his way, he made friends, he slept under trees and at inns, but most of the time he simply observed the people, the landscape, the language, the customs. This book is his account of that time, written thirty years later.

In a lyrical yet lucid style he paints a fresh and captivating picture of a beautiful country, then unfamiliar to most foreigners. To anyone who knows Spain, his account rings true. He describes the hospitality and real kindness of the people, but also the widespread poverty of the time. He evokes the brilliant light, the aridity of the central plains, the bustle of the larger towns, and the threat of imminent civil war. Above all, he is a master at creating atmosphere. There is an exotic, primitive spirit about the heart of Spain which is endlessly fascinating, and Laurie Lee gets it spot on.

In a memoir you might expect the narrator to set himself up as the main character, but here he tends to deflect attention away from himself, his own thoughts and feelings, and towards the people and events he observes. We feel that he is effacing his own personality, wherever possible, in favour of his real subject – Spain.

There are other characters who are described in the book, but we do not see them for long enough to retain a strong interest in them. It was the journey itself, and the place, that counted for Laurie Lee.

In a way, the book is like an Impressionist painting – an inspirational creation of colour and feeling, based on reality but seen through the eyes of an unsophisticated young man. His encounter with Spain and her people changed his life, and the vividness of his perceptions has made this book popular with millions of readers.

A Complete the review by choosing the correct phrases from the box.

You have been asked to write a **review** for your college magazine, in 220 – 260 words, of *On Beauty* by Zadie Smith. Explain why you think the author chose this title, and say whether or not you would recommend the novel to other students.

sharp observation	looking for links	in the right way
easy read	sift through	idea of fairness	at first glance
key question	incredibly perceptive	feuding families

ON BEAUTY

Set in New England and London, this is the story of two 1) _____ , the Belseys and the Kippses. It's both wonderfully funny and 2) _____ about what makes families tick, and it delves fearlessly into the characters' personal relationships. There is 3) _____ here, and truly believable dialogue – Levi's street talk, in particular, is impressive.

Art is a theme which runs through the book, so 4) _____ one might think that's the beauty referred to in the title. However, it seems that the author borrowed the title and some inspiration from Elaine Scarry's essay called 'On Beauty and Being Just', so the concept of beauty, for Zadie Smith, might include the 5) _____, the appropriate way of doing things. Carl is an example of this – he has physical good looks, but more importantly he wants to do things 6) _____. There's also Claire's poem about beautiful people – do they suffer more than the rest of us? Is life harder for them? Perhaps the 7) _____ that Zadie Smith is asking throughout the book, though, is, what makes life beautiful?

There's so much to think about, so many layers to 8) _____ – I'd recommend this book to anyone who likes to read something a bit complex. It isn't an 9) _____, but a worthwhile one. And of course Zadie Smith acknowledges being influenced by E. M. Forster, especially his novel *Howards End*, so it's interesting 10) _____ between the two works.

B Put the nine sentences or paragraphs in the correct order to complete the article, starting with A.

A bookshop website has asked for articles to be sent in on *The Falls* by Joyce Carol Oates. Write an **article**, in 220 – 260 words, first describing the importance of Niagara Falls in the book, and then saying which character you felt most sympathy for.

LOVE AT THE FALLS

A In 1950 Ariah Erskine is taken by her new husband Gilbert to Niagara Falls for her honeymoon.

B As far as the characters go, Ariah herself doesn't strike me as sympathetic at all.

C It's his basic integrity and sense of justice which involves him in the contentious court case that ultimately leads to his death.

D No, personally I feel most sympathy for Dick Burnaby. He sincerely loves Ariah and does his best for her and the children.

E As she mourns and waits for his corpse to be returned by the waters, a local lawyer, Dirk Burnaby, falls in love with her, and not long afterwards they marry.

F She's too opinionated to be a good mother, and her strong convictions lead her to defy society's conventions and her family's expectations.

G It's also the place where Dirk eventually dies, and it forms a continual backdrop to the action, constantly threatening with its power to cause death and destruction.

H Niagara Falls, then, is the place where Ariah loses her first husband and finds her second. It's the town where she lives for most of her life, first with Dirk and their three children, and later alone, as she separates from Dirk, and her children grow up and move away.

I Unexpectedly, Gilbert's suicidal plunge into the raging waters of the Falls leaves her a widow.

C Complete the letter by putting **one** word in each space.

A library is about to have an exhibition on writing about Africa, and has asked the public for some suggestions. Write a **letter** to the library staff, in 280 – 320 words, recommending that they include *The No. 1 Ladies' Detective Agency* by Alexander McCall Smith in the exhibition. Give a brief description of the book and its main character, Precious Ramotswe.

Dear Sir or Madam,

I am writing to recommend Alexander McCall Smith's *The No. 1 Ladies' Detective Agency* for your exhibition. 1) _____ I expect you know, this is the first in a series of novels by this author, set in Gaborone, Botswana.

The main character is a woman called Precious Ramotswe, 2) _____ decides to set up a private detective agency with a legacy from her father, 3) _____ help people solve their problems. 4) _____ the course of her investigations, Mma Ramotswe deals with many difficult and occasionally dangerous situations. 5) _____, she almost always achieves a successful outcome, 6) _____ using her common sense and powers of observation.

7) _____ makes this book particularly suitable for your exhibition, in my view, is that Mma Ramotswe often comments on the fine qualities of the country of Botswana and its people, landscape and traditions. As an African, she is proud of her culture and heritage, and loves her country. She is content to drink her red bush tea in the company of her friend, the garage owner Mr J.L.B. Matekoni, 8) _____ discussing the day's events, or to sit on the verandah of her house in Zebra Drive, thinking her own thoughts. She sees nothing to be ashamed of in being 'a traditionally built African lady' (dress size 22), 9) _____ does she envy other nations or individuals.

Various characters in the book show the same pride in their country. Obed Ramotswe (Precious's father) says, 'I love our country, and I am proud to be a Motswana. There's no other country in Africa that can hold its head up as we can.'

The author shows us 10) _____ welcoming and warm-hearted Africans can be. In 11) _____, he lays stress on the importance of family values and morality as perceived by them. It seems to me that this story, told with such simplicity and humour, carries the strong message 12) _____ traditional cultures may have a deep, indestructible understanding of what matters in life. We should learn from them.

I hope you will consider my recommendation favourably.

Yours faithfully,
Louisa Rizzi

D Now write this **report**, in 220 – 260 words.

Write a report, for your class to read, on a book you have recently read. Briefly outline the plot, give your opinion of the main character(s), and say whether or not you would recommend the book to others. (See **Unit 83** for guidance on reports.)

Competition entries

A **competition entry** is written for a judge or panel of judges. You are expected to provide a response to a question or statement, or complete a task. This may take the form of nominating someone or something, or of proposing yourself for selection, or of expressing your opinion in an appropriate way.

Your entry needs to catch the reader's attention, and should include a strong final paragraph. Use the language of persuasion, and give reasons for your choices.

Sample question and answer
You see this notice at your school or college. Write your **competition entry**, in 220 – 260 words.

> WRITING COMPETITION
> Yes, it's here again – our annual competition!
> Great prizes offered for the five best entries.
> The subject this year is: *The person I most admire.*
> Open up your laptops and get writing!
> Entries must be in by the end of term.

BIG BROTHER'S WATCHING ME!

There's only one person who fits the bill, and that's my big brother Mike. For as long as I can remember he's been around to take care of me, keeping an eye on me and my brothers and sisters to make sure we don't get into trouble. My mum died when I was little, and my dad's pretty busy just earning enough to make ends meet, so Mike's made it his responsibility to keep the family together.

He's eighteen now, and you might think he'd be out in the evenings with his friends, leading his own social life, not wanting to be bothered with us kids. Well, you'd be wrong. There's a great atmosphere at home once we all get back from school. Mike's in the kitchen, getting us all to do the chores. One of us peels the vegetables, another sets the table, and so on. He says it's good discipline for us, teaching us to manage for ourselves. But he makes it fun too – that's the reason we all do it without grumbling.

The great thing about Mike is that we don't worry about things, because we know he's there. Sometimes I think he's taken all our anxieties onto his own shoulders, and maybe that's a lot for him to cope with. But you'd never guess that to look at him – he's always cheerful and smiling. That's why he's the person I most admire and look up to. I hope I'll be just like him when I grow up.

Here is some useful language for persuasion.

There's no doubt that ...	I hope you will agree with me that ...
It seems indisputable that ...	That's why ...
It's evident, to me at least, that ...	That's the reason I approve of ...
There's no one else who ...	It's by far the best ...
There's nothing else which ...	What could be more valuable than ...?
I would like to suggest that ...	My favourite ... is ...
I am nominating/putting forward ...	Furthermore, ...

A You see this announcement in an international student magazine. Complete the **competition entry** by choosing the correct words or phrases from the box above.

GREATEST 20TH CENTURY INVENTION

We are planning a TV programme in which we ask viewers to vote on the greatest invention of the 20th century. Write to us with your nomination, in 220 – 260 words, giving reasons for your choice, and you may be selected to present your views on the programme.

THE WONDERS OF THE WORLD WIDE WEB

There's no 1) _____ that there are a number of strong contenders for the title of greatest invention of the 20th century, but in my view it seems 2) _____ that the World Wide Web (or web for short) was by far the greatest invention. That's why I am 3) _____ it.

The web is a system of interlinked documents accessed via the internet, and it was invented in 1989 by Tim Berners-Lee, an English computer scientist and internet pioneer. There's no one 4) _____ who has made such a large contribution to methods of global communication. Thanks to Berners-Lee, we can view web pages from a huge variety of sources, and navigate easily between them using hyperlinks.

It's 5) _____, to me at least, that the benefits the web brings to researchers in every field of endeavour are incalculable. The reason I 6) _____ of it so strongly is that almost any question can now be answered in a matter of minutes, or even seconds, by referring to the web, thus obviating the need to travel to a library or keep reference books at home. What could be more 7) _____ as a resource?

8) _____, there is no hierarchy among web users. Anyone who has a web browser on a computer connected to the internet can access the web, and participate freely in the global information revolution.

Therefore, I hope you will 9) _____ with me that the World Wide Web is truly the greatest invention of the 20th century.

B You see this announcement on a language school website. Read the **competition entry**, and the judges' comments which follow. Some of the comments do not apply to this entry. Tick those which do apply.

FREE TUITION

Do you want to study for free? Well, if you win our competition, you can! The prize is a month-long intensive language course at our award-winning school. Tell us, in 220 – 260 words, exactly why you think you deserve a free language course. Just send in your entries by the end of June, and we'll publish the name of the winner on this website. Good luck!

Hello. First of all, I must explain something to you. I'm entering the competition on behalf of my best friend, Anna. I can afford to pay your fees, but she can't. I think you should let her have the free course. This is why. She is a good, hardworking student. If you don't give her the prize, she will have no chance of improving her language. And it's important for her. She has a plan for the future. It's to become a teacher. And for that she must speak and write much better English. She asked me to write to you. She thinks her English is too poor to express herself well. You see how you could help her? I think you will understand and be kind and let her win. It will be good for her. It will be good for you too. She will tell her friends what a good school you are. Then you will have more students coming to your school and paying your fees!

Judges' comments

1 There are spelling mistakes.
2 Some of the sentences are too short.
3 There are grammar mistakes.
4 There are not enough linking words.
5 There should be more than one paragraph.
6 No reasons are given.
7 The entry has too few words.
8 The entrant should be applying for him/herself.
9 The register is inappropriate.
10 There is a poor range of vocabulary and structure.

C Now write a **competition entry**, in 220 – 260 words, in response to this announcement in a wildlife magazine.

CALLING ALL WILDLIFE ENTHUSIASTS

What's the most interesting bird, animal, flower or insect you've seen this summer? Write and tell us all about it – where you saw it and why it was so special for you. The entry we judge to be the best will win one of our wildlife tour packages (see our website for more details).

Contributions to longer pieces

You may be asked to write a **contribution to a longer piece**, such as a book on international customs or traditions. You should concentrate on providing information and opinion. It is important to match the style of your contribution with that used in the longer piece of writing; for example, a collection of people's philosophical ideas may be written in a discursive style, whereas a guidebook is likely to be more factual.

Use a paragraph for each bullet point in the question, to make sure you are giving a complete answer.

Sample question and answer

You have been asked to write a contribution to a book which is being written about theories and methods of learning languages.

Your contribution should:
- describe your experience of learning a foreign or second language
- identify the most favourable language learning environment for you personally
- recommend a method of language learning that you have found successful.

Write your **contribution to the book**, in 220 – 260 words.

For me, the experience of learning a foreign language started at school, when I was introduced to some of the elementary phrases needed for getting around in France. This was just the beginning of what was to become years of study, learning language rules in class and then going on international exchanges to practise what I had learnt. I found language learning addictive – I soon took German as well, and later Spanish. It is hard to describe the feeling of jubilation when you find you are able to participate in a proper conversation with native speakers.

As far as I am concerned, there is simply no comparison between learning a language at home and learning it in the country where it is spoken. Being surrounded by the language all the time makes it almost painless to assimilate. There is the added benefit of contact with all the culture and customs of a different country, something impossible to learn from a textbook. And because you are away from home, it even feels like a holiday, which means you relax enough to be receptive to new information.

Nevertheless, I have recently discovered a successful language learning method which can be fitted in between daily activities at home. A language course on CDs, as long as it does not require you to read at the same time, can be followed in the car, on the train or on the bus. The key is to listen to it regularly. I found it went a long way towards improving my language level.

A Read the task, then answer the questions which follow.

You have been asked to write a contribution to a book which is being written about childhood memories. Your contribution should:
- describe a childhood memory which you remember vividly
- say why you think you remember it so well
- give your opinion on the value of retaining memories from childhood.

Write your **contribution to the book**, in 220 – 260 words.

1 How many paragraphs should you use? Tick one answer.
Four / Three / Two / One

2 Which style should you use? Tick two answers.
humorous   discursive   persuasive   ironical
colloquial   objective   descriptive   factual

B Complete the **contribution to the book** about childhood memories by putting sentences B – D of each paragraph into the right order. Each sentence A is already in the correct position.

Paragraph 1

A The thing I remember best about my childhood was going to visit my grandmother, which we did every summer holiday.

B She'd come to the door to greet us, saying 'You're here! You're here!' as if she could hardly believe it.

C That long journey seemed to last for ever, but we forgot all about it as soon as we arrived.

D She lived about six hours' drive away from us, so you can imagine the fuss and commotion as the five of us packed the car to the roof and then clambered in.

Paragraph 2

A The reason I remember it so well is that we never had such fun anywhere else as at Grandma's.

B And when we came in for supper in the early evening, you wouldn't believe how much food she had ready for us.

C She had a huge, overgrown garden we could run wild in, with an ancient plum tree to climb and a rustic summerhouse to play in.

D She must have thought we needed feeding up!

Paragraph 3

A I'm determined to hold on to memories of my childhood like this one.

B If you're lucky enough to have had a happy childhood, I think it gives you a certain confidence and the ability to make other people happy.

C Because when I look back, I see it as a golden time.

D Why is this important for me?

C Read the question below. Then read the answer and the editor's comments which follow it. Some of the comments do not apply to this contribution. Tick those which do apply.

You have been asked to write a **contribution to a book**, in 220 – 260 words, about international cuisine. Your contribution should:

- describe a food or dish which is typical in your country
- explain its cultural or traditional significance.

There's a cake I often make which always turns out reely well. You could hardly call it typical, I supose, but it's one of my favourites. It's a coffee and wallnut cake, and this is the recipe.

Ingredients

50 g chopped wallnuts	175 g flower	half teaspoon baking powder
100 g butter	100 g sugar	1 tablespoon instant coffee
2 medium eggs	3 tablespoons milk	half teaspoon salt

Method

Mix all the ingriedents together in a bowl or food processor. Bake in an 18 cm square tin for 40 minutes at 190° C. Once it's cool, cut it in half (to make two layers) and sandwitch it wiht buter icing.

It's so easy – I'm sure you'll love it!

Editor's comments

1 It is supposed to be a typical dish.

2 Giving a recipe is not an adequate description.

3 There are punctuation mistakes.

4 Part of the question has not been answered.

5 The contribution is not long enough.

6 Only one dish should be described, not two.

7 The wrong register has been chosen.

8 There are spelling mistakes.

Help with writing tasks

PREPARATION

1 Familiarise yourself with a wide range of types of writing, including advertisements, articles, emails, leaflets, reports, surveys, etc.

2 Practise the language functions which are required in CAE and CPE writing tasks: comparing, describing, giving opinions, giving advice, narrating, persuading, recommending, evaluating, presenting arguments.

3 Practise writing within the word limits.

4 Practise writing without consulting a dictionary (you can't use one in CAE or CPE examinations).

WHEN STARTING TO WRITE

1 If in doubt about which question to choose, go for a topic that appeals to you – you are more likely to produce a good answer.

2 Read the question carefully, and work out a clear and logical plan for your answer, making notes of headings, key ideas and useful phrases.

3 Check who the target reader is: your boss, a magazine editor, your classmates, the general public, your tutor, etc. This will help you to decide which register (formal, informal or neutral) to use.

WHILE WRITING

1 Adopt the most appropriate layout, style and register for the task.

2 Use a separate paragraph to address each point in your answer. Make sure that you devote equal space to each point.

3 Use your own words. Don't lift chunks from the input text.

4 Write straight on to the paper in ink (there isn't time to write a rough draft in pencil first).

5 Link your ideas from one paragraph to another with discourse markers, so that your answer reads smoothly and a reader can follow your argument or train of thought.

6 In an examination, keep a close eye on the time you are allowed, and save time at the end for corrections.

7 Be prepared to describe your personal experiences and express your own opinions, which will make your answer more interesting to read.

8 Don't be afraid of attempting complex structures or using sophisticated vocabulary. You will be given credit for this, even if you make mistakes.

AFTER WRITING

1 Read through your answer and check that it makes good sense.

2 Correct any spelling or grammar mistakes by crossing out once and writing the correction above the word(s).

3 Check that your answer isn't too long (the part beyond the word limit will not be taken into account) or too short (you will be penalised).

4 And finally, ask yourself these questions:
Will my answer have a positive effect on the target reader?
Will the reader get the information that I have been asked to convey?
Have I answered every part of the question?

APPENDIX

1 Verbs which do not usually take the continuous form

dislike, like, hate, love, wish, prefer, want, hear, sound, understand, suppose, remember, recognise, realise, mean, know, imagine, guess, doubt, believe, astonish, satisfy, surprise, please, impress, belong, concern, consist, contain, possess, own, owe, matter, need, depend, deserve, fit, include, involve, lack, appear, resemble, seem

(See Unit 2, Present tenses)

2 Verbs which can be used in simple or continuous tenses, with different meanings

look, see, smell, taste, feel, think, measure, weigh

(See Unit 2, Present tenses)

3 Verbs which are usually followed by a gerund (*-ing* form)

admit, appreciate, avoid, consider, contemplate, delay, deny, detest, dislike, dread, endure, enjoy, escape, excuse, face, fancy, feel like, finish, forgive, give up, can't help, imagine, involve, leave off, mention, mind, miss, postpone, practise, put off, recollect, resent, resist, risk, can't face, can't stand, suggest, understand

(See Unit 7, Gerund and infinitive)

4 Verbs which are usually followed by the infinitive with *to*

want, would like, would prefer, ought, have, be able, appear, seem, decide, attempt, intend, plan, hope, expect, arrange, manage, fail, pretend, dare, afford, tend, teach

(See Unit 7, Gerund and infinitive)

5 Verbs and expressions which can be used with either a gerund or an infinitive, with different meanings

remember, forget, regret doing: a past action or state
• *I'll never forget seeing the World Cup final.*

remember, forget, regret to do: information to be remembered or passed on
• *I regret to inform you ...*

stop/go on doing: stop or continue doing the same action

• *He decided to stop smoking.*

stop/go on to do: the current activity is stopped, and a new one started
• *He stopped to light his cigarette.*
• *She went on to explain how it had happened.*

be interested in doing: keen on (a hobby or an interest)

be interested to do: would like to do
• *I'm interested to know what you thought of the film.*

try doing: use a technique in order to achieve something
• *Try soaking it in salt water to loosen the stain.*

try to do: attempt something, usually unsuccessfully
• *He tried to persuade her to go with him.*

need doing: an object (usually) needs something done to it
• *The house needs painting.*

need to do: a person (usually) needs to do something
• *Gregory needs to find a job.*

be/get used to doing: be or become accustomed to certain actions or situations

used to do: habitual actions in the past, but not now

like/enjoy/love/hate/prefer doing: any action generally liked/enjoyed/hated etc.

would like/enjoy/love/hate/prefer to do: an activity chosen or rejected for a particular occasion

allow/advise/forbid/permit doing: general permission/advice etc.
• *The doctor advises giving up smoking.*

allow/advise/forbid/permit someone to do: permission/advice etc. for a particular person
• *I forbid you to climb that wall.*

mean doing: involve/entail/signify something
• *Love means being able to forgive.*

mean to do: plan/intend an action
• *I didn't mean to hurt you.*

(See Unit 7, Gerund and infinitive)

6 Structures used after reporting verbs

1 verb + *(not)* to do:
• *We refused to have anything to do with the plan.*
• *He threatened not to come.*
promise, agree, refuse, threaten, offer

2 verb + someone + *(not)* to do:

- *He advised her to say nothing about it.*

warn, beg, remind, recommend, tell, persuade, advise, encourage, instruct, order, invite

3 verb + *that* + verb clause:
- *She pointed out that she had been there first.*

claim, state, explain, add, report, boast, complain, point out, agree, confirm, estimate, promise, insist, admit, deny

4 verb + preposition + doing:
- *He insisted on seeing the manager.*

apologise (to someone) for, accuse someone of, insist on, object to someone, congratulate someone on, blame someone for, thank someone for, charge someone with

5 verb + someone *(that)* + verb clause:
- *They assured me that there was nothing to worry about.*

assure, inform, tell

6 verb + doing:
- *He admitted having sent the letter.*

admit, deny, regret

7 *suggest* + doing/*suggest that* someone should do something

(See Unit 11, Reported speech)

7 Adverbs and adjectives used adverbially

(All meanings given below refer to adverbial usage only.)

close (to): near
- *We live very close to the hospital.*

closely: intimately
- *She's closely related to the archbishop.*

direct: without stopping or making a detour
- *We're going direct to Paris.*

directly: a) immediately
- *He'll do the shopping directly.*

b) frankly
- *The producer spoke honestly and directly to the cast about the play's future.*

easy: in a relaxed way
- *Take it easy!*

easily: with no difficulty
- *You can easily go in for that competition.*

fair: according to the rules
- *Play fair!*

fairly: a) justly, honestly, correctly
- *He was fairly judged and punished.*

b) quite, not very
- *It was fairly good weather, but not as good as last week.*

fine: well
- *She's feeling fine now.*

finely: in tiny pieces, in meticulous detail
- *Chop the onions finely.*
- *The lines of the pen-and-ink sketch were finely drawn.*

flat: a) completely, outright
- *They turned me down flat.*

b) lower than the correct musical note
- *She always sings flat.*

c) in an exact or short time
- *He arrived in four minutes flat.*

flatly: a) completely
- *He flatly refused to help me.*

b) in a dull, lifeless way
- *'What's the point?' she asked flatly.*

free: a) without paying
- *He was allowed in free*

b) at liberty
- *They let the dog roam free.*

freely: willingly, as much as desired
- *They partook freely of their hosts' generous hospitality.*

hard: with great energy
- *His father has always worked hard.*

hardly: scarcely, only just
- *You'll hardly have time to get to the bank.*

high: at or to a height
- *She jumped high over the bar.*

highly: to a high degree
- *The professor's work is highly respected at Oxford.*

late: opposite of early
- *They arrived at the meeting very late.*

lately: recently
- *The neighbours have been making a lot of noise lately.*

near: close to
- *Does your boss live anywhere near us?*

nearly: almost
- *They nearly had an accident this morning.*

pretty: quite, fairly
- *They're pretty good at carpentry.*

prettily: nicely, charmingly
- *The little girls were prettily dressed for the party.*

right: correctly (normal adverbial use)
- *Do it right, for heaven's sake!*

rightly: correctly (referring to a whole clause)
- *He had assumed, rightly, that no food would be provided.*

sharp: punctually, on the dot
• *They turned up at ten sharp.*
sharply: brusquely, crossly
• *'Don't do that!' she said sharply.*

short: suddenly, just before the end
• *He stopped short.*
• *She cut him short.* (= she interrupted him)
shortly: soon
• *News of the takeover will be released to the press shortly.*

sound: deeply (with *asleep*)
• *He was sound asleep.*
soundly: deeply, thoroughly
• *He was sleeping soundly.*
• *They were soundly punished.*

tight: in a close, firm way
• *Sit tight.* • *Hold tight.*
tightly: firmly and securely
• *The mast was tightly lashed to the deck.*

wide: a) a long way away, far from the target
• *The parents searched far and wide.*
• *The arrow fell wide of the target.*
b) fully open
• *Open (your mouth) wide!*
c) completely (with *awake*)
• *The children were wide awake.*
widely: in many places, all over the world
• *Those theories are widely accepted.*

(See Unit 14, Adverbs)

8 Prepositional phrases

above
all, average (size/height), -mentioned, suspicion, freezing(-point), zero

over
a cup of tea/coffee/a meal, all ~ the world, and above the call of duty, pull the wool ~ someone's eyes, the odds

beneath
contempt, marry ~ you

below
sea-level, the belt, freezing(-point), zero

under
age, contract, control, guarantee, his/her etc breath, pressure, stress, suspicion, the circumstances

at
all costs, a loose end, a loss, a profit, any rate, best, first, first sight, hand, heart, high speed, large, last, once, peace, present, random, risk, sea, short notice, the beginning, the end, times, war, worst, someone's disposal

by
accident, all means, chance, cheque, day, degrees, far, force, hand, heart, mistake, night, oneself etc, plane/taxi/train etc, post, return, rights, sight, surprise, the way, your own admission

between (usually two people or objects)
you and me, jobs

among (more than two people or objects)
the bushes/trees, themselves, others

in
advance, all likelihood, any case, bed, cash, conclusion, control, danger, debt, detail, doubt, due course, fact, full, future, general, good/bad condition, hand, ink, pain, particular, person, public, reply, retrospect, short, tears, the end, the long run/term, time, trouble

on
a diet, approval, a visit, behalf of, business, call, duty, earth, fire, foot, guard, holiday, horseback, land, offer, your way home, paper, purpose, second thoughts, the contrary, the mend, the other hand, the whole, time, your own, your own admission

out of
breath, control, danger, date, doors, focus, hand, luck, reach, order, pocket, practice, sight, stock, the question, work

(See Unit 21, Prepositions)

9 Adjectives/nouns with dependent prepositions

admiration for
advance on
advantage in/over/to
angry about/at/with
appeal to
attack on
attitude towards
aware of
benefit to
chance of
change in/from
concerned about/in/with
confidence in
confident of
confined to
conscious of
contrary to

convinced of
critical of
crowded with
curious about

damage to
danger of/to
dealings with
death from
delay in
deprived of
deterioration in
developments in
devoted to
difficulty in doing
disappointed at/in/with
disposed towards
doubt about

eligible for
envious of
essential for/to
exception to
expert in/on
faith in
familiar with
famous for
fed up with
foreign to
free from/of
friendly towards
good at/for/with
greedy for
guilty of
habit of
honest with
hope for/of
hungry for
ignorant of
ill (in bed) with
important for/to
impression on
improvement in/on
incapable of
increase in
independent of
indifferent to
indignant at
influence on/over/with
intention of
interested in
involved in
jealous of
keen on
key to
lacking in
likelihood of
limit to
missing from
need for
(be) news to
noted for
obstacle to
occupied with

opinion about/of/on
opportunity of/for doing
opposed to
particular about
patient with
peculiar to
pleasure in
point in
poor in/at
popular with
possibility of
preferable to
pride in
qualified for
question of
reason for
relationship between/
   with
relief from
reputation for
responsible for/to
restricted to
restrictions on/to
result of
revenge for/on
rich in
rise in
safe from
satisfied with
self-sufficient in
sensitive to
solution to
strict about/with
substitute for
success with
superior to
surprised at
suspicious of
sympathetic towards
sympathy for/with
threat of/to
typical of
victory over
views on

(See Unit 24, Dependent prepositions)

10 Verbs with dependent prepositions

accuse someone of
agree on/to/with
allow for
amount to
apologise for
appeal for/to
apply for/to
approve of
attend to

bargain for/with
beat someone at
benefit from
blame someone for, something on
boast about/of

care for
change into
charge someone for/with
cheat someone out of
compete against/with/for/in
compliment someone on
concentrate on
condemn someone to
confess to
confide in
conform to
congratulate someone on
consent to
contribute to(wards)
convince someone of
cure someone of

deal with
decide between/on
declare war on
depend on
deprive someone of
die for/from/of
differ from
disapprove of
discourage someone from

end in/with
enter into (an agreement etc)
equip someone with
excuse someone for/from

feed someone/sth. on
fish for
fit someone/sth. with
fool someone into
force someone into
forgive someone for

grow in/into
guard against

have pity on
have sympathy for
help oneself to
hint at
hold sth. against someone

impress on someone
impress someone with
inform someone of/about
insist on
insure against
interfere in/with
invest in
involve someone/yourself in

keep something to yourself
know of

listen (out) for
live by/for/on/up to

make someone/sth. into
make up your mind about
mean something by
mistake someone/sth. for

object to

part with
plead guilty to
prevent someone/sth. from
profit from
provide for/with
puzzle over

reason with someone
reduce something by, someone/sth. to
resort to
restrict something to
result from/in
rob someone of

sacrifice someone/sth. for/to
seethe with
share something with
show mercy to(wards)
speak of
specialise in
struggle against/with
succeed in
suffer for/from
supply someone with
surrender to
suspect someone of

take advantage of
think about/of
threaten someone with

trust someone with
turn someone/sth. into

warn someone about/against
wait on
watch (out) for
work at a job etc/on a project etc
worry about

(See Unit 24, Dependent prepositions)

11 Article (Unit 82, C)

FITNESS FOR LIFE

In today's health-conscious society, more and more attention is being paid to the benefits of exercise, a balanced diet and a healthy lifestyle. Of course we all want to maintain our fitness throughout our lives. For some, that means a radical change to the habits of a lifetime, while others (the lucky ones!) will merely continue their present healthy lifestyle.

To start with a tough message – habits harmful to health should be controlled. Not only can cigarette smoking cause bronchial disease and lung cancer, but even passive smoking can do the same. Excessive alcohol consumption can cause liver disease, and alcohol is also addictive, so it's better to limit yourself to a 'safe' number of units per week.

We are what we eat, and therefore it is essential to maintain a well-balanced, varied diet. We all know that vitamins provided by fruit and vegetables help to give resistance to infection, while more fibre in the diet makes for better digestion and helps to avoid bowel cancer. In addition, it is important to cut salt and fat intake, in order to reduce the likelihood of heart disease and circulatory problems.

A further factor to consider is stress, which can contribute to heart disease and stress-related disorders such as migraine. People may have to change their lifestyle, if it is producing excessive stress. However, there is a partial solution in the form of physical exercise and relaxation therapy. Exercise can be both enjoyable and healthy, as it controls the appetite, gives a feeling of well-being, reduces susceptibility to disease, and helps to eliminate stress. Many types of relaxation therapy are both popular and effective.

So it seems that no matter how fit we imagine ourselves to be, there's always room for improvement. Cutting nicotine and alcohol intake, establishing a balanced diet, and incorporating both exercise and relaxation into the daily routine would be beneficial for most people.

(318 words)

12 Article (Unit 82, D)

Speaking volumes

My idea of heaven is reading *Far From the Madding Crowd* in a hayfield in summer, with rolling wooded downs around me. Or it might be *A Christmas Carol* in front of an open fire, with the curtains tightly drawn to keep out the cold. You can take a book anywhere with you, to read on the train on the way to work, or at the airport while waiting for your flight, or to sunbathe with on the beach. It is the most portable form of entertainment, and comes in all shapes and sizes. And because you do not have to concentrate all your senses on reading (there is no flickering screen to watch, or disembodied voice to listen to), your surroundings can add to the reading experience. You are almost unconsciously aware of the jolting of the train, or the scent of wild flowers, or the warmth of the sun on your skin. This gives an extra dimension to your reading, and you may in future associate butterflies with *Nineteen Eighty-Four,* or the smell of Ambre Solaire with *War and Peace,* or freshly ground coffee with *The Hound of the Baskervilles.*

Radio and television have their place as purveyors of current affairs, international events, educational information and light entertainment, but for me books are simply a source of endless delight. Who can read of the deaths of famous literary characters such as Sydney Carton, Piggy, Lord Jim or Heathcliff without emotion? Only the written word has the power to inspire as well as to move.

(259 words)

13 Report (Unit 83, B)

Report on LinguaShow Conference

Where, when and why

This report is intended to summarise my feedback from the 15th annual LinguaShow Conference, which took place in Aberdeen from 8th – 11th April. I attended as a delegate to help the company keep abreast of developments in teaching methodology, and in order to make recommendations for implementation in our many language schools around the world.

Positive aspects

It was extremely useful being able to sit in on seminars and workshops led by some of the best-known language practitioners in the world. The huge variety of sessions available had to be seen to be believed. In addition, the conference provided excellent opportunities for networking.

Negative aspects

At peak times, the refreshment facilities were overstretched and had difficulty in coping with the large numbers of delegates. It was often hard to find a quiet space for a conversation, or to mull over what had been said.

Recommendations

It is clearly crucial for our language schools to keep up with teaching innovations. It is recommended that, as a matter of urgency, we investigate the feasibility of installing interactive whiteboards in every classroom, and ensuring that staff are fully trained in how best to use them.

Conclusion

It is interesting to note that there is now interactive web coverage of parts of the conference. However, on balance I think it is far more beneficial to the company to send a delegate in person. Attending the conference is an immensely valuable experience.

(247 words)

14 Proposal (Unit 84, B)

Changes to the office timetable

The proposed scheme

The proposal for a flexible working timetable has been considered by the entire staff, and approved by almost all personnel. Only the receptionist (MW) is not in favour, but this may not affect the success of the scheme, as she will almost certainly have to maintain her normal 9 to 5 working day in any case.

Core time

The Design Department (JA and MS) suggest a core time of 10 to 2. They envisage working from 8 to 4 if the scheme is introduced. However, the Accounts Department (JG, RN and SB) propose a longer core time of 9.30 to 3. They also point out that it is essential for cover to be provided in each department for the whole working day.

Negative feedback

The Marketing Department (PH and AV) have reservations about the scheme because of the impact it may have on customers. Nevertheless, they would personally welcome flexitime.

Recommendation

As there are so few objections, I recommend that a core time should be fixed, and the scheme tried out on a experimental basis for one month, to be reviewed after that time.

(192 words)

15 Information sheet (Unit 85, A)

First Aid? Why do I need it?

It could be *your* loved one who needs your help.

Don't you think you owe it to them to get some basic know-how?

Don't worry if you know nothing about first aid.

In only two hours the Heartbeat course will show you how to

- deal with someone who's choking
- deal with someone who's unconscious
- control serious bleeding
- check if someone is breathing
- recognise a heart attack
- check if the heart has stopped
- deal with a person whose heart has stopped.

So what should you do next?

Well, our highly trained professional paramedics are leading the next public training session in April. Phone 676444 now to book your place on our course. You won't regret it. You might even save a life. Wouldn't that be worth a couple of hours of your time?

(194 words)

16 Essay (Unit 86, C)

Both texts deal with the issue of whether people should eat meat or not. The first text presents a forceful case against meat-eating, claiming that our methods of farming and killing livestock are cruel and inhumane, and that animals do feel pain, however much we might like to ignore the fact. Humans are seen as grasping and mercenary, making use of animals for profit; the text urges us to turn vegetarian in order to allow animals a more comfortable existence.

The second text maintains that the human body is designed to digest all types of food, not just vegetables, and that meat is a valuable, even necessary food for us. Interestingly, this text also takes a very negative view of intensive farming practices, not from the perspective of animal welfare, as the first text does, but from the 'green'

angle. Individual consumers are encouraged to buy their meat only from farmers with a more traditional, ethical approach, who rear their animals outside and feed them on grass.

I agree that we should not keep animals in unpleasant conditions or cause them unnecessary pain. Personally I am not in favour of raising livestock for meat; I am a vegetarian, and I believe that every life-form is entitled to a decent, dignified life and death. Moreover, there are implications for the planet if we continue to use so much land for livestock, when we could produce far greater quantities of cereals in the same space. However, if people find it hard to give up meat, I think it is important for them to source it from environmentally friendly farmers, who seem likely to have more respect for the animals in their care.

(280 words)

17 Contribution to a longer piece (Unit 90, B)

The thing I remember best about my childhood was going to visit my grandmother, which we did every summer holiday. She lived about six hours' drive away from us, so you can imagine the fuss and commotion as the five of us packed the car to the roof and clambered in. That long journey seemed to last for ever, but we forgot all about it as soon as we arrived. She'd come to the door to greet us, saying, 'You're here! You're here!' as if she could hardly believe it.

The reason I remember it so well is that we never had such fun anywhere else as at Grandma's. She had a huge, overgrown garden we could run wild in, with an ancient plum tree to climb and a rustic summerhouse to play in. And when we came in for supper in the early evening, you wouldn't believe how much food she had ready for us. She must have thought we needed feeding up!

I'm determined to hold on to memories of my childhood like this one. Why is this important for me? Because when I look back, I see it as a golden time. If you're lucky enough to have had a happy childhood, I think it gives you a certain confidence and the ability to make other people happy.

(222 words)

KEY

Unit 1

A 1 The, –
2 –, –, the
3 the, the, a
4 the, a, a, –, a
5 –, –, –, a, the, –
6 –, –, a, a, the
7 a, an
8 a, –
9 –, –, –
10 a

B 1 the Himalayas
2 ✓
3 the Lake District
4 ✓
5 to Kathmandu
6 the Annapurna region, the Nepalese
7 ✓
8 The group leader, the River Trisuli
9 the world's, of Mount Everest
10 the group, simple village rooms, the Nepalese
11 the group, the Himalayas
12 the most exciting, to Nepal, the very first

C 1C 2U 3U 4C 5U 6U, C 7C 8U

D 1D 2E 3B 4G 5F 6I 7A 8H 9J 10C

Unit 2

A 1i 2g 3h 4a 5d 6c 7b 8e 9d 10f 11i 12c 13a 14d 15g 16f

B 1 ✓
2 ✓
3 ✓
4 Do you understand what the lecturer said?
5 I think that they made a mistake.
6 ✓
7 The police don't know why he came here.

8 ✓
9 ✓
10 He's commuting to Paris every day this week.

C 1 You look very worried. What are you thinking about?
2 Listen, he's climbing the stairs! What's he doing now? He's ringing the bell!
3 Thank goodness Barbara is taking more exercise these days! She seems much fitter, don't you think?
4 When water boils, it gives off steam.
5 Alex never breaks a promise or lets down a friend.
6 The house stands on its own, on a hill that overlooks the park.
7 I know her husband is looking for a new job at the moment, but I don't suppose he will find one quickly.
8 When you heat the pan, the fat begins to sizzle.
9 The Foreign Ministers of several EU countries are currently meeting in Luxembourg, where they are attempting to negotiate a solution.
10 He's always spilling coffee on his shirt! It makes me furious!
11 At weekends she frequently drives up to her mother's in Liverpool, and spends an evening with her sister on the way back.
12 I'm a bit worried about Greg. He's working too hard in his present job. He really needs a holiday.

D 1 I have been studying English here since August.
2 ✓
3 We met several fascinating people at the conference last week.

4 Once upon a time a beautiful princess lived in a castle ...
5 ✓
6 I've owned this answerphone for three years.
7 They haven't sold all the tickets for the Cup Final yet.
8 My friends have been married for a long time now.
9 ✓
10 A light plane has crashed in the French Alps.
11 I've already spoken to the delegates three times.
12 ✓

E 1 I haven't had time to do any typing since Monday.
2 Nobody has heard from Amanda since she went to the Seychelles.
3 She's worn/been wearing the same old clothes for a week.
4 He hasn't ridden a bike since 1970.
5 I don't think I've seen you since the sales conference.
6 It hasn't snowed here for ages.
7 They've lived/been living in that house since it was built.
8 My neighbour hasn't spoken to me for more than two years.
9 I haven't bought a new battery since last year.
10 She's been waiting for you for an hour and a half.

Unit 3

A 1 dare   5 be able
2 should   6 have
3 used   7 ought
4 May   8 will

B 1 Did you have to ...?
2 ... ought to have given you ...

3 The President can't be
re-elected for a fourth term.

4 ✓

5 I might have returned the
book.

6 Will you be able to help me ...?

7 They couldn't have a picnic
because of ...

8 ✓

C 1 needn't
2 has to
3 must
4 have to
5 had to
6 didn't need to
7 needn't have bothered
8 mustn't

D 1d 2e 3d 4f 5c 6a 7d 8f

E 1D 2G 3A 4C 5H 6E 7B 8F

F 1 couldn't   5 couldn't
2 would   6 were able to
3 could   7 could
4 used to

G 1 can we?
2 oughtn't I?
3 will/won't you?
4 wouldn't you?
5 mustn't he?
6 mightn't it?
7 didn't they?
8 will you?
9 shall we?
10 don't you?
11 had I?
12 couldn't we?

Unit 4

A 1B 2A 3C 4E 5F 6D

B 1 won't
2 'll/will, ✓
3 Shall
4 will, ✓
5 will

6 Shall
7 won't
8 ✓, ✓
9 ✓, 'll

C 1 ✔
2 'What are you doing/going
to do tonight?' 'Oh, we're
having a barbecue.'
3 By this time next week I'll
have filled in my tax forms.
4 I promise I'll support you
whenever you need me.
5 You won't see him this
summer. He'll be doing his
military service then.
6 I'm going to be an architect
when I finish my studies.
7 ✓
8 Will you come/Are you
coming to dinner with me
tonight?
9 I think he'll/he will probably
marry the girl next door.
10 What will you be doing
at 3 o'clock next Sunday
afternoon?

D 1 If you don't object, we'll ask
the committee to approve
the proposal.
2 By the time Juan finishes/
has finished his maths
project next week, he'll be
exhausted!
3 What will our world be like
in the year 2050?
4 Anne won't be happy until
she sees/has seen the doctor
this afternoon.
5 This time next year I'll
probably be living on the
other side of the world.
6 I'm not going to watch
the horror film that's on
tonight. I know it will give
me nightmares.
7 By the end of this week
we'll have raised over £800
for the children's charity.
8 I swear I'll do my best from
now on. Things will be
different, you'll see.

Unit 5

A 1b 2a 3d 4b 5d 6a 7b 8d
9c 10a 11a 12b 13d 14a 15b
16c 17d 18b 19a 20c 21d
22b 23c

B 1 taste   5 article
2 touch   6 turned
3 dare   7 pressed
4 heavy   8 hold

C 1 has
2 been
3 the
4 as
5 to
6 an
7 the
8 its/a
9 will/may
10 has
11 a
12 the
13 is
14 may/could
15 in
16 which/that
17 If
18 surround
19 continuing
20 have

D 1 can   6 to   11 are
2 a   7 the   12 ✔
3 do   8 being   13 be
4 from   9 should   14 are
5 ✔   10 ✔   15 ✔

Unit 6

A 1 had received/had been
receiving, told
2 made, had been
3 had tried, met, fell in love
4 found, wanted, had
graduated
5 (had) asked, was not, had
gone
6 arrived, realised, was still
breathing

7 spent, had finished

8 hit, were playing, were having

9 was raining, beginning, set out

10 was, wanted

11 recognised, had been

12 opened, felt, had been ringing

13 went back, were still quarrelling

14 did not answer, was trying

15 did you get

16 (had) worked, moved

B 1 My aunt (had) worked in London before she moved to Norwich.

2 ✓

3 ✓

4 The judge brought the trial to an end yesterday.

5 ✓

6 Pierre owned a sailing boat for several years.

7 The company were thinking of giving ...

8 ✓

9 ... just before the British team arrived.

10 A police car almost knocked me over as I crossed/was crossing the road.

11 ✓

12 'Oh, a group of students who arrived in Oxford a week ago.'

13 ✓

14 ✓

15 The mountain seemed very high ...

C 1 defeated

2 killed

3 was

4 had been

5 were

6 aimed

7 were

8 was

9 had murdered

10 disappeared

11 were

12 was

13 had had

14 had seized

15 (had) wanted

16 was

17 had arranged

18 succeeded

D 1C 2E 3G 4J 5F 6I 7B 8A 9D 10H

Unit 7

A 1 Taking regular exercise ...

2 I don't mind being interviewed ...

3 ✓

4 ✓

5 ✓

6 You can go sightseeing ...

7 In addition to losing all my money ...

8 ✓

9 It's no use telling me ...

10 ✓

11 Most cats enjoy being stroked.

12 I'm afraid I just can't face going into the witness box and telling ...

B 1 They didn't ask me to leave early.

2 The army made him complete his training course.

3 ✓

4 Try not to keep interrupting the speaker this time.

5 ✓

6 ✓

7 ✓

8 In my view parents should not let their children watch too much television.

9 He enrolled at a language school in Pisa to learn basic Italian.

10 ✓

11 She didn't want you to go to all this trouble for her.

12 ✓

C 1 being

2 to enter

3 to know

4 seeing

5 to reduce

6 reviewing

7 to stir up

8 being, going

D 1C 2B 3C 4D 5A 6A 7A 8B 9D 10D 11A 12A 13A

Unit 8

A 1 make

2 hadn't eaten

3 have

4 had been

5 is

6 take

7 leave

8 asked

9 had dropped

10 were

11 would have been/would be

12 are

13 Were

14 happens

15 broke down

16 like

B 1 ... go on defying instructions, there will be/we will take ...

2 ... to change your mind, we would be ...

3 ... turn out to be true, I'll hand ...

4 ... passes the final examination, he'll be ...

5 ... had been muzzled, it wouldn't/couldn't have bitten ...

6 ... been presented, the prisoner might/would have been ...

C 1D 2E 3B 4A 5C 6G 7F 8H

D 1 come
2 had just landed
3 didn't agree
4 are
5 end up
6 had spotted
7 receive
8 hadn't gone
9 hadn't come
10 weren't
11 hadn't heard
12 find

E 1 I wish he weren't/wasn't so boring.
2 I wish I hadn't accepted that job.
3 I wish they hadn't all heard about it.
4 I wish I had shares in the company.
5 I wish he would contribute his opinions more tactfully.
6 I wish I had gone to the conference.
7 I wish I could remember Myra's address.
8 I wish it would stop snowing.

Unit 9

A 1 was originally used
2 being put
3 is known
4 was/has been successfully deployed
5 is involved
6 be laid out
7 was ended
8 were punctured
9 has been established
10 be caught

B 1 were/had been found
2 were/had been discovered
3 were pronounced
4 were only made
5 be carried out
6 were nevertheless thrown
7 was arranged

8 were published
9 were/had been composed
10 be regarded

C 1 ✓
2 The whole community was/were told the news.
3 ✓
4 ✓
5 I have been given a lucky mascot ...
6 She will be awarded a postgraduate diploma ...
7 He is being refused a chance to participate ...
8 ✓
9 ✓
10 The officials in charge of the institution at the time seem to have been offered a bribe.

D 1 ... are expected to be announced ...
2 ... are understood to be going up ...
3 ... is said to have had ...
4 ... are feared (to have been) lost ...
5 ... was considered/thought/judged to be ...
6 ... cannot be denied/is true/is undeniable that mistakes were ...
7 ... was reported to have been helping ...
8 ... was alleged that the accused had ...

E 1 put away
2 slept in
3 ✓
4 put off
5 ✓
6 brought up
7 made out
8 taken down

Unit 10

A 1a 2c 3b 4c 5d 6b 7c 8a 9c
10b 11d 12c 13b 14d 15a
16c 17b 18c 19b 20a 21d 22c

B 1 see   4 catch
2 free   5 form
3 reach   6 threw

C 1 the
2 were
3 order
4 being
5 was/became
6 should
7 to
8 did (were/was)
9 succeed (successful)
10 would
11 A
12 with/involving
13 one
14 The/This
15 solved/resolved
16 would/could
17 were
18 for
19 All
20 towards

D 1 survivors
2 fascinating
3 treatment
4 dangerously
5 natural
6 unscientific
7 Eventually
8 recovery
9 appreciative
10 prescription

Unit 11

A 1D 2B 3A 4H 5C 6E 7G 8I
9J 10F

B 1 She boasted (that) she had had better marks than anyone else all term.
2 She accused me of stealing her watch.
3 She threatened to hit me if I didn't give her my money.

4 She apologised for not getting round/not having got round to writing earlier.

5 She suggested (that) we should all go for a drive in the country/going for a drive in the country.

6 She insisted on seeing the manager at once.

7 She begged me not to tell anyone I had/I'd seen her.

8 She confirmed (that) my flight was taking off at midnight.

9 She reminded me to bring the binoculars.

10 She estimated that Mexico City had about 20 million inhabitants.

C 1I 2L 3A 4K 5J 6H 7C 8F 9D 10G 11B 12E

D 1 He pointed out that it was already five o'clock.

2 He agreed to help.

3 He assured me (that) there would be no difficulty.

4 He thanked me for bringing the flowers.

5 He advised me to keep it under my hat.

6 He added (that) there would be a 2% surcharge.

7 He denied robbing/having robbed the old lady.

8 He refused to make a speech.

9 He warned me to be careful when I crossed the road.

10 He congratulated me on passing the test first time.

11 He blamed Charlotte for letting them down.

12 He admitted causing/having caused/(that) he had caused the accident.

E 1 She said that if she had known, she would have come earlier.

2 He said that unless John told the truth, somebody would get hurt.

3 She said (that) she really thought (that) I should join the tennis club that summer.

4 Her teacher said that if she practised more, she might be able to make a career out of music.

5 He said that he wouldn't have had the accident if the brakes had been repaired properly.

6 The magistrate said (that) he would be sent to prison if he committed a further offence.

7 He said (that) I could stay there as long as I liked.

8 Maggie said (that) she wished Bob would buy himself a new suit.

F 1 I asked how far it was to the station.

2 ✓

3 She asked me if I could do the shopping for her.

4 Her father asked if what she had told him was true.

5 ✓

6 The traffic warden asked why I had parked there.

7 I asked the old man what his recipe for long life was.

8 We wondered how our neighbours managed to keep their garden so neat.

9 The officials asked him what he wanted.

10 ✓

G 1A 2C 3E 4H 5B 6D 7F 8G

H 1 ... congratulated me on passing ...

2 ... apologised for forgetting to ...

3 ... (that) Jim should put off his ...

4 ... me to put/enclose a cheque in ...

5 ... me to run through my speech ...

Unit 12

A 1 In spite of revising/having revised/ In spite of the fact that he (had) revised hard for his exams, he didn't pass.

2 ✓

3 All the same, he doesn't know what he's talking about.

4 ✓

5 ✓

6 ✓

7 ✓

8 Quiet though this spot seems now, ...

9 'Try a bit harder!' 'But I don't want to!'

10 ✓

11 In spite of/Despite your lack of agreement, ...

12 Even though his creditors are baying for satisfaction, ...

B 1 aware
2 Deprived
3 Alone
4 Because
5 Sad
6 for
7 Surprised
8 Told
9 Horrified
10 Due
11 Embarrassed
12 Disgusted

C 1 The matter is important enough for you to deal with yourself.

2 She didn't study enough to pass the end-of-term test.

3 The door was too narrow for us to squeeze through/ wasn't wide enough for us to squeeze through.

4 She had too little energy/ She didn't have enough energy to keep going all day.

5 The leisure centre is too inaccessible/isn't accessible enough for tourists to find.

D 1 They had so little money (that) they couldn't afford to run a car.

2 There was such a lot of food (that) we could have fed ten hungry men with it!

3 You're such an experienced worker (that) you should know what to do.

4 He has had so little acting experience that we can't give him the part.

5 I draw so badly that I can't do a very good sketch map.

E 1 ever needed/should ever need

2 see

3 is

4 has got lost

5 spots, tries

6 was selected

7 don't get

F 1 the undersigned

2 are as follows

3 respectively

4 The former

5 The latter

6 In terms

7 aforementioned

8 hitherto

9 the above address

10 twice

11 Gourlays

12 Merryford

13 a complaint about the closure of a village bank and a request for the bank to reconsider its decision

14 the undersigned, the former, the latter, the aforementioned, hitherto

Unit 13

A 1 There's the woman who sold me the oranges.

2 This is my brother, whose wife's French.

3 ✓

4 I don't like people who talk too loudly.

5 ✓

6 I know a little taverna where you can get a wonderful meal.

7 ✓

8 I suppose that's the house where we'll have to stay.

9 ✓

10 ✓

11 What I can't stand is queuing in the rain.

12 Have you any idea who I'll be speaking to?

13 Is that the school where/ at which you studied/which you studied at?

14 Deirdre will show the new students what to do.

15 You'd better tell me the reason why he didn't turn up.

16 That's the old chap (who) ...

17 ✓

18 ✓

B 1a She was only interested in going to Strasbourg, and let other trains pass until the Strasbourg train arrived.

1b She took the first train to arrive. It happened to be going to Strasbourg.

2a Everybody was caught unawares because they hadn't seen the forecast.

2b Only some people (the ones who hadn't seen the forecast) were caught unawares.

3a All the food was bad, so we couldn't eat it.

3b Some of the food was bad, so we couldn't eat that part.

4a I only have one cousin. He/ She happens to live in New Zealand.

4b I have several cousins. One of them lives in New Zealand.

5a They only picked some of the fruit – the fruit that had ripened.

5b They picked all the fruit. By the way, it had all ripened.

C 1 The bus that goes up Edward Avenue doesn't stop at the railway station.

2 The debate the backbenchers had demanded went on all night.

3 The escaped convicts stashed away the gold bars they had stolen in an earlier bank raid.

4 It was the dream cottage she had always wanted.

5 They booked into the hotel where they had stayed on their honeymoon.

6 The bodyguards who were flanking the King had revolvers concealed inside their jackets.

7 It wasn't their dog but their cat I was taking care of.

8 They cut down the tree that had died.

9 That's the cruise I've always wanted to go on.

10 I think it was the manager I was speaking to.

D 1 It's the tallest building I've ever seen.

2 ✓

3 ✓

4 ✓

5 He'll be playing with the same racquet he always plays with.

6 Next Tuesday I'll have to visit the dentist again, which I detest.

E 1 She had invited a hundred guests, none of whom I knew.

2 Growling in the corner were two big dogs, both of which looked extremely dangerous.

3 The manager called in my new colleagues, one or two of whom I had met already.

4 There were several large holes in the road, three of which had to be repaired urgently.

5 There were some vegetables left over, a few of which I was able to use in some soup for supper.

6 The talk was attended by over two hundred delegates, most of whom took notes.

7 The researchers reported back on the questionnaires, the most interesting of which showed a marked change in leisure habits among older people.

8 He comes from a large family, all of whom now live in Australia.

Unit 14

A 1 gracefully
2 well
3 importantly
4 fully
5 straight
6 hard
7 heavily
8 cruelly
9 timidly
10 illegally
11 inevitably
12 fast
13 noisily
14 in a jolly way
15 increasingly

B 1 Tomorrow the boss is having a day off/The boss is having a day off tomorrow.
2 She likes watching videos at home very much/She very much likes ...
3 ✓
4 ✓
5 Yesterday they mowed their lawn/They mowed their lawn yesterday.
6 ✓
7 Suddenly he slammed the book down on the table.
8 Alma stamped out of the office angrily/Alma stamped angrily out of the office.
9 I always make sure I do my homework every day.

10 We frequently go for a picnic in the forest.
11 The foreman always gives the workmen a ticking off.
12 ✓

C 1 With hindsight/In retrospect
2 in the wake of
3 by ... %
4 in monthly instalments
5 Without more/further ado
6 at the expense of
7 With reference to
8 by no means

D 1 at the end
2 eventually
3 at the beginning
4 actually
5 at last
6 finally

E 1 close   11 free
2 easy   12 fair
3 finely   13 flat
4 pretty   14 direct
5 shortly   15 late
6 tight   16 flatly
7 highly   17 sound
8 hard   18 short
9 widely   19 nearly
10 sharp   20 right

Unit 15

A 1a 2b 3c 4a 5c 6d 7b 8c 9c 10d 11c 12d 13b 14a 15c 16c 17a 18b

B c, e, a, d, b

C 1 ... being blamed for ...
2 ... causing/having caused harm to ...
3 ... a shortage of ammunition, the battle was won ...
4 ... your scheme is, it is doomed to ...
5 ... enjoy/like her company, I find her/I think she's ...

6 ... is rumoured to be planning ...
7 ... were awarded without more ...
8 ... cut me short/cut in halfway ...

D 1 by
2 may/might/could
3 which
4 have
5 which/that
6 they
7 Recently/Newly
8 to
9 order/detail
10 could
11 producing
12 could
13 which/that
14 spreading/transmitting
15 wake/light
16 is
17 will/may

E 1 what
2 where/because
3 whom
4 While/Whilst/Whereas
5 who
6 Provided/Providing
7 however
8 as/when/whenever
9 or
10 well

Unit 16

A 1 Seldom had they participated in such a fascinating ceremony.
2 In vain did I plead with him. He was adamant.
3 Under no circumstances will Miss Weaver be offered the job.
4 Should the film be a box-office success, there may be a sequel.
5 So surprised was he to be addressed by the Queen that he didn't answer at once.

6 Had they confirmed by phone, the airline could have warned them.

7 Hardly had he entered the house when the police arrested him.

8 Never for one moment did I think the consequences would be so far-reaching.

9 Rarely has she travelled more than fifty miles from her village.

10 On no account must you lift heavy weights like that again.

11 Scarcely had I put the phone down when it rang again.

12 In no way did the defendant express his misgivings.

13 So difficult was the task that expert assistance was required.

14 Had they accepted our offer, we would have moved house by now.

B 1C 2E 3B 4A 5D

C 1 Over I fell, and broke my leg.

2 'So would I.'

3 Not only did she twist her ankle, but she also dropped her purse.

4 ✓

5 ✓

6 ✓

7 Up the stairs puffed the plump old housekeeper.

8 ✓

9 Right through the underwater tunnel she swam.

10 ✓

11 ✓

12 There stands the famous statue of Admiral Lord Nelson.

13 Only last week did I find the information I'd been looking for.

14 Here come the police! Someone must have called them.

D 1 ... is it worth giving his suggestion any ...

2 ... was his disgust at her behaviour that ...

3 ... hard Adele tries, she gets ...

4 ... did the volunteers attempt to ...

5 ... was I ever shown how to make ...

6 ... before had such a lavish celebration/such lavish celebrations been ...

7 ... did the minister admit to an error ...

8 ... you wish to accept the offer, put a ...

9 ... may have to be turned ...

10 ... had the date been chosen when/before the ...

11 ... than four helpers are needed to enable ...

12 ... been for his father's advice, he might be ...

13 ... a full bonus would satisfy ...

14 ... should/must this computer data be revealed ...

Unit 17

A 1 like
2 As
3 As
4 as
5 like
6 as
7 as
8 as
9 as
10 As
11 as
12 like
13 Like
14 like
15 Like

B 1 She's nothing like as good at tennis as her friend.

2 ✓

3 Have as many potatoes as you like.

4 His hand is as steady as a rock.

5 ✓

6 ✓

7 ✓

8 ✓

9 The dictionary wasn't nearly as helpful as I had hoped.

10 ✓

11 Laurie drank half as much beer as Hugo.

12 Their offer is every bit as acceptable as yours.

C 1 That's the same formula (that) ...

2 ✓

3 ✓

4 That's the same man that ...

5 ✓

6 The rules are the same (as) in my country.

7 ✓

8 Did you pay the same as I did?

D 1 The more you work, the more money you earn.

2 The more difficult it is, the harder he tries.

3 He's been working longer than you.

4 This meat's tougher than yesterday's.

5 ✓

6 You're the most infuriating person I've ever met.

7 He's by far the best boxer in the world.

8 ✓

9 My cousin is much/far/a lot taller than me.

10 ✓

11 I think the driver is a bit tireder/more tired than me.

12 ✓

13 The more, the merrier.

14 ✓

15 It was the dreariest hotel I'd ever had the misfortune to stay in.

16 That one's the slowest train.

17 ✓

18 Your work's more impressive than anyone else's.

19 ✓

20 ✓

Unit 18

A 1 Having
2 annoyed/shocked
3 exciting/interesting/gripping
4 broken
5 Supposing
6 Feeling/Being
7 asking/enquiring
8 Having
9 Taking
10 bored
11 carrying/bearing/bringing
12 Being/Feeling
13 Coming
14 Judging
15 looking/feeling, smoking

B 1 close
2 repairing
3 cooking
4 bang
5 standing
6 well
7 throw
8 open, take

C 1 Once
2 since
3 When
4 After
5 On
6 as

D 1 When I booked a room for myself and my wife ...
2 Looking at my diary, I saw (that) there were several double-booked appointments.
3 ✓
4 I hope you've mentioned this to the people concerned in the matter.
5 As I had not written about the required topic ...
6 ✓
7 While I was working in California ...
8 As it was such a sunny day ...
9 ✓
10 Do you know anyone who's been to the Canary Islands?
11 ✓
12 ✓
13 ✓
14 Once he was ensconced in his comfortable armchair ...

Unit 19

A 1 asleep
2 alone
3 frightened
7 live
8 open
4 blazing
5 awake
6 burning
9 afloat

B 1 pale
2 ✓
3 ✓
4 ✓
5 ✓
6 angry
7 ✓
8 ✓
9 ✓
10 unconscious

C 1 for the disabled.
2 a two-hour lecture.
3 for the blind.
4 ✓
5 ✓
6 The French negotiated with the Spanish ...

D 1 I saw a sweet little green silk scarf.
2 There was a huge mediaeval stone castle on the hill.
3 A beautiful white sailing ship was moored at the quay.
4 There is a battered old leather suitcase on the table.
5 They live in an ancient fisherman's cottage by the sea.
6 She was carrying a heavy striped canvas shopping bag full of vegetables on her arm.
7 She was introduced to a remarkably handsome young executive.
8 He was wearing a smart grey business suit with a jazzy waistcoat.
9 She only makes cakes with the best unsalted Danish butter.
10 He has just bought an extremely exotic oriental carpet.

E 1H 2O 3B 4J 5A 6D 7K 8F
9L 10E 11G 12M 13N 14C
15I

F 1 blatant
2 insatiable
3 abortive
4 fierce
5 mere
6 gruelling
7 innovative
8 heinous
9 burgeoning
10 sworn
11 dire
12 lucrative
13 contemporary
14 primary
15 first-hand

Unit 20

A 1b 2b 3b 4a 5c 6d 7c 8c 9a
10c 11c 12c 13a 14d 15a
16b 17a 18b 19d 20c

B 1D 2C 3B 4B 5A 6C 7D 8A
9B 10D 11C 12A

C 1 until/before
2 directives/laws
3 another
4 who
5 as
6 provided
7 have
8 which
9 By
10 chance/opportunity
11 such
12 without
13 increasingly/extremely/very/too
14 focus/area

D 1 first-hand
2 disregard
3 assumption
4 household
5 uproar
6 respective
7 apologise
8 carefree
9 overwork
10 despite

Unit 21

A
1 under age
2 above suspicion
3 under guarantee
4 under control
5 above-average height
6 Above all
7 below the belt
8 under contract
9 under his breath
10 beneath contempt
11 above-mentioned
12 below zero/below freezing (-point)
13 over a (cup of) coffee
14 over the world
15 below sea level
16 under stress/pressure
17 over my eyes
18 over the odds

B 1H 2E 3N 4P 5A 6G 7C 8J 9M 10O 11F 12D 13K 14I 15L 16B

C
1 out of
2 Between
3 out of
4 between
5 among
6 out of
7 over
8 out of
9 among
10 between
11 out of
12 over
13 out of
14 among
15 out of
16 out of
17 among
18 out of
19 out of
20 out of

D
1 On
2 by
3 in
4 by
5 on
6 In
7 by
8 on
9 in
10 on
11 by

E
1 On
2 By
3 in
4 in
5 in
6 in/during
7 at
8 on
9 with
10 by
11 with
12 by
13 of
14 In
15 in

Unit 22

A
1 doing
2 makes
3 make
4 done
5 make
6 do
7 do
8 makes
9 made
10 doing
11 do
12 make
13 making
14 do
15 making
16 does
17 do
18 making
19 make
20 do

B
1 told
2 talked
3 said
4 tell
5 speak
6 Tell, say
7 tells
8 talking
9 speaking
10 said
11 tell
12 say
13 told
14 tell
15 say
16 speak

C
1 rise
2 ✓
3 risen
4 ✓
5 ✓
6 ✓
7 ✓
8 arise
9 rise
10 ✓

D
1 laid
2 lain
3 laid
4 laying
5 lying
6 lying
7 laid
8 lay
9 lay
10 laying
11 lies
12 laid
13 lies
14 lies

Unit 23

A 1E 2I 3J 4H 5A 6B 7D 8C 9G 10F

B
1 The prisoner gave an honest answer to the question/was honest in answering the question.
2 He is reputed to have been born in Segovia.
3 We were about to finish/ We had just about finished when Isabel arrived.
4 Their recent behaviour has been very strange.
5 His medical treatment appears to have seriously affected his mental state.
6 On his arrival at the stage door, the star was (immediately) surrounded by screaming fans.
7 The staff have always held the headmaster in very high esteem.
8 The electrician's advice (to me) was to have the wiring checked.
9 The guided tour takes place at hourly intervals.
10 By/On her own admission, she is rather selfish.

C 1F 2J 3I 4A 5D 6B 7C 8E 9H 10G

D
1 She is by no means a good cook.
2 I was unaware (that) it was a breach of protocol.
3 The store should definitely refund (you) your money/ give you a refund.
4 The castle made a great/a big/the greatest/the biggest impact on the tourists.
5 Building societies will not be able to rest on their laurels.
6 They're on the horns of a dilemma.
7 Taxpayers had to foot the bill for the privatisation plan.
8 I did my utmost to expedite the matter.
9 Juliet could only long for his return.
10 By the time we all sat down to dinner, there was still no sign of the Morrises.
11 I think you've got the wrong end of the stick.
12 Thanks to Gerry's advice, the firm didn't go bankrupt.
13 A relaxing break would do you good/It would do you good to have a relaxing break.
14 With the advent of the assembly line, five hundred workers were dismissed.

15 It came as a shock to his colleagues to hear of Ahmed's illness/The news of Ahmed's illness came as a shock to his colleagues.

16 Alan does nothing but complain (all the time).

17 She stands a good chance of winning first prize.

18 The policeman drew our attention to the speed limit sign.

E 1 exclusive
2 household
3 lacked
4 quandary
5 deadlock
6 grain
7 shed
8 justice
9 economical
10 tendency

Unit 24

A 1 for
2 in
3 of
4 to
5 from
6 about
7 in
8 of
9 in
10 with
11 to
12 of
13 of
14 in
15 in
16 of
17 in
18 for
19 of
20 for
21 in
22 of
23 of
24 of
25 in

B 1 apologise
2 worry
3 to
4 on
5 keep
6 depends
7 insist
8 for
9 applied
10 hold
11 for
12 in
13 to
14 in
15 with

C 1G 2H 3J 4I 5F 6B 7C 8A 9E 10D

D 1 about
2 doubt
3 for
4 in
5 for

6 responsible
7 in
8 in
9 working/concentrating
10 in
11 with
12 of
13 suspected/accused/guilty
14 damage

Unit 25

A 1a 2b 3c 4b 5b 6d 7c 8b 9a 10d 11b 12d 13a 14d 15a 16b 17b 18a 19d 20b 21a 22c 23b 24a 25c

B 1 ... lacked in numbers, they made up for ...
2 ... no difference of opinion between ...
3 ... was left to foot ...
4 ... own admission, he (has) ...
5 ... point (in) shedding tears ...
6 ... bore/took the brunt of ...
7 ... nothing but sit in the office ...

C 1 of
2 was
3 the
4 which
5 by
6 had
7 than
8 For
9 over
10 to
11 has
12 which
13 as
14 the
15 that/the
16 leading
17 were
18 so
19 be
20 lies/waits/is

D 1 resignation
2 breakdown
3 application
4 utmost
5 strength
6 indecisive
7 achievement
8 conclusion(s)
9 widespread
10 molehill

Unit 26

A 1 sat down
2 closed down
3 going/coming down
4 broke down
5 pouring/pelting down
6 slammed the book down
7 play down
8 put down
9 fell down
10 got me down
11 calmed down
12 tore down the notice from/ tore the notice down from

B 1 slow
2 pull/tear
3 squatted
4 blew/tore
5 tone
6 marked
7 narrowed
8 tracked
9 bring
10 cut
11 tumble
12 noted

C 1 Family traditions have been handed down through the centuries.
2 Jeremy is forever running down his wife's achievements.
3 The man in a business suit flagged down a taxi.
4 With two small children, she's rather tied down at the moment.
5 The preservation order will prevent them from chopping down the tree.
6 I listened to the lecture and jotted down the professor's points.
7 The authorities are cracking down on fraud everywhere.
8 After the interview I turned down the job they offered me.

9 When Steve wouldn't help, I felt badly let down by him.

10 The holiday gave us a chance to wind down properly.

Unit 27

A 1D 2J 3E 4I 5M 6N 7H 8O 9B 10F 11A 12C 13K 14G 15L

B
1 set about
2 call back
3 pay, back
4 go, back
5 look after
6 set about
7 turn/go back
8 went about
9 called, back
10 holding/keeping back
11 get back
12 fall back

C
1 We are campaigning to bring about a change in the law.
2 You'll have to take back what you said about him.
3 A passer-by went after the pickpocket.
4 I'll ring you back when I get home.
5 How are you going to go about raising the money?
6 A severe frost could set my roses back by several weeks.
7 Sometimes a certain smell can bring back memories of a person or place.
8 For the children's sake he held back his anger.

Unit 28

A
1 F carefully aim at and shoot one of a group
2 F live with money or food provided by
3 T
4 F leave
5 T
6 T
7 F display boastfully, to draw people's attention to
8 T
9 T
10 T

B
1 put/turned
2 gone
3 telling
4 give
5 cordon
6 worn
7 wrote
8 send
9 fight/shake/throw
10 Come
11 be
12 come

C
1 She called it off (the party)
2 I'm sure he'll pull it off (his job/task)
3 –
4 Turn it off, please (the light)
5 –
6 I'll drop it off (a letter/parcel/present etc)
7 to scrape it all off (mud/paint etc)
8 –
9 I just laughed it off (their opinion)
10 Noel will shave it off (his beard or moustache)
11 the moment had come to break it off (her relationship)
12 –

D
1 The plane will be taking off in two hours' time.
2 Fortunately Zoë got off very lightly in the accident.
3 The factory will be laying off 500 workers until after the summer.
4 I don't think his gamble will pay off as he is hoping.
5 Her family cut her off without a penny.
6 The boys let off fireworks in their garden.
7 The rain kept off during the cricket match.
8 James refuses to be put off by what people say.
9 The effects of our holiday wore off all too quickly.

10 We'll have to set off before first light.

Unit 29

A 1I 2O 3F 4G 5J 6K 7E 8A 9L 10D 11M 12B 13N 14C 15H

B Across: 1 see   4 fish for   7 pull   8 check   10 by   11 account   12 get   13 look
Down: 2 ask   3 go   4 fall through   5 fall   6 run   7 put   9 care   10 break

Unit 30

A 1b 2a 3c 4d 5c 6a 7b 8d 9c 10a 11c 12a 13c 14b 15d 16c 17a 18c

B get by: manage with little money
look for: try to find
sit down: take a seat
apply for: ask for
go about: approach, start, tackle
jot down: write down quickly
send off: post
see through: not be deceived by
turn down: reject
pull off: manage to do (something difficult)

C 1E 2A 3G 4D 5C 6B 7F

D
1 as
2 with
3 Unlike
4 enabling/allowing
5 by
6 While/Whereas/Although
7 feeding
8 most
9 seldom/rarely/never
10 another
11 Even/When
12 whose
13 makes
14 So

15 put
16 until/before
17 least
18 what
19 despite
20 no

Unit 31

A 1E 2H 3A 4B 5L 6C 7I 8D
9K 10F 11G 12J

B 1 cheered me up
2 tied the dog up/tied up the dog
3 ate her food up/ate up her food
4 bottle up his emotions/ bottle his emotions up
5 split/break up
6 give up
7 gets up
8 filled up
9 sealed up
10 went up
11 took up
12 pick you up

C 1 picked   7 held
2 build   8 blowing
3 shut   9 grew
4 keep   10 ended
5 fix   11 Hurry
6 cut   12 turned/showed

D 1 We should look Lorenzo up if we pass through Rome.
2 The taxi pulled up in front of the hotel.
3 The boy was told to clear up his room before doing his homework.
4 Tom's grandmother brought him up on her farm in Cornwall.
5 Prices simply shot up last month.
6 I didn't expect that topic to crop up at the meeting.
7 I can easily put you up if you need to stay overnight.
8 The story was obviously made up, if you ask me.

Unit 32

A 1 T
2 F make tired, make unfit or useless through wear
3 T
4 T
5 F separate from a larger group, find a solution to, organise
6 T
7 T
8 T
9 T
10 T
11 F exclude
12 F discover
13 T
14 T
15 F choose, identify
16 F extend your activities

B 1 eat   8 passed
2 taking   9 pulled
3 dropped   10 hand/give
4 turned/came   11 let
5 laid   12 come
6 lock   13 stick/put
7 point   14 throw

C 1 to try it out (a computer/ car/camera etc)
2 measure it out (food or drink)
3 get it out (the diary)
4 –
5 –
6 Rub it out (my name)
7 thought it out (your plan)
8 we can share it out (the work)
9 Could you check it out (the information etc)
10 I'll look it out for you (the Kingman family file)

D 1 ruled   6 coming
2 sort   7 sticking
3 drop   8 pick
4 try   9 handed
5 put   10 branch

Unit 33

A 1D 2H 3M 4E 5L 6F 7A
8K 9B 10G 11C 12N 13J
14I

B 1 part with
2 came apart
3 go/run over
4 boiled over
5 tell, apart
6 fighting with
7 look over
8 deal with

C 1 The engine finally turned over the fourth time I tried it.
2 The state airline took over the small private company.
3 My sister has always identified with the feminist cause.
4 Everyone was quite bowled over by the success of the plan.
5 I expect it will cloud over later on today.
6 The newly-weds could do with some financial assistance.
7 Sally could only toy with the food on her plate.
8 It was a long time before she got over her tragic loss.

D 1 boiled   5 dealing
2 taking   6 do
3 reason   7 toying
4 sided   8 blown

Unit 34

A 1F 2I 3D 4H 5G 6J 7C 8A
9E 10B

B 1 put on
2 hold/hang on
3 went/carried/kept on
4 switch/turn on
5 rambled on
6 let on
7 added on
8 having me on?

C 1 catch   7 getting
     2 try   8 moved
     3 touch   9 let
     4 live   10 passed
     5 count   11 call
     6 Hang/Hold   12 put

D 1 For no apparent reason, the professor turned on his unsuspecting assistant.
     2 The workers decided to soldier on without a pay rise.
     3 Philippa is getting on well in her new job.
     4 The new boy was picked on to clean the whiteboard.
     5 Car manufacturers have carried on their business for 100 years now.
     6 Dave's nervous breakdown was brought on by overwork.
     7 Her mail is being sent on to the new address.
     8 Be careful not to take on too much extra work.
     9 We'll have to keep on advertising until we find someone suitable.
    10 There was a loud party going on somewhere in the street.

Unit 35

A 1a 2c 3d 4b 5c 6a 7d 8c 9c 10a 11b 12b 13d 14c 15d 16c

B dress up: put on smart clothes

turn up: arrive

find out: discover

point out: indicate, draw attention to

go on: continue

get on: make progress

do with: find useful

think over: consider

apply for: ask for (a job)

let on: reveal information

cheer up: make someone feel happier

C 1 We haven't entirely ruled out the possibility of a cure.
     2 The competition judges picked out the best display.
     3 The little boy's ears stuck out from under his school cap.
     4 Tracy's boyfriend took her out to the disco.
     5 The steam train pulled slowly out of the station.
     6 The royal servants laid out the banquet in the palace.
     7 The farmer found it hard to keep foxes out of the chicken shed.
     8 I can't quite make out Marcella's handwriting.
     9 When my favourite sweater wore out, I bought another one just like it.
    10 Just as we set out, there was a clap of thunder.

Unit 36

A 1 T
     2 F donate or give as a gift, prize etc
     3 T
     4 T
     5 F leave
     6 T
     7 T
     8 T
     9 T
    10 F die
    11 F act or play irresponsibly
    12 T

B **Across:** 1 gamble 4 pass 6 hang 8 Take 10 die 11 throw 14 pull 15 come 16 send 17 look 18 break

Down: 1 give 2 blaze 3 clear 5 stow 7 get 9 crowd 12 scare 13 get 14 put 16 shop

Unit 37

A 1L 2H 3A 4J 5B 6C 7I 8E 9F 10G 11D 12K

B 1 ran/bumped
     2 sank
     3 tuned
     4 sent
     5 talk
     6 taken
     7 drop/pop/call
     8 settle
     9 turned
    10 dig/break
    11 barge/burst
    12 show
    13 phase
    14 paid

C 1 plug it in (the hairdryer)
     2 –
     3 –
     4 Hand it in (the report)
     5 –
     6 –
     7 take it all in (the information/situation)
     8 –
     9 break it in (the horse)
    10 –
    11 –
    12 fill it in (the form)

D 1 On her aunt's death Karin came into a fortune.
     2 Burglars have broken into the isolated house.
     3 Daisy burst into tears as she waved goodbye.
     4 It's no good. You can't fool me into believing you!
     5 Don't you think we should check in before we have dinner?
     6 Is your sister moving in soon?
     7 Think about it. Don't rush into anything.

Unit 38

A 1 T
     2 T
     3 T
     4 F get rid of, abolish

5 T

6 F find time to

7 F consider another person inferior

8 F become too big for

9 T

10 T

11 F complete a course of action

12 T

B 1 looks up to

2 go ahead with/go on with/ carry on with

3 go along with

4 cut down on

5 caught up with/kept up with

6 got out of doing

7 settled up with the hotel

8 walked out on

9 got rid of/done away with

10 keeping up with

C 1 put up

2 write off/send off/write away/send away

3 got on/along

4 feel up

5 get round

6 came up

7 come down

8 get down

9 live up

10 getting up

11 run out

12 faced up

D 1 Sarah was disappointed at missing out on such a good opportunity.

2 The boss always lets Fred get away with murder!

3 The President has come in for a great deal of criticism lately.

4 Many people would like to do away with the monarchy.

5 The baby's ill: she came out in spots yesterday.

6 You should hang on to those stamps. They're valuable.

7 Rachel decided she couldn't go through with the wedding.

Unit 39

A 1 comedown

2 lookout

3 handout

4 breakdown

5 breakup/breakdown

6 castaway

7 breakthrough

8 go-ahead

9 dropouts

10 grown-up

11 outlook, upbringing

12 let-up

13 outburst

14 getaway

15 lay-offs, cutbacks

16 stopover

17 turnout

18 onlookers

B Across: 3 standby 5 takeover

7 sell-out 10 in 11 on

12 stowaway 13 hold

14 layout 19 outbreak

20 setback 21 together

23 hangover

Down: 1 stand 2 let-down

4 break 6 knockout 8 lay-by

up 15 onset 16 check

17 goings 18 get 22 in

Unit 40

A 1c 2a 3b 4c 5d 6c 7a 8b 9d
10c 11a 12d 13b 14c 15a 16a

B rule out: exclude, consider ineligible

go on: continue

close down: cause to stop working

get over: recover from

look for: try to find

take on: employ

put up with: tolerate

take off: depart (a plane)

join in: take part in

lay off: dismiss

give up: stop

go back: return

C 1 There was an impressive turnout for the by-election.

2 Police investigated the goings-on at the student hostel.

3 The culprits made their getaway in a stolen car.

4 Please fasten your seatbelts ready for take-off.

5 The hospital closures are the result of government cutbacks.

6 Their ticket to Sydney allows them a stopover in Hong Kong.

7 The accused's antisocial behaviour was blamed on his upbringing.

D 1 The plain-clothes policeman hung around outside the star's home.

2 Josephine came across a rare coin among her loose change.

3 The fire blazed away, completely out of control.

4 Eventually he owned up to having started the rumour.

5 News of their affair will get around pretty fast.

6 She'll never talk him into giving up golf.

Unit 41

A 1 search engine, a newsgroup, chat room, social networking

2 attachment, virus, delete

3 crash, back up

4 cursor, icon, double-click

B 1B 2D 3B 4C 5A 6A 7B 8A
9D 10B 11A

C 1 computers

2 data

3 exchange

4 cable

5 satellite

6 smartphone

D 1 desktop
2 organisers
3 e-readers
4 cables
5 web
6 package
7 ISP
8 router

E 1 customers
2 website
3 transfers
4 public
5 fraud
6 password
7 online

Unit 42

A 1 slogans/jingles
2 jingles/slogans
3 commercials
4 brand
5 subliminal
6 pressure groups
7 disseminate
8 posters
9 hoardings
10 press

B 1D 2B 3H 4A 5C 6E 7G 8F

C 1 critic
2 commentator
3 censorship
4 coverage
5 circulation
6 catchy

D 1 rehearsing
2 stage
3 series
4 characters
5 channel
6 on location
7 role
8 review

E 1 box-office success
2 standing ovation
3 soap opera
4 final curtain
5 subtitles
6 low-budget
7 prime-time
8 supporting roles

Unit 43

A 1 ambition
2 jet set
3 Rising
4 best-seller
5 Success
6 achieve
7 potential
8 expanding
9 rocketed
10 whizz-kid
11 reap
12 respected
13 market
14 public

B 1 prodigious
2 dedicated
3 ruthless
4 (un)skilled/skilful
5 notorious
6 (un)successful
7 ephemeral
8 stressful/stressed
9 celebrated
10 legendary
11 renowned
12 talented

C 1 prodigy
2 lights
3 stardom
4 infamous
5 champion
6 status
7 autograph
8 failure
9 invasion
10 reputation
11 posthumous

12 big break
13 posterity
14 gap
15 winnings
16 celebrities

Unit 44

A 1 experiments
2 animal rights
3 widespread
4 blood sports
5 activists
6 tested
7 consumers
8 vivisection
9 opposition
10 climate
11 entertainment
12 cruelty
13 free-range
14 battery hens
15 factory farming
16 livestock

B 1 H bookworm
2 D stag party
3 J dark horse
4 A puppy fat
5 B zebra crossing
6 C pigeon-hole
7 E crocodile tears
8 I dog collar
9 G wolf whistle
10 F cat's eyes

C 1 fly
2 frog
3 butterflies
4 bird's
5 parrot-
6 dog
7 wild goose
8 horse
9 wolf
10 rat
11 whale
12 sardines

D 1E 2A 3B 4F 5D 6C

Unit 45

A 1 authors
2 Translation
3 dialect
4 translators
5 allusions
6 nuances
7 original
8 colloquial
9 Evoking
10 literal

B 1F 2I 3J 4H 5A 6G 7C 8E
9D 10B

C 1 spoonerism
2 slang
3 alliteration
4 onomatopoeia
5 palindrome
6 jargon
7 malapropism
8 tongue-twister/
alliteration
9 pidgin
10 limerick

D 1 lecture
2 sermon
3 quarrel
4 speech
5 accent
6 debate
7 pronunciation
8 anecdote
9 sentence
10 riddle

Unit 46

A 1 policy
2 bypass
3 consultants
4 collapses
5 emergency
6 cardiac
7 heavy smokers
8 surgery
9 interim
10 patient

11 medical
12 treatment
13 addicts
14 transplants
15 National Health Service

B 1 under the weather
2 disease
3 surgeon
4 side effects
5 ward
6 donor
7 surgery
8 clinic
9 first
10 diets
11 theatre
12 prescription
13 casualty
14 transfusion
15 sling

C 1 T
2 T
3 F cannot resist infection
well
4 F specialises in children's
illnesses
5 T
6 F means being excessively
fat/overweight
7 F a means of inserting a
drug with a needle
8 T
9 F treating patients with
small amounts of drugs
that would cause
symptoms in a healthy
person
10 T

Unit 47

A 1E 2H 3J 4L 5I 6A 7K 8C
9G 10F 11D 12B

B 1 narrow escape
2 run the risk
3 safe and sound
4 been swept overboard
5 sheer folly

6 peace of mind
7 bear a charmed life
8 take sensible precautions
9 risk life and limb
10 a false sense of security
11 raise the alarm
12 odds are heavily stacked
against

C 1D 2A 3E 4B 5I 6L 7K 8C
9F 10G 11H 12J

D 1 hardships
2 foolhardy
3 funding
4 sponsors
5 provisions
6 survivors
7 hazardous
8 jeopardising
9 intrepid
10 determination
11 endurance
12 casualties

Unit 48

A 1 rugged
2 construction
3 irrigation
4 drought
5 source
6 developing
7 environmental
8 scale
9 damage
10 tribal
11 obliterated
12 environmentalists

B 1 world
2 land
3 countryside
4 pick
5 sky
6 coast
7 eradicate
8 fumes
9 resources
10 lake

C 1 tropical
  2 global
  3 urban
  4 rural
  5 (un)natural
  6 scenic
  7 mountainous
  8 coastal
  9 regional
  10 protective/protected
  11 congested
  12 coniferous
  13 polluted
  14 climatic
  15 disastrous
  16 (ir)replaceable
  17 disposable
  18 biodegradable
  19 (in)soluble
  20 (un)productive
  21 problematic
  22 polar

D 1F 2D 3I 4H 5G 6E 7C 8J
  9K 10A 11L 12B

Unit 49

A 1H 2F 3I 4B 5D 6J 7C 8G
  9A 10E

B 1 rival
  2 accused
  3 hoodwinked
  4 espionage
  5 loyalty
  6 devious
  7 blame
  8 integrity
  9 traitor
  10 reproached
  11 disgrace
  12 bribed
  13 corrupt
  14 conscience

C 1 integrity
  2 traitor
  3 loyalty

  4 devious
  5 reproached
  6 hoodwinked

D 1 (dis)honourable
  2 (un)ethical
  3 suspicious
  4 petty
  5 bankrupt
  6 scandalous
  7 fraudulent
  8 deceitful
  9 vicious
  10 sinful
  11 sacrificial
  12 treacherous

E 1 tax evasion
  2 looted
  3 offence
  4 bribing
  5 culprit
  6 shortcomings
  7 amoral
  8 betrayed

Unit 50

A 1 wealth
  2 poverty
  3 increase
  4 income
  5 satisfaction
  6 level
  7 economists
  8 material
  9 expenditure
  10 factors

B 1I 2E 3A 4B 5G 6C 7F 8J
  9D 10H

C 1 T
  2 F buys from the producer
    and sells to the retailer,
    who sells to the public
  3 F before tax
  4 F a period of economic
    decline
  5 T

  6 F *impecunious* means short
    of money
  7 T
  8 T
  9 T
  10 F the opposite
  11 F you are borrowing money
    from someone
  12 T
  13 F an extra payment in
    addition to your salary
  14 T

D 1 direct debit
  2 mortgage
  3 will
  4 in arrears
  5 creditors
  6 competition
  7 profit
  8 bounced
  9 expense
  10 cash
  11 receipt
  12 discount
  13 fare
  14 priceless
  15 within their means
  16 proceeds

Unit 51

  1a 2d 3a 4b 5c 6a 7c 8b 9a
  10d 11a 12b 13a 14b 15d
  16a 17c 18d 19a 20b 21a
  22c 23d 24a 25b 26c 27d
  28c 29a 30d 31b 32d

Unit 52

A 1A 2D 3C 4B 5A 6D 7A 8C
  9B 10C 11D 12B 13D 14A
  15A

B 1G 2C 3E 4A 5I 6B 7D 8F
  9H 10J

C 1 electorate, general election
  2 candidate, constituency
  3 MP
  4 Opposition

Unit 53

A 1E 2F 3A 4L 5I 6J 7C 8G
9H 10D 11B 12K

B 1 feud
2 antagonise
3 motive
4 wreak
5 warfare
6 reconciliation
7 reprisal
8 vindictively
9 victims
10 rancour
11 retaliated
12 aggressive

C A *8 down*
B *12 across*
C feud
D victims
E vindictiveness
F *5 across*
G motive
H *10 down*
I *1 across*
J *2 down*
K *13 down*
L reconcile
M wreak
N antagonise
O warfare
P rancour

Unit 54

A 1M 2D 3C 4F 5B 6L 7K 8I
9H 10N 11E 12G 13J 14A

B 1 revenue
2 system
3 PCs
4 integrated
5 compatible
6 rivals
7 monopoly
8 consumers
9 market
10 growth
11 investing

12 digital
13 encoded
14 lucrative
15 initiative

C 1 robot, remote control
2 electromagnetic field
3 anti-nuclear
4 solar
5 closed-circuit
6 security tags
7 streamline
8 white goods
9 microchip
10 optimum efficiency
11 central locking
12 programme

D 1 T
2 F a small piece of
equipment, not
necessarily electrical
3 T
4 F usually four-wheeled
5 T
6 T
7 F a device on a wall into
which a plug can be
inserted to make an
electrical connection
8 T

Unit 55

A 1F 2I 3G 4B 5D 6E 7H 8J
9A 10C

B 1 overtime   5 redundant
2 candidates   6 living
3 benefit   7 loan
4 sabbatical   8 syllabus

C 1c 2a 3b 4a 5d 6a 7b 8c 9d
10a

D 1 on the dole
2 enter the labour market
3 on-the-job training
4 achieve his potential
5 wage dispute
6 picket line

Unit 56

A 1M 2C 3N 4I 5F 6J 7K 8L
9D 10H 11E 12A 13B 14G

B 1 renovation
2 cottage
3 habitation
4 belongs
5 bare necessities
6 evict
7 demolish
8 plight
9 polarised
10 support
11 sympathise
12 victimising
13 threats
14 brave

C 1 T
2 T
3 F someone who wants to
acquire/possess many
things
4 F Affluence is wealth.
5 T
6 T
7 T
8 T
9 F the first, most important
things to think about
10 F a young person, usually a
girl, who goes to a foreign
country to learn the
language while staying
with a family and helping
to look after their children
11 T
12 T

D 1 boom
2 beyond their means
3 suburbs
4 second-hand
5 rat race
6 investment
7 security
8 sophisticated
9 apart
10 image

11 entertaining

12 debt

Unit 57

A 1D 2J 3F 4I 5B 6K 7G 8L 9C 10E 11H 12A

B 1 F usually of an unwelcome event

2 T

3 T

4 T

5 F the study of the movements of the stars, interpreted in terms of their influence on human behaviour

6 T

7 T

8 F someone who can predict the future or see what is happening out of sight

9 T

10 T

11 T

12 T

13 T

14 F someone who believes there is no God

15 T

16 T

17 T

18 T

C 1 mirage

2 medium

3 mythical

4 monster

5 Magic

6 miracle

7 mesmerised

D 1b 2a 3c 4d 5a

Unit 58

A 1D 2E 3I 4A 5B 6F 7H 8C 9J 10G

B 1 reminisce

2 a total blank

3 lasting

4 souvenirs

5 prevaricated

6 nostalgia

7 absent-minded

8 haunted

9 historical

10 ancient

11 memorising

12 contemporary

13 sooner or later

14 on the dot

15 forecast

16 on time

17 at the end

18 refresh

19 recognise

20 elderly

C 1 tip

2 rack

3 sieve

4 Ages

5 predecessor

6 prehistoric

7 high

8 passage/passing

9 flies

10 documents

11 posterity

12 hindsight

Unit 59

A 1H 2F 3A 4J 5B 6C 7I 8E 9G 10L 11D 12K

B 1 F is an electronic device fitted to an aircraft for collecting and storing information about the flight

2 T

3 T

4 T

5 F is a bed or a bunk on a ship or train

6 T

7 F records a vehicle's speed on a journey, and how far it has travelled

8 F a plan for a journey to different places

C 1 brochure

2 range

3 resort

4 facilities

5 cruise

6 luxury

7 lounging

8 spectacular

9 self-catering

10 picturesque

11 cuisine

12 excursions

13 inclusive

14 accommodation

D A *7 across*

B bypass

C villa

D *10 down*

E roundabout

F cabin

G *8 across*

H package

I safari

J via

K *4 down*

L ticket

M brochure

N overland

O *17 across*

P journey

Q Tube

R *16 across*

S exhaustion

Unit 60

A 1 copyright

2 proofs

3 phrasebook

4 plot

5 browse

6 dust-jacket

7 edition

8 imagination

9 key

10 paragraphs
11 rhyme
12 literally
13 page
14 thrillers
15 library

B 1 hardback
2 translated
3 engrossed
4 best-seller
5 chapter
6 author
7 prose
8 biography
9 copy
10 illustrated

C 1F 2K 3A 4B 5J 6H 7C 8E
9D 10I 11L 12G

Unit 61

A 1E 2A 3J 4B 5C 6D 7I 8F
9G 10H

B 1 charged
2 offence
3 stand
4 plead
5 court
6 jury
7 evidence
8 witnesses
9 lawyers
10 sum up
11 reach a verdict
12 defendant
13 pass sentence
14 acquitted
15 committed
16 criminologists
17 offenders
18 deterrent

C A court
B wrists
C *6 across*
D excuse
E magistrate

F riot
G *13 down*
H *1 down*
I deterrent
J acquitted
K authorities
L *9 down*
M jail
N judge
O delinquent
P barrister
Q *7 across*
R *17 across*
S fine
T mug

Unit 62

A 1b 2c 3c 4c 5b 6c 7d 8a 9c
10a 11d 12b 13a 14b 15b
16c 17b 18c 19a 20b 21c
22a 23b 24c 25c 26d 27d
28a 29b 30c 31a 32a 33b

B 1D 2C 3A 4B 5A 6C 7B 8C
9D 10B 11D 12A 13B 14D

C 1 saved   4 stand
2 pose   5 backed
3 held

D 1 worldwide
2 digital
3 financial
4 background
5 correspondence
6 personal
7 password
8 confidential
9 security
10 streamline

Unit 63

A 1 Refuse   7 dressing
2 pride   8 skate
3 crane   9 trunk
4 Hailing   10 spotted
5 branch   11 spirits
6 spring   12 scales

B *Possible answers:*
1 Why don't you have one then?
2 Only another few minutes, sir.
3 Flowers, perhaps, or chocolates?
4 Delicious, thank you.
5 When it's a French window.
6 They don't want people to get tangled up in them.
7 Mostly vegetables.
8 Oh, he was in Wellington's army, was he? (*At the Battle of Waterloo in 1815, Napoleon was defeated by the Duke of Wellington's and Field Marshal Blücher's armies. Waterloo is also a well-known railway station in London.*)
9 It is part of their migration pattern.
10 Certainly, sir, including lobster.
1G 2J 3E 4F 5A 6C 7D 8B 9H 10I

C 1 red/read
2 boar/bore
3 cheetahs/cheaters
4 crypt/script
5 tiers/tears
6 carrots/carats
7 moose/mousse
8 twirly/too early
9 ewe/you

D 1 Hair today, gone tomorrow!
2 an unidentified frying object
3 by Norse code
4 No time like the present!
5 drop him a line
6 to make ends meet
7 He wanted to make a clean getaway.
8 He took a very dim view of things.

E 1 unprovoked
2 wonderful
3 playwright
4 thoughtfully
5 enclosing
6 unfortunately
7 unable
8 updated
9 politician
10 long-term
11 sworn
12 apparently
13 whereupon
14 wittily
15 ahead

F 1F (*by Friday* could mean a time deadline, or it could refer to the person, Man Friday, who did the chores for Crusoe in Daniel Defoe's novel)

2E (*ham* is cooked pork, and *-let* can be used as a diminutive)

3A (a pun on the word *vessel*)

4G (a pun on the word *skeleton*)

5D (a pun on the word *wave*)

6B (sounds are transposed)

7C (a deliberate confusion of *meters* and *meteors*)

Unit 64

A 1 make a mountain out of a molehill
2 pulling my leg
3 out of the question
4 a bone to pick
5 down in the mouth
6 takes the biscuit
7 give them the slip
8 tongue in cheek
9 got her own back
10 on the tip of my tongue
11 watch your step
12 takes her/it for granted

B 1H 2A 3L 4F 5B 6D 7C 8K 9E 10G 11J 12I

C 1 bee in his bonnet
2 sort out the sheep from the goats
3 flogging a dead horse
4 get the lion's share
5 let the cat out of the bag
6 putting the cart before the horse
7 dark horse
8 lame duck
9 red herring
10 barking up the wrong tree
11 whale of a time
12 dog-eared

D 1D 2F 3J 4C 5A 6B 7I 8E 9H 10G

E 1 chain
2 Dutch
3 pitch
4 close
5 bone
6 song
7 tail
8 shop
9 house
10 bell
11 day
12 loggerheads
13 wall
14 cake
15 thoughts

Unit 65

A 1J Too many helpers cause confusion.

2A People have different tastes and interests.

3G The first one to apply often gets the job/prize/bargain etc.

4F Don't rely on something happening until it is certain.

5B Eat fruit to stay healthy.

6I Think carefully before you decide to marry.

7C Whoever is paying the bill has the right to choose.

8E It's better to be sure of having a little than only the possibility of having more.

9D Enjoy yourself while you can.

10H If you put off doing a necessary job or repair, it may take longer in the end.

B 1B 2D 3E 4C 5A

C 1 mouth　　6 Rome
2 stone　　7 summer
3 dogs　　8 spots
4 dangerous　9 dog
5 No　　10 milk

D 1I Office juniors/employees/pupils don't concentrate on their work if the boss/teacher is away.

2A Look at your own faults before criticising others.

3B Don't anticipate success, because many things can go wrong and prevent you from succeeding.

4C Even a setback or disaster has some good in it for somebody.

5H You have to take some risks to make progress.

6D If you do something too fast, you may do it badly and have to do it again, which will take more time.

7F There's a little truth in every rumour.

8J A tiny extra burden/annoyance can be the final factor causing breakdown/dispute etc.

9E People of the same type usually associate with each other.

10G A job is done faster if there are a lot of helpers.

E 1 unflappable
2 well-behaved
3 without shame
4 very pale
5 tough
6 defunct
7 extremely short-sighted
8 healthy
9 hard of hearing
10 crazy
11 obvious
12 ancient

F 1 as sound as a bell
2 as red as a beetroot
3 like a bull in a china shop
4 like a fish out of water
5 as thick as two short planks
6 as thin as a rake
7 as sober as a judge
8 as stubborn as a mule

G 1G 2A 3F 4B 5D 6E 7C

H 1C 2F 3B 4G 5J 6H 7A 8D 9I 10E

Unit 66

A 1 top   8 woo
2 wed   9 cut
3 rock   10 net
4 clash   11 clear
5 axe   12 dog
6 name   13 go
7 up   14 flee

B 1 Three people have been rescued from a dangerous cliff.
2 The number of people killed in a motorway crash has gone up.
3 The Prime Minister has promised to create more jobs.
4 The police have stated that long hair is not allowed.
5 There is still no explanation why an explosion happened in a fish shop.
6 Railway workers' attempt (to improve working conditions?) is expected to fail.
7 A large amount of drugs has been discovered at Heathrow Airport.
8 The Government's position has been weakened by a recent corruption case.
9 Help is being sent to victims of an earthquake.
10 A dangerous situation is likely to arise in a coal mine.

C 1 weapons
2 negotiations
3 employment
4 ambassador
5 disappointment
6 election
7 angry outburst
8 hurried visit

Unit 67

A 1 vice versa
2 coup d'état
3 bona fide
4 curriculum vitae
5 faux pas
6 persona non grata
7 post-mortem
8 blasé
9 non sequitur
10 contretemps
11 née
12 spiel
13 ad lib
14 alibi

B 1J 2H 3G 4I 5A 6K 7B 8E 9D 10L 11F 12C

C 1 carte blanche
2 ad infinitum
3 alfresco
4 tête-à-tête
5 in camera
6 aplomb
7 kamikaze
8 quid pro quo
9 entrepreneur
10 macho
11 incognito
12 verbatim

Unit 68

A 1 common   6 coach
2 initial   7 suit
3 surgery   8 trip
4 pound   9 plot
5 very   10 degree

B 1 coach   5 very
2 common   6 trip
3 surgery   7 plot
4 pound   8 initial
9 suit   10 degree

C 1 firm   8 bill
2 arms   9 plant
3 letter   10 novel
4 club   11 like
5 spell   12 book
6 trunk   13 quite
7 file   14 sole

D 1 serve   5 show
2 carry   6 broke
3 roll   7 concern
4 take

Unit 69

A 1 judicious   8 illegible
2 continually   9 advise
3 gaol   10 suit
4 childish   11 corpse
5 humane   12 diary
6 effect   13 moral
7 economic   14 principal

B 1 classical   7 officious
2 practical   8 credulous
3 stationary   9 troop
4 respectively   10 dessert
5 ✔   11 infer
6 Loath   12 ✔

C 1 pare   17 core
2 ore   18 coarse
3 gilt   19 isle
4 gamble   20 fair
5 medal   21 suite
6 wave   22 pier
7 course   23 horse
8 corps   24 canvass
9 tears   25 gambol
10 canvas   26 oar
11 meddle   27 fare
12 peer   28 tiers
13 pair   29 waive
14 guilt   30 bier
15 beer   31 hoarse
16 aisle   32 sweet

Unit 70

A 1 hurries
2 ✓
3 wholly
4 installing
5 ✓
6 ✓
7 flapping
8 ✓
9 separating
10 ✓
11 ✓
12 ruining
13 ✓
14 played
15 ✓
16 bowing
17 comfortably
18 friendly
19 ✓
20 ✓

B 1 separate
2 dependent
3 interested
4 receive
5 lose
6 developed
7 responsibility
8 advertisements
9 any more
10 definite
11 than
12 embarrassing

C 1 their   7 whether
2 been   8 which
3 ✓   9 review
4 know   10 whole
5 too   11 reigned
6 ✓   12 ✓

D Plans for a spectacular pop concert in Falmer Park, just outside Portsmouth, have been submitted to Hampshire County Council. The open-air event, featuring the singer Neil Silver and his backing group The Raiders, is planned for Wednesday 6th July and Friday 8th July, to coincide with Portsmouth Arts Festival as well as the Tour de France. The organisers, Gigs Unlimited, say the show will have a French theme to fit in with the cycle race. The proposal will be considered at a special meeting on Thursday 12th May.

Local people are divided on the issue. While some welcome the influx of visitors and the increase in trade that the concert will bring to Portsmouth, others are predicting an invasion of New Age travellers. Hampshire's Chief Constable Edward Lang-Jones is, however, confident that he has adequate manpower to deal with any disturbance that may occur.

E 1 aunt's a
2 isn't a
3 Brown's b, teachers' b
4 1920's c
5 He's a, i's c, t's c
6 James's b
7 children's b
8 Celia's b, can't a
9 Bennets' b, Joneses' b
10 Tom's b, won't a, father's b

F 1b 2b 3a 4c 5c 6a 7b 8c

Unit 71

A 1 the lion's share
2 Many hands make light work.
3 Nothing venture, nothing gain.
4 the sheep from the goats
5 ✓
6 Waste not, want not.
7 A stitch in time saves nine.
8 ✓
9 The early bird catches the worm.
10 Make hay while the sun shines.
11 a close shave
12 before they're hatched
13 blow your own trumpet
14 Birds of a feather flock together.
15 down in the mouth
16 An apple a day keeps the doctor away.
17 out of the blue
18 Every cloud has a silver lining.
19 kicked the bucket
20 ✓

B 1 alfresco
2 rapport
3 ad infinitum
4 cuisine
5 eligible
6 aplomb
7 paparazzi
8 waive
9 siesta
10 cache

C 1 suit   8 coach
2 trip   9 very
3 plot   10 degree
4 initial   11 arms
5 surgery   12 sole
6 common   13 trunk
7 pound   14 race

D 1 as white as a sheet
2 ✓
3 as mad as a hatter
4 like a fish out of water
5 as like as two peas in a pod
6 as cool as a cucumber
7 ✓
8 as strong as an ox
9 as bold as brass
10 as old as the hills
11 ✓
12 like hot cakes
13 as red as a beetroot
14 ✓

E 1 online
2 overdraft
3 apprehensive

4 disgrace
5 poverty
6 unflappable
7 recession
8 humorous
9 leaflet
10 criticising

Unit 72

A 1 quits   6 day
2 tune   7 a halt
3 mind   8 names
4 celebration 9 bluff
5 question

B 1 first   6 make
2 shed   7 face
3 travelling 8 years
4 let   9 In
5 come   10 set

C 1 in the heat of the moment
2 a heated discussion
3 blowing hot and cold
4 piping hot
5 take the heat off you
6 hotting up
7 hot under the collar
8 get into hot water
9 a hot potato
10 just so much hot air
11 hot off the press

D 1D 2A 3C 4D 5B 6A 7B 8C
9A 10B 11D 12A 13B 14C

Unit 73

A 1 cutting edge
2 user-friendly
3 keyhole surgery
4 healthcare
5 number cruncher
6 dotcom
7 biodiversity
8 raves
9 text messages
10 asylum seeker
11 counsellor
12 sell-by dates
13 grassroots

14 proactive
15 name of the game

B 1 PIN (personal identification number) *This is the true acronym.*
2 TLC (tender loving care)
3 RSI (repetitive strain injury)
4 OTT (over the top)
5 aka (also known as)
6 asap (as soon as possible)
7 PC (politically correct)
8 BSE (bovine spongiform encephalopathy)

C 1 camcorder (camera + recorder)
2 biopic (biography + picture)
3 docusoap (documentary + soap opera)
4 psychobabble (psychology + babble)
5 sitcom (situation + comedy)
6 heliport (helicopter + port)
7 guesstimate (guess + estimate)
8 blog (web + log)

D 1 a bad hair day
2 big time
3 cherry-picked
4 been there, done that
5 gobsmacked
6 drop-dead gorgeous
7 to die for
8 the full monty
9 a couch potato
10 vegging out

E 1J 2H 3C 4E 5B 6G 7A

Unit 74

A 1 mosquitoes
2 pianos
3 avocados
4 volcanoes
5 mottoes
6 casinos
7 shampoos
8 ghettos

9 rodeos
10 tomatoes
11 echoes
12 potatoes
13 heroes
14 studios
15 concertos
16 videos
17 kangaroos
18 radios
19 biros
20 solos

B 1 leaves   12 postmen
2 geese   13 beliefs
3 deer   14 halves
4 feet   15 wolves
5 wives   16 sheep
6 children 17 lives
7 houses   18 lice
8 mice   19 knives
9 roofs   20 selves
10 teeth
11 hooves/ hoofs

C 1 S/P   11 S
2 S   12 P
3 P   13 P
4 S   14 S
5 S   15 S
6 S/P   16 S
7 S   17 S/P
8 P   18 S
9 S   19 S
10 S   20 S

D 1 bunch   7 swarm
2 flight   8 herd
3 pack   9 pack
4 gang   10 flock
5 flock   11 bunch
6 shoal   12 swarm

E 1 nuclei
2 formulae/formulas
3 boyfriends
4 press-ups

5 take-offs
6 aquaria/aquariums
7 brothers-in-law
8 bonuses
9 stimuli
10 criteria
11 circuses
12 cacti/cactuses
13 breadwinners
14 operas
15 diagnoses
16 viruses
17 appendices
18 larvae
19 bacteria
20 automata

F 1 heiress
2 fiancée
3 masseuse
4 nun
5 niece
6 actress
7 sculptress
8 empress
9 heroine
10 widow
11 doctor
12 manageress
13 hostess
14 barmaid
15 bride
16 aunt
17 landlady
18 cousin
19 headmistress
20 stewardess

G 1D 2C 3I 4J 5G 6A 7E 8H
9F 10B

Unit 75

A 1 unattainable
2 non-existent
3 illegitimate
4 irresistible
5 inaccessible
6 unprepared

7 unaware
8 inexpensive
9 unconscious
10 intolerant
11 unlikely
12 improbable
13 dissatisfied
14 impatient
15 uncomplicated
16 unable
17 incapable
18 unenthusiastic
19 illegible
20 irrational
21 imperfect
22 non-resident

B 1 undo
2 disapprove
3 anticlockwise
4 misunderstand
5 dis/mis/unused
6 debriefing
7 miscast
8 unwrap
9 disembark
10 decentralise
11 anticlimax
12 disprove
13 declassify
14 disincentive
15 unconfirmed
16 dismount
17 undamaged
18 uncommon
19 unemployment
20 depersonalise
21 misfire
22 anticyclone

C 1 co-worker
2 over/counterbalance
3 co-pilot
4 counterclaim
5 co-author
6 overpriced
7 counterattack
8 overestimate

9 overreact
10 co-director
11 co-operate
12 overanxious
13 counter-espionage
14 overboard
15 oversimplify
16 coeducational
17 overdue
18 overdose

D 1 outpouring
2 ex-wife
3 outlast
4 outvote
5 redirect
6 undercooked
7 reorganise
8 ex-boyfriend
9 re-elect
10 undermine
11 outsize
12 redistribute
13 underexposure
14 outstay
15 reclaim
16 reunite
17 reassure
18 underclothes
19 underachiever
20 reintegrate

E 1 hyperactive
2 amoral
3 malnutrition
4 neo-Nazi
5 malformation
6 apolitical
7 hypersensitive
8 monosyllable
9 neoclassical
10 hypercritical
11 malfunction
12 asymmetrical
13 maladjusted
14 hypermarket
15 monotone

F
1 foggy
2 helpful/helpless
3 destructive
4 friendly/friendless
5 hateful
6 childish/childless/childproof
7 tragic
8 fireproof
9 humorous/humourless
10 magical
11 homely/homeless
12 washable
13 nostalgic
14 quarrelsome
15 graceful/gracious/graceless
16 hopeful/hopeless
17 imaginative
18 reliable
19 dramatic
20 realistic

G
1 departure
2 entertainment
3 betrayal
4 piety
5 behaviour
6 attraction
7 arrival
8 emancipation
9 darkness
10 patience
11 satisfaction
12 rudeness
13 pleasure
14 maintenance
15 advertisement
16 theory
17 delivery/deliverance
18 widowhood
19 availability
20 tolerance

H
1 horrify
2 widen
3 straighten
4 realise
5 categorise
6 lengthen
7 heighten
8 intensify
9 idealise
10 shorten
11 criticise
12 redden
13 pacify
14 falsify
15 computerise

I
1 international
2 reviewed
3 disgrace
4 innocence
5 likelihood
6 irregularity/-ies
7 illegal
8 horrified
9 unbelievable
10 unacceptable
11 realise/-ize
12 succeeding

Unit 76

A 1B 2B 3B 4A 5A 6A 7B 8A
9B 10A 11B 12A 13B 14B
15B 16A 17B 18A

B
1 birthday   5 waistcoats
2 aerial   6 opinion
3 insulated   7 bench
4 crisps   8 bargain

C
1 warehouse: large shed for storing goods

department store: large shop selling clothes, furniture etc.

2 recipe: method of cooking a dish

receipt: proof of purchase

3 block: large chunk of wood, stone etc, or building containing flats or offices

notepad: paper for taking notes, attached to a piece of thick card

4 smoking: action of consuming tobacco

dinner jacket: man's evening suit

5 costume: special clothes, e.g. traditional or national costume suit: matching two or three-piece outfit

6 congealed: having become thick or solid (of blood, fat, cold food)

frozen: below 0°C, hard and solid like ice

7 salute: give a military greeting

wave to: raise the hand in casual greeting to a friend

8 pensioners: elderly people who do not work and who receive a state pension

boarders: pupils who live at their school

9 deranged: mentally unbalanced

disturbed: confused, bothered

10 prove: show that something is true

test: try out something

D
1 fish and chips
2 women and children
3 pen and ink
4 bed and breakfast
5 bread and butter
6 dead and buried
7 rules and regulations
8 shoes and socks
9 in and out
10 pros and cons
11 rights and wrongs
12 law and order

E
1 figures   6 about
2 mortar   7 wide
3 bone   8 dry
4 fro   9 proper
5 sound   10 span

F
1 song and dance
2 wear and tear
3 pins and needles
4 chalk and cheese
5 odds and ends
6 cut and dried

7 flesh and blood
8 sick and tired
9 tooth and nail
10 head and shoulders
11 cock-and-bull
12 hard and fast
13 chop and change
14 ins and outs
15 neck and neck

Unit 77

A 1 ramble
2 wade
3 toddle
4 marched
5 limp
6 shuffled
7 stroll
8 staggered
9 tiptoe
10 plodded

B 1E 2I 3A 4H 5J 6B 7D 8F 9C 10G

C 1 whisper
2 moaning
3 express
4 snaps
5 utter
6 gossip
7 lectured
8 discussing
9 called
10 stammer

D 1 glimpse
2 peering
3 glanced
4 recognised
5 examined/scrutinised
6 peep
7 gazed/stared
8 watching
9 noticed/observed
10 spot

E 1H 2F 3D 4A 5G 6B 7E 8C

F 1 laughed off
2 Don't make me laugh
3 a laugh a minute
4 had the last laugh
5 laughing all the way to the bank
6 laughable
7 laughing up my sleeve
8 laugh on the other side of your face
9 laughed in his face
10 Don't laugh
11 no laughing matter
12 laugh her out of it

Unit 78

A 1 tow 5 wrench
2 tugged 6 lugging
3 drag 7 haul
4 jerk 8 drew

B 1F 2N 3A 4P 5G 6B 7E 8M 9L 10I 11D 12K 13O 14H 15C 16J

C 1 a concept, the nettle, at straws
2 a flower, up courage, your eyebrows
3 your fists, your teeth
4 an audience, your passport nervously, someone's imagination
5 forty winks, a bag away from an old lady
6 power, someone's imagination
7 at straws, your passport nervously
8 his long-lost brother to his heart, your passport nervously
9 the enemy soldiers, someone's imagination
10 a flower, someone's brains, your teeth

D 1 dazzled
2 glistened
3 glittering
4 glimmer
5 glare
6 flash
7 shimmered
8 flickered
9 sparkled
10 beam

E 1I 2H 3D 4F 5J 6A 7B 8E 9G 10C

F 1 glow
2 embers/ashes
3 spark
4 blaze/burn, flames/sparks
5 scorch/burn
6 scald/burn
7 steam
8 swelter/boil
9 ashes
10 smoke

G 1 drew 4 streaming
2 glow 5 flared
3 grip

Unit 79

A 1 actual 7 boss
2 bargain 8 boarder
3 bench 9 scales
4 review 10 recipes
5 notorious 11 opinions
6 imagination 12 private

B 1 buried (completely over, past)
2 dance (a fuss)
3 mortar (property, buildings)
4 cons (advantages and disadvantages)
5 blood (family)
6 bull (improbable)
7 wide (over a wide area)
8 neck (absolutely even in a race)
9 tear (damage through use)
10 ends (miscellaneous items)
11 dry (stranded, abandoned)
12 cheese (two very different things or people)
13 dried (already decided)
14 needles (prickly feeling in cramped limbs)
15 nail (fiercely, violently)

C 1C 2D 3A 4B 5D 6A 7C 8B 9B 10D

D
1 exemplified
2 childhood
3 opposition
4 remainder
5 underlying
6 relationships
7 outstanding
8 foreshadowed
9 identification
10 prestigious
11 withholding
12 unmistakeable
13 instinctively
14 universal

E
1 rough
2 ground
3 trunks
4 struck
5 spring
6 make

Unit 80

A 1b 2a 3a 4b 5a 6b 7a 8b

B The Sales Manager
Randalls Ltd
75 Central Drive
Northampton NN4 1SW

Dear Sir or Madam,

I saw your advertisement for the PC 386SX in last week's edition of PC Direct. Please send me further details of this model, as well as other PCs you are currently offering, with prices. Please confirm that you can deliver.

Thank you for your attention. I look forward to receiving your prompt reply.

Yours faithfully,
Jerome Walsh

Unit 81

A 1C 2J 3A 4G 5D 6I 7B 8E 9F 10H

B Dear Susie,

Thanks very much for doing that babysitting last week. The kids *really enjoyed* it, and also it gave me the chance to get on with my work with fewer interruptions *than* usual. I've just started an interesting new project on attitudes towards *recycling*, which the council are paying (*me*) *for*. All very useful income, now *that* Paul's only working part-time.

I may have to ask you to look *after* them again. It could be next week, but the one after is more likely. I'll let *you know* soon. What *would* I do without a friend like you?!

By the way, you know that little tax problem I mentioned to you? Well, in the end I rang up the tax office, and you wouldn't believe how helpful *they were*! They sorted it all out in no time. I'll try them again next time *I get* in a muddle.

Anyway, must dash. Hope you have a great time at Martha's. Will be in touch.

All the best,
Laura

C *Model answer:*
Dear Fred,

I thought I'd drop you a line, as this is really very important, and I'm not sure you people up at St Anne's Hall understand how the man in the street feels.

Oxley Park is the best park we've got in Rugley. You can go there any afternoon, and find people walking, playing tennis, football or cricket, having an ice cream or a coffee, sailing or rowing boats, paddling canoes ... Well, you know what it's like – a wonderful place we've all grown up with, and I for one want it to be there, unspoilt, for my kids too.

Now Haslers have come along and made their bid to build luxury flats at the south end. If you agree to that, you can say goodbye to the tennis, cricket and football, secretaries sunbathing in their lunch hour, and staff from the offices sitting on benches eating their sandwiches. For Heaven's sake, that's where you and I used to run when we were training for the marathon we were misguided enough to enter! I was eighteen and you were nineteen. Seems centuries ago now.

Anyway, people are getting very steamed up about it.

Please give the whole thing a bit of thought, and get your Planning Committee to look at the application again.

Let me know what you've decided.

All the best,
Gerald Portland

Unit 82

A 1D 2A 3E 4B 5F 6I 7J 8C 9H 10G

B E, A, F/G, G/F, C, H, D, B
Possible heading: A MEDIC, A MODEL AND A MYTH

C *Model answer on page 238 of the Appendix.*

Unit 83

B
1 intended
2 make
3 useful
4 addition
5 recommended
6 urgency
7 note
8 balance
Subheadings:
Where, when and why
Positive aspects
Negative aspects
Recommendations
Conclusion
Complete answer on page 239 of the Appendix.

Unit 85

B 1 A utility company, supermarket or other retailer, trying to make consumers think about ethical issues, but also possibly trying to forge stronger links between themselves and their customers.

2 A holiday company or hotel, advertising short holidays.

3 A company, informing its shareholders or the public about its financial performance.

4 An educational institution, hoping to encourage people to participate in the courses it runs.

5 The local council or police, warning residents to beware of people calling at the door, pretending to be tradesmen or officials, when in fact they are looking for an opportunity to steal things.

6 A company, announcing the prize(s) for a competition it is running.

7 The local council, a school or the police, warning people of the dangers that exist on the town's streets.

8 An action group, trying to gain support from the public for its campaign to stop the closure of a local hospital.

9 A voluntary organisation, charity, hospital, school or old people's home, hoping to recruit unpaid helpers.

10 An employer, or an official body such as a tax office, stating that some information must be sent or some action taken by a specified date.

Unit 86

A 1C 2F 3E 4A 5B 6D

B *Possible answers:*

1 Celebrities seek publicity, so they are to blame for their loss of privacy. The public has the right to know about their lives, as the public is paying (through match tickets, film tickets, etc) for their lifestyle.

2 Privacy is everybody's right. Celebrities just happen to be famous for doing their job, so that shouldn't affect their private lives.

3 Celebrities should be realistic and accept that fame brings disadvantages as well as advantages. Each individual is entitled to a certain degree of privacy, but famous people should expect the public to be interested in their lives.

4 Paragraph 1: Introduction – short statement of the central issue

Paragraph 2: Main section – points for and against

Paragraph 3: Conclusion – summary and personal view

Unit 87

A 1C 2F 3I 4B 5G 6L 7K 8J 9D 10H 11E 12A

B *Positive:* unusual, informative, brilliant, successful, fantastic, stunning, original, witty, fine, outstanding, thrilling, amazing, superb, great
Negative: boring, awful, amateurish, conventional, unimaginative, hopeless, predictable, dreadful, horrible, pathetic, dull

C 1 review
2 directors
3 script
4 interval
5 special effects

Unit 88

A 1 feuding families
2 incredibly perceptive
3 sharp observation
4 at first glance
5 idea of fairness

6 in the right way
7 key question
8 sift through
9 easy read
10 looking for links

B A, I, E, H, G, B, F, D, C

C 1 As
2 who
3 to
4 During/In
5 However
6 by
7 What
8 while
9 nor
10 how
11 addition
12 that

Unit 89

A 1 doubt
2 indisputable
3 nominating
4 else
5 evident
6 approve
7 valuable
8 Furthermore
9 agree

B 2, 4, 5, 7, 8, 9, 10

Unit 90

A 1 Three
2 discursive and descriptive

B A, D, C, B
A, C, B, D
A, D, C, B

C 1, 2, 4, 5, 7, 8